ALL THE WORLD'S A STAGE

By the same author

Novels
ALL THE SAME SHADOWS
THE GUILT MERCHANTS
THE GIRL IN MELANIE KLEIN
ARTICLES OF FAITH
THE GENOA FERRY
CÉSAR & AUGUSTA
ONE. INTERIOR. DAY.
Adventures in the film trade (Short stories)

Biography
SIR DONALD WOLFIT C.B.E.
His life and work in the unfashionable theatre

Screenplay (and introduction)
ONE DAY IN THE LIFE OF IVAN DENISOVICH

Plays
A FAMILY
THE ORDEAL OF GILBERT PINFOLD (from Evelyn Waugh)
THE DRESSER
AFTER THE LIONS

Essays
A NIGHT AT THE THEATRE (Editor)

ALL THE WORLD'S A STAGE

RONALD HARWOOD

SECKER & WARBURG
BRITISH BROADCASTING CORPORATION

For my friend and publisher
Tom Rosenthal
who had the idea for the television series
and for this book

First published in England 1984 by
Martin Secker & Warburg Limited
54 Poland Street, London W1V 3DF
and the British Broadcasting Corporation
35 Marylebone High Street, London W1M 4AA
© Ronald Harwood 1984
British Library Cataloguing in Publication Data

Harwood, Ronald
   All the world's a stage
   1. Theatre-History
   I. Title
   792'.09   PN2101

   ISBN 0-436-19132-6
   (Secker & Warburg Ltd)
   ISBN 0-563-17932-5
   (British Broadcasting Corporation)

Set in 10/13 Trump Medieval by Tradespools Limited, Frome,
and printed in Great Britain by
Collins of Glasgow and London

CONTENTS

In the television series on which this book is based the principal members of the BBC crew were as follows:

Executive Producer: Richard Cawston

Producer: Harry Hastings

Directors: Keith Cheetham, Harry Hastings, Misha Williams

Unit Manager: Paula Leonard

Researchers: Christopher Hesketh-Harvey, Brent McGregor

Picture Research: Maggie Colbeck Rowe

Production Assistants: Eve Cowdrey, Maggie O'Sullivan, Yvonne Robinson, Carol Snook, Cassie Braban

Assistant to Ronald Harwood: Sarah Lillywhite

Production Managers: Tom Kingdon, Nicholas Mallett, Stephany Marks, Harry Rankin, Katherine Thomas

AFM's: Jacmel Dent, Barbara Simonin

Editors: Mike Crozier, Malcolm Daniel, Andrew Page, Sue Spivey

Dubbing Editor: Ken Hains

Cameramen: David Bennett, Elmer Cossey, John Daley, John Else, Remi Adefarasin, David Gray, Brian Hall, Peter Hall, John Hooper, Paul Houlston, Ken Lowe, Bill Matthews, John McGlashan, Nigel Meakin, Ian Punter, John Sennett, Fintan Sheehan, Mike Southon, Nick Squires, Ben Wade, Colin Waldeck, Nigel Walters, Ken Westbury

Camera Assistants: Dave Bennett, Bill Broomfield, Doug Campbell, Mike Darby, Terry Doe, Graham Frake, Chris Hartley, John Keating, Niall Kennedy, Christopher Kochanowicz. Victoria Parnall, Stephen Plant, Martin Shepherd, Philip Sindall, Nigel Slatter, Adrian Smith, Alan Smith, Lorraine Smith, Roger Twyman

Sound Recordists: Ron Brown, Malcolm Campbell, Bruce Gallaway, John Hooper, David Jewitt, Dick Manton, Stuart Moser, John Murphy, Bob Roberts, Ian Sansam, Robin Swain, Dave Brinicombe

Sound Assistants: Clive Derbyshire, Jim Greenhorn, Gordon Lester, Richard Merrick, John Paine, Mike Spencer, John Taylor, Eric Wisby

Grips: Denis Balkin, Roy Caney, Roy Carley, Tex Childs, Joe Felix, John Phillips, Steve Phillips, Roy Russell, Stan Swetman, Alfie Williams

Gaffer:Archie Dawson, Gerhardt Dedlow, John Gracey, Vic Marshall, Tommy Moran, Charles Mowatt, Alan Muhley, Des O'Brien, Joe Shearer, Ken Shepherd, Derek Stockley, Sam Taylor, Bob Turner, Dickie Wood

Sparks: Ian Cooke, Dave Child

Designers: Jim Clay, Barrie Dobbins, Ken Ledsham, David Myerscough-Jones, Austin Ruddy, John Stout, Michael Young

Costume Designers: Odette Barrow, Richard Croft, John Hearne, June Hudson, Rupert Jarvis, Irene Whilton

Make-up: Toni Chapman, Marianne Ford, Shaunna Harrison, Eileen Mair, Tommy Manderson, Jenny Shircore, Sally Sutton, Sylvia Thornton, Maureen Winslade

Visual effects designers: John Brace, Mickey Edwards, Peter Logan

INTRODUCTION

As far as I know there is no previous incidence of insanity in my family. The attempt to recount on television and in this book the history of the theatre represents the first serious lapse in what so far has been a psychologically unremarkable if slightly highly-strung breed. The facts speak for themselves: covering the drama's history from Athens in the fifth century BC until the present day would require a compression rate of roughly three theatre-years to one television-minute. Thirteen hours of television on a subject like the theatre would probably take at least three years to make, and longer to plan. The theatre, by its nature, gives rise to the most vehement enthusiasms and hostilities: it would be hard to reach agreement about making such a series, and impossible to satisfy the legion of critics, both theatrical and academic, that the series would confront.

The madness which possessed me when I agreed to embark on the journey can be traced, I suppose, to my love of the theatre, which has been part of me for as long as I can remember. Having, after some hesitation, said yes to the idea, I had only to rely on my own life-long enthusiasm for the subject in order to grapple with some of the difficulties to which I have just referred. The problem of the time scale was the easiest: it was quite insoluble, which meant that it could be respectfully ignored. Devising scripts that would satisfy not only myself but also producers, directors, actors and the great corporate entities of the BBC and Time-Life Inc., who were also involved, would force me to give a persuasive account of my own ideas about the theatre. Going to the places where the theatre had been born and where it has flourished would match the ideas to their physical context. Satisfying the critics was another insoluble problem, and in any case I realized that *All the World's a Stage* would have to be made in the main for and about the audience, the people whose needs created the theatre and have kept it alive. I wanted to make a long advertisement for the theatre and what it represents.

This book and the series were conceived at the same time, early in 1976, but I decided then that the book I would write at the end of the project would have to stand or fall on its own merits, independent of the series itself, but complementing and if possible counterpointing it. That decision has been reinforced by the circumstances of writing the book, so it may be helpful to give a brief account of what they are. Before we started work we had 'The Concept', which began as thirteen headings – Origins, Greece, Rome, Middle Ages and so on – which then shuttled back and forth across the Atlantic while it was examined, re-examined and reconceived. After countless enjoyable and rewarding discussions we had a Final Concept which had survived examination by the executives in the BBC and Time-Life Inc. who had to approve the financing of what was bound to be an expensive project. Full-time work on the scripts began in 1979, and filming in 1980, to continue into 1983 – rigorous demands which have squeezed the writing of the book into the few months between completing and launching the series. These circumstances put a writer under an inhuman time pressure, but conversely they contain a hidden and splendid advantage. By now he is saturated in the material he has been working on for so long. His knowledge and convictions have been tested and enriched by the working process itself. This labour was in every sense an unexpected pleasure.

One conviction which has withstood the exhaustive testing of the last four years is that the drama, no matter when it was originally created, is brought to life by each succeeding generation. The moment a play is performed by living actors before a living audience, it becomes a contemporary experience. It is that insight which frees the series from being an extended historical study of the way the past is reflected in the present. I came to realize that no purpose would be served by demonstrating the influence of, say, *Hamlet*, or *The Oresteia*, because each time those plays are performed, their world becomes, or should become, the world of the audience. Directors and actors create the playwright's landscape, which the audience is invited to share. Current attitudes and ideas will inevitably colour the landscape, and in that sense the drama is timeless. If it lives, it lives in the present, not in the past. What counts in the theatre is the pulse of life, the imaginative charge which can be generated when actors and audience come together. That is the theme of the series, and of this book.

All the same, those readers who see the television series will notice broad discrepancies between it and the present book. They are deliberate. There seemed to me no point in writing 'the book' of a series which – given my theme – depended on being able to show the theatre at work, with plays performed, if not in their original settings, then in reconstructions as accurate as we could devise, and using actors trained in a similar tradition. Some of the illustrations are stills from the series, but most are drawn from those sources which do not work very well on television because they do not move, but which represent our only form of visual knowledge about the theatre before the advent of film and video.

This book covers a time span which reaches from the theatre's beginnings, more than two and a half thousand years ago, to the present day. It attempts to trace the way the theatre has survived as a live tradition by repeatedly proving its own necessity, changing according to the patterns of life and often influencing their shape and colour. The theatre manages to juggle with two apparently opposite qualities, and keep both of them up in the air. It depends on being an ephemeral art of style and performance, yet it must also be, and has always been, a potent force in society and an arena where people are able to explore themselves and the world they live in. Considering how easy it is for officialdom to interfere with theatres, and if necessary even close them down, and considering the theatre's immoral and subversive reputation over the centuries, its mere survival is a measure of the unique and vital function which it has to perform. It needs to be as free to entertain as it is to offend.

Except for the Balinese ritual of the Barong dance, I have not ventured outside the Western theatre, nor do I pretend to offer anything like a comprehensive account of the history of Western drama. My aim has been to focus on the theatre at some of its greatest moments, and particularly on those which have left a permanent mark. I have looked for enduring themes, styles or methods, and for plays which are still performed and enjoyed long after their own time. Here again I have set out to extend the view presented in the series by sketching in more of the social backgrounds where the theatre has flourished, and giving more detailed attention to its growth and development.

I came to the series as a playwright and former actor who has been involved in the theatre as writer, performer and spectator, and for whom the mystery of what brings players and playgoers together is also a practical working concern. Consequently I want to make it clear that I am not interested in the drama as literature. Plays live and breathe in the theatre: only if they can no longer be re-created there should they become the property of the scholars and the literary critics. It is extraordinary that so much of what has been written about drama and the theatre has been produced from the one-dimensional viewpoint of the academic study. After that kind of introduction it is a wonder that any schoolchild or older student can ever avoid looking for hidden meanings, forget about sub-texts and literary influences, and get down simply to experiencing the drama in performance. Plays need to be experienced before they are studied – that is what they are written for.

More and more, present-day culture puts the audience at the end of a long technological chain, far removed from the original performer and creator. My special plea for the theatre is that it brings us together as people and away from our separate bookshelves and loudspeakers and TV screens. It also gives us a role: our presence changes the performance, just as it changes us. I know of few more exhilarating experiences. The hours spent reading this book will be wasted time if they do not persuade the reader out into the audience and into the chancy, dangerous dimension of the drama.

ACKNOWLEDGMENTS

The idea for the television series and this book was put to me in November 1975. The final editing and dubbing of the last episodes will probably still be in progress when the series begins to be televised. The real difficulty of so vast an enterprise is not the actual labour involved, although that was demanding enough, but rather keeping faith with what has been undertaken. Over the eight years from start to finish, I was in constant need of sustenance and to those who made the work possible and pleasurable this inadequate token of gratitude is made.

During my employment by the British Broadcasting Corporation I have seen come and go two Directors-General, two Managing Directors of television, three Controllers of BBC-2, and two Heads of the Music and Arts Department under whose aegis the series was made. Of these, I must single out Humphrey Burton who, when in charge of Music and Arts, proved to be both a wonderful colleague and a friend, as is his successor, Richard Somerset-Ward, who has been closely concerned with the wellbeing of the series.

Other BBC personnel from the upper echelons (some no longer with the Corporation) to whom thanks are due include John Selwyn Gilbert, who guided me through the earliest stages, William Slater and Peter Wineman, who helped the programmes take their first faltering steps in front of the camera.

Once the commitment to make the series had been given, I was empowered to choose my own small staff. If I succeeded in nothing else, my appointments proved to be inspired. My assistant, Sarah Lilywhite (who typed all the scripts more than once and most of the chapters), protected and supported me calmly and firmly. The research was shared by two men. Brent McGregor (whom I was honoured to witness receive his doctorate from the University of Oxford) reduced half of the material to pithy, staccato sentences that made the vast amount of required reading manageable. This done, he rightly moved on to more demanding employment. The other half fell to Christopher Hesketh-Harvey, who, once the major filming began, carried the main burden of research and was invaluable in the preparation and writing of this book. He turned out to be not only first-rate at what he was paid to do, but also, and more importantly from my point of view, a serene, witty and delightful companion who kept my spirits buoyant in good and less good times.

The series was realized for the screen by two young and talented directors, Keith Cheetham and Misha Williams, whose gifts turned my scripts into films. I hope the series serves them as well as they served the series. Their assistants, Maggie O'Sullivan and Yvonne Robinson, were responsible for organizing my complicated schedules and it was my good fortune to be associated with two people of such efficiency, integrity and sweetness. Besides their other arduous duties, they saw me into motorcars, aeroplanes and railway trains; they rose at dawn in a score of locations and helped shepherd me through the day's filming; they kept track of what I wore and what I said. They must have been thoroughly sick of me, but never once, over the entire period, did they show me anything but courtesy and, if they will allow me to say so, affection which I hope they know I return in spades.

The making of thirteen hour-long programmes would not have been financially possible without the partnership of Time-Life Inc. As it turned out, Haidee Grainger, the Time-Life executive whose concern we were, was more than a partner: she was a staunch ally and a loyal friend who, apart from being an endless source of encouragement, helped to cajole a great many distinguished Americans into appearing before our cameras.

In the writing of this book, I owe special thanks to my editor, Stephen Cox, who is a literary alchemist. He rearranged, rewrote and transformed my first drafts, and in so doing made me believe that the light at the end of the tunnel was not another train approaching. I want also to thank Laura Morris of Secker and Warburg, Linda Blakemore and Stephen Davies of BBC Publications whose diligence and enthusiasm made the preparation of this book both pleasurable and exhilarating. I thank, too, Evelyn Ford for her precision and concern in composing the index, as I do Maggie Colbeck Rowe for the illustrations.

I have kept two of the largest bouquets for last. First, I owe a debt of gratitude that can never properly be repaid to the Executive Producer, Richard Cawston, whose qualities both as a man and as a producer gave me strength when I was in need of it and expertise where I was lacking. I hope he will allow me to call him a friend. He, I know, will not mind if I reserve star billing for the producer, Harry Hastings. The day-to-day burden was his and, given the length and complexity of this series, a heavy burden it proved to be. If anything was achieved in the making of *All the World's a Stage*, then the greatest credit is due to him. Above all, he is a golden man with whom I was honoured to work.

Ronald Harwood
Liss, September 1983

MAKERS OF MAGIC

The theatre is one of man's most ingenious compromises with himself. In it he performs and entertains, shows off and amuses himself, and yet it is also one of his most powerful instruments for exploring and attempting to understand himself, the world he lives in, and his place in that world. The theatre can be controversial or reassuring, subversive or conservative, diverting or enlightening: if it chooses it can be all of these, and more. It can dazzle the eye and ear, and hold an audience spellbound. More important, in creating that special atmosphere it is able to provoke deep, often subconscious emotions, and to embody those drives and forces in the human mind which set both individuals and society most at risk. Presumably that is why, throughout its history, there have been so many attempts to tame or to outlaw the theatre. And if these have always failed it is because the theatre is something that people need.

Human beings have a permanent, never-sated appetite for seeing and recognizing their own image, enacted live, in all its possibilities. In the theatre, this is a communal experience. Audiences are much more than the sum of their parts – anyone who has ever been in an audience knows that. At the same time, a theatre performance is very much more than author, actors and directors can know or control in advance, and somewhere in the reciprocal exchange between these two groups, in all their daily differences, lies the special absorption and excitement which belong to the theatre. Over the centuries, it has contained a vast panorama of some of the most sublime and – it follows – the most ludicrous moments of the human imagination.

According to Peter Brook, 'the theatre and life are the same thing and aren't the same thing. They are made up of the same ingredients, yet the theatre wouldn't exist as a form if something different didn't take place.' Because the theatre is like life and about life it can never be reduced to a simple formula. In its thousands of years of history it has remained stubbornly amorphous. When it has become too crystallized in one place it has emigrated to another. Whenever a society has over-defined it, it has been likely to turn into whatever it was not supposed to be. Its history is punctuated with extraordinary explosions of new vitality, changes of every kind around the nucleus of actors and audience.

Yet the evidence of the theatre's history is often infuriatingly sparse. We do not know exactly what an ancient Greek theatre from the classical age looked like, or how Greek actors played, and we are ready to put up with our ignorance because after all we are dealing with the events of two and a half thousand years ago. But shift the focus to only four hundred years ago, and we do not know quite what Shakespeare's Globe theatre looked like, nor is there one surviving portrait of Shakespeare which was done in his lifetime. Medieval woodcuts are a rich source for historians, but there is hardly one surviving which shows actors going about their business, and the painters of the Renaissance likewise seem to have shunned the stage. Written evidence is equally hard to find until the last two or three hundred years.

Perhaps the theatre's existence has been simply taken for granted as an obvious need, too familiar to need recording or discussing. That will not do for the twentieth century, which has built vast theoretical superstructures over these obscure beginnings. All the same, for someone whose work is in the theatre, some of the questions are practical ones. Why the need for theatre, expressed when it first burst into life, and in all those later regenerations? Why do we have a theatre at all, with its buildings, actors, playwrights, directors, critics? Most crucial of all, why do we have audiences? Why do people go to the theatre? This book attempts to approach these questions by visiting the theatre at some of the focal points in its history, but it does not make the visits empty-handed. Some of its assumptions will emerge along the way. One of them can be stated at the start.

The theatre has the alarming power to embody problems that are fundamental to existence but which frequently defy solution because, historically, the theatre has been a medium more of emotion than of rationality, finding a language and a setting in which to express what otherwise must have remained hidden or suppressed. Theatre has invaded areas of existence, countries of the mind, which are by nature resistant to rational exploration, and it has done so in order to make a home there, not to destroy, or to analyse. When actors and audience come together and jointly commit themselves to a collective experience, a necessary mystery takes place.

Another kind of mystery surrounds the origins of the theatre, mysterious in the more commonplace sense that they lie where they can't be excavated, in one of the permanent locked rooms of the distant past. Multiplied together, these mysteries of past fact and present understanding have given birth to all sorts of schools of thought. None of them can offer proofs, but the one which offers the most food for the imagination argues that the theatre's roots grow out of ancient ritual. Another school insists that the evidence for any religious beginnings is inadequate, improbable and furthermore puts a straitjacket on the understanding. This school goes on from arguing that it is now impossible to discover the origins of the theatre to propose that all theories of its genesis are irrelevant. I make an altogether contrary point: acknowledging a connection between the archaic past and the present day ought to enrich the understanding not only of the theatre but also of the societies it serves.

An alternative theory of the theatre's sources would have us accept a closer resemblance to games and sports than to rituals and religious mysteries; much is made of the word 'play' being common to both activities. Where games and sports are pastimes, I would argue that this theory is demonstrably false: that the excitement and passion generated by a sporting contest are superficial and short-lived in comparison to the abiding emotional and social impact which the theatre is capable of producing. Where performance in a game or sport becomes a test of the whole person, and where the notion of a 'game' can be extended back into the same distant past where the performance of the hunter or the farmer becomes bound up with ritual itself, the connections become harder to disentangle. What matters in the present is that games and sports represent alternatives to the pressures and concerns of our daily lives, while the theatre – though it may also work in this way – has the essential but exactly opposite function of helping us remember who we are and where we are. In that sense its ties to religion are unbroken.

It is another of the assumptions of this book that imagination is more important than knowledge. The kind of academic rigour which requires mechanistic proofs or verifications at every level of existence is in direct conflict with the springs and sources which feed theatrical life. (I do not make the same accusation against science in general, whose highest levels are habitually enlivened by the most extravagant speculations, apparently of necessity.) One dare not fight shy of making imaginative leaps or of calling on intuition, because these ordinary human faculties are, and have always been, part of the fabric of the theatre. The very idea that magic and the making of magic might still be connected to what is now a thriving modern pursuit, often conventional, often tainted by ruthless commercialism, is bound to be viewed with deep suspicion by contemporary eyes. So it is helpful to recall that magic itself represents another attempt to deal with the hidden part of the psyche, and to create a vocabulary for it. This is the domain of the theatre too.

Even so, the connection may still seem tenuous, especially if it is pointed out that many of today's theatres stand somewhere in the middle of great busy cities and seem to offer the most vulgar and garish of neon wares. I would like to meet this objection head-on by arguing that theatres, if they are truly to be of service, ought to stand at the centre of things, where life is encountered at fever-pitch. All elements of society have to be present, respectable or not, fashionable or not. The notion of festivals in idyllic pastoral surroundings smacks too strongly of escape from that daily reality into an artificial enclave of cultural isolation. Theatre thrives most where it is ready to stand the contrast between itself and its surroundings and to create an experience which is plainly at a heightened level of existence. It must satisfy the human need to undergo strains and tensions, to witness conflicts of good and evil, might and right, chaos and order. To do that, it has to possess the audience, and be possessed by it. That is the essential requirement: both actors and playgoers are obliged to lose a sense of themselves, or, if you like, to gain a broader identity, if the drama is to do its work.

To illustrate my belief that the contemporary theatre is linked to the sacred rituals of primitive societies, I shall quote the director Peter Brook:

... at the beginning of a performance you have a number of people – fifty, five hundred, two thousand people – all of whom are self-contained fragments with no natural flow going between them ... each one of us is like a car rushing along a highway and even when one comes into a traffic-jam, one is completely cut off from the flow of life; one is in one's own little box and that is, in a very crude way, the way we live most of the time.

One comes into a special surrounding which is an amphitheatre. An amphitheatre has only one virtue, it brings people together. And one sees the more different the people ... the better the result. And then through a number of steps, through ... the rhythm ... the work of the actor, perhaps the presence of the actor, all these gradually attract a common interest. So already there's a common factor: these people, very different from one another, who have come together, begin to share a common interest. Now, that becomes dynamic because the common interest turns into a common process. Something begins, begins to unroll and flow, shared by everyone. And then you have, like water coming to the boil ... a change of state.

And that particular phenomenon, which happens in love between two people, happens in an act of communion when a number of people are gathered together ... through the intense involvement in an action stemming out of life.

A surrounding special because 'it brings people together', the actor, communion – Brook states the terms of reference. He also talks of 'a change of state', and I have made the claim that the theatrical mystery works when actor and audience jointly surrender their conscious workaday selves to the event. It possesses them, something other than their conscious selves possesses them, and this is one of the major clues that lead into the heart of the mystery. The earliest cave-paintings show human beings impersonating creatures other than themselves. To be something else, or somebody else, is a notion that seems always to have absorbed us. In the Trois Frères caves in southwest France, for example, paintings daubed on the walls by men who lived there many thousands of years ago depict humans impersonating animals. It is thought that this is the earliest form in which people took on the identity of others.

The reasons for these imaginative mutations are speculation, and always will be. The guesswork tends to be informed by the guesser's own sense of humanity in the world, and it is another of my own assumptions that here the more rational suggestions are by definition the more suspect. These concern primitive man's underdeveloped linguistic skills, and his resultant need to tell what happened during the hunt by re-enacting the adventure. Another guess is that early hunters dressed in the skins of animals as a form of camouflage, enabling them to get close to the prey undetected. These interpretations are deficient because they offer an account of early man as a kind of simple-minded modern, exercising a makeshift common sense, rather than living in a mental world as complex as our own, but governed by instincts and highly developed intuitions. They also ignore the presence of magic in the primitive world, the supernatural forces created by the human need to account for that world, and the human talent for drawing analogies and for seeing things simultaneously as themselves and as symbols.

We are entitled to deduce, from what we know of the rituals still practised by the 'primitive' peoples of our own time, that the cave paintings of early man were not just a form of narrative art but in themselves part of a magic ritual: In Colin Wilson's words: 'The pygmies of the Congo draw in the sand a picture of the animal they intend to hunt, then fire an arrow into its throat;

Cave paintings near Salt Lake City, Utah, depicting a horned huntsman.

Tungus carve an animal they intend to hunt; Yeniseis make a wooden fish before going fishing, and so on.' 'Capturing' the prey in wood, or on sand or stone, becomes the necessary preliminary to its capture in reality. The cave drawings showing men in the guise of beasts extend this process of re-creating the prey into capturing the animal in man's own person. These are the first known instances of impersonation, and they place it at the start of drama. Yet the word 'impersonation' is not strictly accurate, because there are grounds for believing that in making the link between himself and what he ate and depended upon, primitive man *became* the animal. He shed his humanity in order to possess the animal's spirit, and for its spirit to possess him.

This is not to say that there was no more immediately practical function of the kind of understanding of animals which cave paintings demonstrate and which the impersonator would need to develop. In 'rehearsing' its movements and behaviour, the hunter must learn more about the prey. In rehearsing the hunt itself, in drawings or as part of the group pursuing the animal made human, the hunter would develop his own responses and intuitions. It was a necessary magic. These animals were the early hunters' sustaining life force, and their instinct was to become one with that force.

In depicting possession, this 'change of state', these paintings recall the ancestry of acting. In time, the actors would use physical aids towards the loss of self, and in order to fortify belief in what was taking place: skins, paint, antlers and, most important for the theme of theatre, masks. The donning of masks is a constant symbol in the origins of theatrical form. What remains to be discovered is how man developed other methods of becoming possessed, of changing his state so as to project his awareness outside himself, into the other worlds which intuition could sense as cohabiting with his everyday reality.

These early drawings and paintings also convey a sense of movement, impressions of a dance, and it is difficult to resist the conclusion that we are seeing glimpses of a transformation in which the hunters not only took on the appearance of the animals they hunted, but also elaborated and formalized the accompanying actions into a dance. The same process happens to this day on the Greek island of Skyros, in a ritual known as the Goat Dance, which has its origins in a time long before Christianity came to the island. The ceremonies mark the end of winter and the coming of spring; in them the men of the village disguise themselves as goats, and dance. It is an eerie and frightening spectacle. Through the animals which are most important to them, they identify with a life force broader than the human animal alone.

In attempting to project the imagination back into our prehistoric past, there is no choice but to look for analogies in the modern world. And to understand what dance may have meant to small hunting communities living in the dawn of human consciousness, it is worth looking at what can be said about the power of dance even in the 'advanced' societies of the twentieth century. Most people can respond to that power. Given a driving rhythm, made by the percussion instruments which certainly produced the earliest form of music other than the human voice, the human body finds rhythms which will follow or answer the tempo and excitement generated by stamping feet, clapping hands, beaten drums, or just the presence of other bodies moving in unison. In these conditions, and no matter if the scene is one of the surviving primitive societies or a metropolitan discotheque, a dancer may lose self-awareness. Abandoned to the music, his body movements are no longer subject to his will but obey an impulse that is only released when he is lost in the activity.

A Sinhalese devil-dancer, photographed in 1903.

Dance seems always to have a means to assist the loss of self. All over the world the phenomenon occurs. The Whirling Dervishes are an obvious example of what may be called ecstatic dance. In medieval Europe the fits of collective dancing mania often associated with the progress of bubonic plague inspired the macabre woodcuts of the Dance of Death. The longing for a state of ecstasy plays a dominant role in the early story of the theatre, and part of that longing was fulfilled by the discovery of this mysterious power of dancing, that it could induce trance. The dancer could enter a state of mind which was other-worldly, a magical sphere where he found himself in touch with forces and perceptions which primitive man may have perceived as belonging to a universe outside himself, or as the outward form of a deep and magical inner transformation. Then as now, when the desired sphere was reached, the dancer lost self-consciousness and the sense of ordinary time. The present was forgotten: he danced in timelessness.

Dance could explore and express what lay outside man's everyday consciousness, long before there was any verbal vocabulary for exploring the powerful forces working both inside and outside himself. If man was going to know his world, he had to embrace its mysteries, and these were bound up with his experience of the loss of self and the sense of timelessness. A component of that fascination was the need to escape, in the sense of not remaining forever confined by his manageable daily reality. But there is another facet which is equally revealing because it springs from our ancient enchantment with the telling of stories. In the world of ritual, it is not just any tale which matters, but one in particular – the story of our beginnings. Throughout the world, this story – these thousands of stories – have been one of our key inventions for keeping contact with both our physical and our spiritual sources, sometimes called gods. The story of evolution half-supplanted these, and is itself in the course of being supplanted. The impulses we are dealing with are not quaint relics of superseded notions of humanity.

Again we are obliged to ask why these impulses have taken the form they have: why this appetite to recreate the birth of time and of life? Anthropologists have noted a widespread, deep-rooted human belief that life was not always as it is now, and that at some time hidden from our everyday view there was a golden age of perfection and harmony, perpetually lost. Another belief, current in many forms, has held that at some climactic moment Death entered that golden world in the form of deliberate murder. Out of that destruction, in the myths of fertility, comes creation. Birth, death and rebirth are seen as a cycle continually recreated, as the seasons are. The rituals which embody these versions of human existence are ways of demonstrating that there must be death so that there can be life. They are attempts by man to recreate that time past, but as if it was happening *now*, in present time.

In the modern Western world, what remains of such rituals has become so fossilized that the word 'ritual' itself conjures up pictures of old men walking in obsolete uniforms, or (in the case of folk dance) young men leaping in outlandish ones. When they began, they were not such rags and bones, observed as curiosities. They were functional: they made things happen, or rather continue to happen. For in the history of ritual, repetitive themes insist on their assertion. Archaic rites suggest a strong link between vegetation and sexuality, the harvest and birth. Life had a precarious hold on the surface of a stony world: to strengthen what sustained it meant performing ceremonies of invocation, and if they succeeded, of joyful celebration. The ceremonies must be as faithful as the processes they hoped to sustain, so they had to be repeated, and exactly repeated, at precise seasonal intervals, if the magic was going to work.

To preserve the fabric of society, ritual also enforced all kinds of social taboos from incest to parricide. At an early stage in his development man acknowledged and ritualized the entry of Death into the world; not unnaturally, he equated it with evil, and sought to counteract its power by literally destroying it. He believed that killing an evil spirit was not only clearly beneficial to the life-force, but also a means of averting all the destructive influences that acted against him. Hence, the emergence of the scapegoat, the transference of evil into an animal or human being whose death, communally performed and dramatized, killed evil too. It seems that man has always been able to persuade himself of the possibility of a perfect world.

By drawing together some of the strands that make up religious ritual, we can begin to detect the form of the fabric that they wove. We have observed hunters who become the animal they hunt, and who wear masks to assist the imagination – both their own and the community's. Dancing assists and elaborates the transformation, because its frenzy in some versions, and its hypnotic repetition in others, is able to induce an ecstatic state of trance. Trance, in turn, allows man to lose consciousness of self and time, or to be possessed by an altered awareness of both. Man's spiritual resources may be renewed and reinforced by the stories of his creation, the golden age eternally debased but never quite obliterated by death and evil. Ritual attempts to recreate original time in the teeth of present mortality. It was also a means of calling on the gods, the sources of life, and of giving thanks for any aid they granted – not only for good hunting or a richer harvest, but for survival. Exact repetition of ritual was necessary for success (and its absence the alibi for failure); success was to be celebrated in full measure, and often excessively.

Many of the themes and forms of ritual prefigure early drama, and continue to reappear sporadically throughout its later history. What both have in common is the ability to elicit the tensions between the human and the divine, one brief and vulnerable, the other detached from death and time. Some of the differences are obvious – that drama can be performed in front of spectators, an audience, whereas for ritual to survive it requires participants, true believers in its mystery; that drama has continually changed, while ritual must stay constant. We cannot know what ancient ritual was, but if we want to guess we need not rely on conjecture alone, because ritual survives in the modern world. But it belongs to its own place, and can't be booked for brief international engagements. It has to be met on its own terms.

One of the oldest surviving rituals performed with masks comes from a cultural tradition outside the focus of this book, but whose key elements put it directly in touch with our theme. The Barong Dance of Bali combines drama and religious rite, possession and performance, and it is performed in a landscape which helps even a Westerner to rid his mind of the technological distractions of the post-industrial world and concentrate on the ritual itself. By taking a television crew to Bali, we ourselves constituted the technological intruders, of course, but Bali seems able to resist its tourists.

The island lies a mile east of Java. It is green, lush and peaceful, its climate is kind, and its inhabitants possess both physical beauty and a temperament which is simultaneously cheerful and serene. Music is part of the atmosphere and day and night the air carries the tinkling sounds of the *gamelan*, the Balinese orchestra consisting of various percussion instruments, a two-string violin and a flute. Bali is alive with religion, superstition and magic. When Islam triumphed over Hinduism in the Malay archipelago, in the sixteenth century, many Hindus – courtiers, priests and artists, as well as craftsmen and farmers – were able to take refuge here. Today it is Indonesia's only stronghold

Above Balinese village girls perform a dance of welcome.
Right the kris dancers turn their daggers in on themselves.

of Hinduism, and Balinese life revolves around its complex religion, which is a blend of the Savite sect of Hinduism, Buddhism, Malay ancestor cult and a variety of animistic and magical practices. Belief in reincarnation is strong. There are countless places of worship, temples large and small. Shrines are dotted along the winding roads, and are recognizable by their traditional drapery of black-and-white checked cloth.

The Balinese appear to have achieved an easy relationship with nature, and a culture that expresses and celebrates it. Hence Bali's legend as a kind of earthly paradise, where it is said that there is a perfect simplicity in attitudes towards sex, and the processes of man's thought have been turned into beauty. The entire human and physical environment conveys the impression of harmony between the spiritual and material worlds. The more curious balance is the relationship between the island and its visitors, because it is to tourists, and – let it be said – to anthropologists, photographers, film and even television crews, that we owe the survival of ancient Balinese ritual. The performances of what may be called dance dramas have been sustained by visitors ever since the Dutch first set foot here in 1597.

Why Bali should have survived the kind of culture shock which has demoralized and enfeebled so many national and tribal self-identities around

the world is another of the island's mysteries. The fact remains that to witness performances which are specially given and paid for does not detract from the event, either for its creators or for its watchers, native or foreign. The lasting image of the Barong imprinted on my memory is of the piety surrounding the performance, and how the two elements, sanctity and drama, combined in an unexpected and terrifying climax.

In the open-air temple precincts of a small village we watched the troupe arrive. Twenty to thirty men and women of all ages stood on the back of an open lorry which bounced along a dirt track road. Among them, as if surrounded by a loyal guard of honour, and bobbing above their heads, we could see the large and magnificent mask of the Barong, a beloved mythological creature with magical powers. Now the first ceremony took place: the mask was unloaded and then carried in procession to a shed at the rear of the temple where it was carefully lifted to hang from a rafter, because the Barong mask must never touch the ground – it is a holy object.

The Barong is a lion figure which probably arrived from China in prehistoric times. For the ritual the mask and body are worn by two men, rather in the style of a pantomime horse in England. To me the Barong resembled a Chinese dragon, but a friendly one, and even slightly comic: brilliantly decorated in scarlet, gold and gleaming white, it has protruding eyes, tusked jaws which clack when operated by the dancer, floppy ears and a beard of human hair plaited with frangipani flowers. In the beard dwells the Barong's magic power. I was told that when a village is threatened by an epidemic, the Barong is called upon and a priest fills a container with water and holds it beneath the Barong's clashing jaws. The ends of the beard are dipped into the water, which at once becomes holy, and endowed with healing powers. Women and children wear strands of the Barong's beard round their wrists for protection.

Once the mask has been suspended above the ground, general preparations begin. The performers retire to a shaded area and begin to dress and make-up while others arrange the space where the event is to take place. The actors and dancers are all trained in their skills; the two men who wear the masks and clothes of the Barong are highly respected, and the role is passed from father to son. For the ritual that unfolds is no spontaneous event, its intricacies have to be taught. The man with these responsibilities is called the *Dah-Lang*, the teacher of ritual. He is the equivalent of a modern theatre director. Fittingly, the *Dah-Lang* of the Barong we saw was the village schoolmaster. His troupe was composed of performers who had talent and had learned necessary skills. The point is that in the development of ritual, the communal act gave way to a ritual enacted by specialists for the good of the whole community. In Bali, their approach was touched with solemnity. The ritual held them just as the drama will hold an actor in the modern theatre. The word 'drama' comes from a Greek root meaning 'a thing done' or 'performed': something was about to be performed, and the sense of theatre could not be mistaken.

The ceremonies proper begin when the village priest emerges to bless the

'The mask is an absolute barrier, and by
wearing it, the actor makes a statement of
total surrender to the part he is playing.'

Above an ornamental Roman mask from the
Casa Fontana Grande, Pompeii.

From the Museo Archeologico Nazionale,
at Naples, a detail from the Pronomos Vase,
which depicts Roman actors with masks as
Hercules and Dionysus.
Right a mask dominates this krater design
from the Museo Eoliana at Lipari: Pan dances
with a maenad.

Two actors, one
masked: the scene is
from a krater at Ferrara.

Left a Roman mosaic
with masks for tragedy
and for a satyr play.
Right the holy mask of
the Barong makes its
ritual entrance carried
by Balinese villagers.

Left from an island off Papua, New Guinea, a ritual mask.

Right since the beginnings of the Japanese theatrical tradition, the masks used in Noh theatre have been treated as objects of veneration.

Below left a mask designed by Miró for La Clacka, a Basque company.

Below right with echoes of *Commedia*, masks were used in the 1977 production of *Volpone* at the National Theatre of Great Britain.

The use of the mask comes full circle in
Peter Hall's 1981 production of Aeschylus'
Oresteia at the National Theatre of
Great Britain.

space where the performance is to take place. Here came another strong echo of the theatrical form, because the Barong Dance is played out in a circle, and the circle is a constant in the story of the theatre. It is a natural shape which provides a sense of community and concentration, and of course in a circle all are more or less equal. The shape emerges over and over again in theatrical architecture, sometimes modified but usually apparent. As we saw in Bali, its use goes back long before the rise of theatre, to religious ritual, which often sees the circle as the sacred centre of the world that is to be created – the *axis mundi*. The priest sprinkled holy water over the area and murmured prayers. Here was a tangible link to Peter Brook's 'special surrounding'.

In this circle, then, the audience gathers. Although we had commissioned the performance, the Barong Dance was naturally attended by the inhabitants of at least two villages – the religious significance aside, it is popularly enjoyed as a form of entertainment. There is no admission charge. If anyone does make a contribution, the money goes to the troupe for the purpose of buying new costumes or musical instruments, or to pay a teacher for further instruction. It is unthinkable for any individual performer to accept payment.

The Barong Dance is a complicated story with a large cast, and I shall not attempt to summarize it, except to say that it shows the influence of the great Indian epics, the *Ramayana* and the *Mahabharata*. A monkey who is comically castrated, a prime minister, robbers and the god Shiva all appear. The *gamelan* music is continuous and lulls the spectator's senses, but it can also be surprisingly ominous and alarming at appropriate moments. Our concern is where ritual and drama meet, especially in the terrifying climax, for the Barong Dance is essentially a fight between Life and Death. Life is represented by the Barong itself, Death by the witch, Rangda, also impersonated by a masked performer, ugly and grotesque, with pendulous breasts and eighteen-inch fingernails. After a series of encounters, the two meet for the final battle in the last scene of the drama.

Because the Barong and Rangda both possess magical powers, neither is able to destroy the other. The skirmish is obviously going to end in stalemate. Suddenly, from the back and sides of the circle, men appear carrying the long knives known as krises. These are the followers of the Barong and they enter the fight on its behalf. They try to kill Rangda, but her power is too great. Either in frustration or because Rangda causes them to, the men turn these long razor-sharp knives against themselves. It is an agonizing moment, for they seem quite out of control. The krises are pliable and deadly, and twitch impatiently in their hands, yet no matter how hard they press the point against their chests – and I witnessed these events at very close quarters – they are unable to pierce the skin. Each man makes frenzied efforts to stab himself, but no blood is shed.

Only then does the newcomer realize that these dancers are in a deep state of trance: they have made contact with another world and no longer suffer the pains of this one. Presently they begin to tire. The scene dissolves. Rangda is gone. Priests come from the temple compound and sprinkle their sweating bodies with holy water to break the spell. The Barong leans over them, its magical beard a restorative force. Live baby chickens are offered as a sacrifice, and as the kris dancers come to, one or two of them bite off the chickens' heads, so that blood runs down their chins. The dance is over. In an instant the audience evaporates. The ritual has served its purpose, to assert and celebrate the victory of the life force, the Barong.

One of the fascinations of the event was the audience. I sensed that the involvement of the spectators in Bali was deep and intense: most were lost in the world that was being created before them. A few showed a marked detachment and gave only occasional darting looks towards the centre of the circle. This look has been described as 'the Balinese sideways glance'; it denotes a form of sophistication, a sense that it is not the done thing to be seen to be too involved. Unfortunately I have observed this very look in theatre audiences all over the Western world, although Western audiences have not lost the capacity to be absorbed in the drama.

Those men who rushed in to attack Rangda were involved at a deeper level. In days gone by, they would have been ordinary members of the audience who so totally believed in the struggle between the Barong and its enemy that they were drawn into a state of trance which took them into battle on the side of the life force. Today the kris dancers are members of the troupe. How they achieve the state of trance was not explained, though the evidence for some form of self-hypnosis was undeniable. The *Dah-Lang* told me of instances where men had been working in the fields some distance from where the dance was taking place. At the moment of danger to the Barong, these workers were possessed – his word – by the compulsion to go to the Barong's aid. They seized krises and attempted to destroy Rangda; when this failed they attempted self-destruction. Again no blood was shed. This, he said, was because the Barong protected them.

This trance and involvement of dancers and audience is essential to the ritual's success. In ritual something actually happens, and it does so because the people believe it to happen. The theatre contains its meaning in words as well as action, and by doing so it necessitates an involvement of the thinking self as well as those parts of our minds which are not accessible to conscious thought and control. Coleridge wrote about the 'willing suspension of disbelief for the moment, which constitutes poetic faith', and this notion of the suspension of disbelief has been taken up to describe the state of mind required by the audience for a theatrical performance. If it denotes a mere intellectual concession, no concept could be more false and detrimental. What Coleridge was attempting to describe was something more positive. We know that what is happening on a stage is not real; we do not want to ignore its fictional character because its invention is part of our enjoyment. At the same time, we are obliged to make believe, to make an act of theatrical faith. Our real and our imaginative perceptions must coexist.

In the kris dancers of Bali my assertion that both audience and actor must lose self-consciousness is borne out. The men who go into trance are both spectators and participants. The theatre echoes ritual. 'When an actor is inhabited by his role,' Peter Brook says, 'if he really and truly plays his part totally . . . you can't see any trace of separation between the him who is not the role and the him that is the role; the two are fused completely so that actually he, at that moment, is the part.' Possession again, and a change of state which is allied to trance: the actor is playing a part, and he *knows* he is playing a part, but the surrender to the part is central. The parallel involvement of the audience is the other half of the agreement. They stand, or sit, and watch, but they also provide the medium of receptive belief in which the performance is planted.

With ritual, we are not yet ready to recognize the actor as an individualized professional performer, but there is another feature of the Barong Dance which relates directly to Brook's 'change of state', and to what happens as a result of that change. It concerns the wearing of masks. We have seen that to both participants and spectators the mask of the Barong is sacred. The dancer who wears it does so in order to become the Barong. He is not playing a part; on the contrary, when he dons the mask he *is* the Barong: that is part of the magic the mask works. And by becoming the Barong the dancer enters the spiritual world in order to make something happen in this world. That is the purpose of ritual. Archaic man performed magic because he wanted the rain to fall, the river to flood, his family or tribe to prosper. He may have celebrated the end of winter and the coming of spring – another image of death and life; he certainly intended to communicate with the unseen forces which he believed to rule all aspects of his existence, from birth to death and beyond.

Ritual also belongs to the worship of gods, who are called upon to avert calamities such as earthquakes, plagues and famine. All sorts of special effects may be employed – smoke, incantations, smells and evocative sounds. Nature is imitated in the form of plants and animals, but also in rain and sun dances, and in movements reproducing the rhythm of the sea. These are kinds of sympathetic magic, which also underlies ritual ceremonies of the sacrament, the eating of the divinity, which have taken place from the earliest times. To take the god into one's physical being was the most vivid outward signal of spiritual communion. Often ritual is conservative: it must keep the world the same, preserve the balance of life and death. Here, its success will often be measured by the ritual itself. That it is performed, and properly performed, is enough. The same may be true of the theatre: the performance itself, the thing done, may be its own fulfilment. If theatre goes further, and is felt to change the state of its audience in some more permanent way, that power may explain why it should have been seen as inherently subversive by some regimes and some philosophers.

Our narrative has not yet reached that point. By trusting not only instinct and imagination but also to the finite evidence of past and present, deep

Ritual belongs to the worship of gods: an African witch doctor dances as intermediary.

connections can be traced between ancient ritual and the theatre. But what is there to justify the claim that one transformed itself into the other, and why did the change occur? Ritual contains the emotional forces in human beings; it existed before the word, before the involvement of language, intellect, ideas. The theatre too contains those forces, but it adds the crucial element of man's growing conscious understanding. What is essential to the theatre but absent in ritual is the presence of an individual creator, the playwright. His emergence catalyses the transformation.

What remains common to both ritual and the theatre as their living source is a special human need, an impulse which exists universally and in many forms – the longing to bring together the real, immediate world and the spiritual world. For many, the real world is the spiritual world. In past times all activity was endowed with spirituality – working the land, preparing food, making love. These are now archaic beliefs. We have made a separation of these elements which diminishes them both. Art is the necessary connection that fills this void, an everyday necessity. If religious ritual was transformed into art, we should be able to observe how it happened, and more specifically, how religious ritual was transformed into the art of the theatre.

ENTER
DIONYSUS

Two and a half thousand years ago, on a hillside in Athens, the drama as an art was born. Never before, and perhaps not since, has so much theatrical energy been released in a single place: its vitality expressed the joy and amazement of a society discovering a means to explore itself at every level – not only the subterranean regions of ritual, but the everyday realms of speech and movement recreated in poetry and dance. Ancient Greek theatre reached its climax in the comparatively brief period of a hundred years or so. In retrospect we see its rise as marking a turning point in human understanding. But what the theatre of ancient Greece meant in its own time, how the plays came to be written, and the way they were staged and acted, are all elusive questions, open to conjecture and interpretation. No wonder that scholars have found themselves compelled to describe what happened as a miracle.

Nothing so important and so widespread in human culture could be free of controversy, of course, and there are specialists who argue that dramatic art germinated several thousand years before the Greeks started writing plays. There is evidence for some elements of theatre flourishing in the Sumerian civilization, which dates from at least 3000 BC. The Sumerians occupied that most familiar ground to archaeologists and schoolchildren, the land between the rivers Tigris and Euphrates, where they developed city states with elaborate palaces and temples. Their chief religious festival was the twice-yearly celebration of the new year. In autumn they expressed the hope that winter, when their god of fertility appeared to die, would not last forever; in spring they enacted their longing for a year of prosperity. At some point a new custom was introduced at the spring festival: a popular king, the lord of misrule, reigned over the city for a day. The Babylonians inherited and elaborated on the culture of the Sumerians. Their new year was celebrated by gorgeous processions, a recitation of the myth of creation, and by perform-ances of mime.

Theatrical claims are also made on behalf of the ancient Egyptians. On the walls of a sealed tomb at Abydos there is a record of what is thought to be a religious drama portraying the passion and death of the god-king, Osiris. The myth of Osiris is fundamental to the way the ancient Egyptians saw their world; at the same time its themes contain fascinating prefigurations of what was to emerge across the Mediterranean in Greece. Like many ancient myths, the events are complicated by a multitude of incestuous relationships. The outline of the passion play reveals that Osiris was murdered and dismembered by his evil brother, Seth. Eventually Isis, the sister of Osiris, and also his wife, seeks out the grisly remnants of the dead king and gives them separate burial, marking each grave with a shrine. The dead Osiris, revived by magic, fathers a son, Horus, whom Isis brings up to avenge his father. Here regicide, fratricide, reconciliation, incest and revenge, obsessive themes of Greek drama, make their archaic appearance. The texts also indicate that in the passion plays priests would impersonate their gods, and this is the ground for describing them as plays at all. But there is not enough evidence for anything more definite than conjecture. The Sumerian and Babylonian civilizations seem not to have extended their rituals into the detached and different form of theatre, nor is there any evidence for any subsequent development of theatre in ancient Egypt. For theatre as a separate form, recognized by its own society, we have to wait for its triumphant genesis in Athens.

There is very little hard fact to demonstrate how the change from ritual to art occurred, and I have already pointed out that we are dealing with an area in which scholarship too has to rely upon imagination and intuition. The term 'art' itself can also be misleading in this context: we are not dealing with works designed for individual contemplation, and plays are not and were not written for reading in studious individual silence. We have seen that ritual was an integral part of archaic society. By the same token, a play implies an audience, and changes with its audience; it lives in performance, not on the printed page. That is why Peter Brook warns of the dangers in thinking of the theatre as different from human life: 'I think it [the theatre] is a very special sort of human experience and unless one is very clear about this one gets lost in art.' Fortunately for the drama, it is poorly designed for acquisition by museums. The theatre needs the groundlings as much as it is needed by them.

Historically, it is as if the Greek drama suddenly existed, fully developed and wonderful. Certainly the appearance of the playwright, the individual creator, is significant of the change, which found expression in three dramatists of monumental achievement: Aeschylus, Sophocles and Euripides. Apart from these men and their plays, we have virtually no record, either written or archaeological, of what, for example, the theatres in the great period of the fifth century BC really looked like. All we know for certain is that the plays were given in competition with one another in the open air, that there was a chorus which sang and danced around an altar, and there were up to three speaking actors who donned masks. We also know the kind of clothes they wore. Given so little evidence, our most rewarding insights are derived from the plays, and central to our understanding of these works and of the society they addressed is one vital ingredient which is common to all Greek drama: the chorus.

Because Athens took the brief space of not much more than two or three centuries to transform itself from a primitive tribal structure into a highly developed civilization, there was a collective, conscious preoccupation with a recent archaic past: ancient religious cults, customs and mysteries which had cemented a different way of life found themselves embedded in a culture which was no longer able to take the social and moral fabric for granted. Anarchy and order were immediate social and individual issues, and the discovery that language could formulate them, and different choices be made, contained as great a potential for evil as for good.

In earlier times the tribes inhabited small villages all over the Greek mainland. The tribe paid its allegiance to the gods, and the villagers sang their praises at harvest festivals, dancing in the circle of the threshing floor, giving thanks for the renewal of life. It was a serious occasion, vital to the health of the little community. These rites began with the dance and the invocation or charm; they celebrated, often crudely, and not mistaking solemnity for reverence, the forces that made life. This floor they danced on, like the sanctified circle in Bali, became a sacred place inside a sanctuary. In the theatre, the word *orchestra* stands literally for a dancing place.

In the course of time, a choric song and dance accompanied or grew out of these harvest rites. The song was called the dithyramb. No early example has survived, and its root meaning is unknown and is probably not even Hellenic. Legend has it that at some point one of the chorus must have stepped forward and started a dialogue with the leaders of the dithyramb. By tradition this innovation is attributed to Thespis, who is also said to have toured the countryside in a cart, giving performances in which he wore masks. He is the first actor for whom we have a name, and his distant descendants are sometimes called Thespians to this day, although nowadays only in poor jokes.

The separation of the individual from the group gives rise to a series of responses, either spoken or sung, which contain a simple form of drama in the inevitable tension (though not yet conflict) between two identities. What makes the dithyramb crucial to this story is that it was the hymn to one god in particular, a god of trance and danger as well as of life and growth.

The entrance of Dionysus into the theatre's evolution is decisive. His nature, the frenzied rites of his followers, and the potential threat he represented to ordered society, underlies the power of the drama from its beginnings until the present day. It has been said of the cult surrounding him that it is the only one in antiquity in which dramatic plays could possibly have evolved. Who he was, what he represented, and why the theatre became his domain, are questions which help to locate the mystery, though they will not solve it. Dionysus is a mythological figure, but what makes his worshippers extraordinary is that they themselves developed myths, and it is in the creation of its own mythology that Dionysiac worship was unique. Mythology is the dream-world language of society's unconscious: individuals dream, and try to interpret their dreams; myths try to make sense of those forces in the world which are beyond the reach of reason. Both dream and myth offer means of taking a symbolic hold, privately or collectively, on realities deeper and more literally unspeakable than those which our everyday lives will contain or represent. In creating the art of theatre, the great Greek dramatists were attempting to give expression to all these coexisting forces in a single communal form.

The myth of Dionysus tells how Zeus, the highest of the gods, slept with a mortal woman, Semele. Because he came to her in his full divinity, instead of one of the lowlier forms he more commonly adopted when he visited mortal women, his power destroyed her, but not before she had conceived Dionysus. Zeus snatched the son who had been made immortal by virtue of the god's unshielded power, and planted him in his own thigh, so Dionysus emerged as a god, even though born of a common mortal. That made him unique both as god and as human, and caused him to be persecuted by both.

Dionysus, also called Bacchus, was a god with many different faces and was to exert great influence over the Athenian mind. He had his origins in Thrace,

Dionysus: a bust found at Herculaneum.

and his worship spread throughout Greece and beyond. He appears in all sorts of forms, some to fear and some to wonder at. He was the god of wine, wearing a garb of grapes and animal skins, and he was a tree god, a bull god, a god of fertility. His attendants, the satyrs, were half-men, half-animal, devilish, sensual, flaunting their sexuality and given to excess. Dionysus could also be seen surrounded by women, his followers, the Maenads; he could be sexually ambiguous, at times more female than male. Because he was a comparative newcomer to the pantheon of gods on Olympus, he liked to be viewed as severe, awesome and sternly bearded, but his true spirit is associated with vegetation, with all sorts of rites enacted to promote fertility, and with the mysteries of death and rebirth. He was the bringer of madness, anarchic and revolutionary, the god of masquerade and a maker of magic, the master of magical illusion. He could induce his followers to see the world as it was not. His worship, like his image, took many forms often connected with sexual abandon, and more significant, with trance. For Dionysus was also the god of possession. He was able to reveal himself directly to the individual. His worshippers were possessed by him, submerged in trance.

In its earliest form the worship of Dionysus was what we would now call a cult, whose aim was to achieve *ecstasis* – the word from which our own word 'ecstasy' is derived. *Ecstasis* could mean anything from 'being taken out of yourself' to a profound alteration of personality. His worship took the form of an orgy, which means simply a secret rite or an act of devotion; the sexual connotation came later. At midwinter the Maenads, the women who followed the god, left their homes and made for a wooded hillside on Mount Cythaeron in search of a mystical and frenzied communion with nature, to achieve a state of ecstatic possession. In his play *The Bacchae*, Euripides has a herdsman describe the scene:

> They were a sight to marvel at
> For modest comeliness; women both old and young,
> Girls still unmarried. First they let their hair fall free
> Over their shoulders; some tied up the fastenings of fawnskins they had
> loosened; round the dappled fur
> Curled snakes that licked their cheeks.
> So we fled, and escaped being torn into pieces by
> Those possessed women. But our cattle were there, cropping
> The fresh grass; and the women attacked them, with their bare hands.

Female ecstasy is central to our understanding of the Dionysiac cult. The rites involved crazed dancing, one of the most ancient methods of losing self-awareness, and always ended with the tearing and eating of the raw flesh of an animal, a fawn, a lion, a lynx, a bull. Originally a human sacrifice was almost certainly offered. The animal was first dressed ritualistically to represent the god, for the worshippers believed that the beast was an incarnation of Dionysus, so that when it was torn apart and eaten they engaged in a sort of unholy communion. Possessed and invaded by the god, they achieved *ecstasis*, losing all sense of themselves. We saw in Bali how the state of ecstatic possession had the power to release forces usually dormant or suppressed in human beings. To the people of ancient times, Dionysus was the incarnation of a cluster of these forces which were present in all men and women, essential to their nature, allied with sexuality, sensuality and natural vigour. I believe it possible to think of Dionysus as the god of Licence, the full expression of instincts normally kept bridled. Admittedly there is a contradiction here, because viewed as a sort of psychological safety-valve, the brief release of instinct, like Sumeria's day of misrule, may be counted as a conservative mechanism, a kind of institutionalized spontaneity. I would argue that these forces are too vital and unpredictable for it ever to be totally 'safe' to give them free expression. The Dionysiac rite differs from most other varieties of religious ritual in the crucial respect that whereas most ritual depends for its effect on exact repetition, the Dionysiac rite called for a kind of spiritual liberation which dictates its own shapes and forms. The worship of Dionysus was dynamic, abandoned and alarming; it harboured the hardy seeds of the drama, the dangerously ungovernable interplay between free participants.

The attributes of the god and the manner of his worship are part of the inheritance of theatre, although it can choose to disregard them (that is part of its own ungovernability). There are degrees of possession, levels of impersonation, which actors control as well as release. Nevertheless it is a further vital assumption of this book that the cardinal point of theatrical experience is the joint loss of self by actor and audience. If the audience is too restless the actor is distracted; if the actor reveals too much of his private personality, as is sometimes the case, especially with star actors, then the audience will fail to obtain a true perception of the reality that is being created. ('Self-expression' is a miniature sort of pastime.)

In the worship of Dionysus there was no separation between celebrants and congregation. We found something similar in the kris dancers of Bali. The followers of Dionysus were possessed by him and surrendered to the collective experience: that is one of the most valuable bequests in our legacy from the god. But the same kind of possession was ascribed to the Nuremberg rallies, and to the medieval outbreaks of mass hysteria which created the image of the Dance of Death. The 'surrender' to a play is not so unconditional: the audience's ordinary responses are to be enhanced not suppressed. This was the step which ancient Greek theatre took, away from total immersion, into an act of communal imagination in which both conscious and unconscious are brought together.

I do not mean to say that the theatre somehow tamed the forces it contained. Loss of self-awareness liberates the personality, and freedom from imaginative restraint detaches the individual from social convention. The followers of Dionysus placed themselves literally outside society, and people who do that are likely to be regarded as a threat to the established order in any age. His worship was dangerous and arousing, and the drama whose patron he became was able to surprise, disturb and shock its audience. To this day, it is the necessary function of theatre to jolt our consciousness, to liberate its audience from taboos and fossilized attitudes.

In the society that Dionysus originally invaded, the old tribes, led by kings and chieftains, were being absorbed by a political system later to become idealized by Western culture. (The fact that its benefits belonged to free citizens, but not to slaves, was a fact that not even the Dionysiac urge could change.) Responsibility was extended to the individual members of the tribe, and Pericles, the great Athenian statesman of the fifth century BC, explained that:

> Our constitution is called a democracy because power is in the hands not of a minority but of the whole people. When it is a question of settling private disputes, everyone is equal before the law; when it is a question of putting one person before another in positions of public responsibility, what counts is not membership of a particular class, but the actual ability a man possesses.

Pericles was articulating the growing stress on the person, as opposed to inherited position. The idea of an individual's uniqueness was exciting and powerful, but conflict was inherent in it, and conflict is the stuff of tragic drama. In Greece, as men formed themselves into larger and larger units cohering eventually into the city state, so obviously a person's place in society altered. The individual began to emerge from the tribe, and yet the archaic past was still uncomfortably close. A pantheon of gods lived on and still had meaning no matter how sophisticated Greek thinking may have become. The Greeks also revered the wealth and symbols of their tribal inheritance. In Delphi stands the ruined Treasury built by one of the Attic tribes to house the relics which recalled the ancient tribal inheritance. Delphi also housed the Oracle which could foretell the future and shed light on the unknown.

So the Greeks carried an awareness of the mysterious past, the unknowable future, and man's fallibility. These themes were dominant in early Greek civilization, and they were echoed in the conflict of educated, rational individuals pitted against the imperatives of a tribal past extending backwards into the night of history. Parricide, incest, ritual obligations to the dead, all were to be examined and re-ordered. Man was seen at the mercy of fate, of the gods, of his own individual freedom.

It seems appropriate that at about the same time that the democratic ideal was being articulated, when Athens under Pericles was at its most confident, actors should have followed the lead of Thespis and stepped out of the chorus to assert their own particular demands. In a society which now required the talents of its individuals, one way to explore and assert these lay in the creativity of mind and feeling which might be expressed in their different forms by a legislator, an architect, an athlete, a sculptor, a playwright. The transformation is symbolized in the visual arts by the difference between the bland and stereotyped features of archaic Greek sculpture and the vigorous human portraits of the classical period.

This movement towards the individual in art was not without strain. The need to be part of a collective society required expression too. As a result, the Greeks displayed anxiety about individuality and society, the one and the many, in all sorts of contexts. And although Athens saw the flowering of logic and ethics and was preoccupied with mathematics, geometry and astronomy, all of them means to rationalize the universe, it did not avoid the irrational. If there were powerful forces in man that resisted rational and logical explanation, they could not be walled up in the past. The Greek drama repeatedly tries to give voice to the mysteries of the human world. What cannot be rationalized demands to be expressed.

The theatre became the medium in which life's tensions were mercilessly exposed – man against the gods, against fate, against the past, and, of course, against himself. It was a form born of practical necessity: the art of drama had to fulfil and extend the function that ritual had performed in the past, enacting the process whereby man, the tragic hero, came to be involved in a new scheme of things, and to question his own role.

The questions were posed by playwrights, not abstractly, but by re-enacting familiar stories with the immediacy of theatre and transforming them by the arts of performance, the power of language, and a new and piercing vision of the world. The conflict which Dionysus himself embodies – half man, half god – stood at the heart of drama, and the playwright was the intermediary between the two. In former times the priest had been the communicator between the people and their gods, making contact through trance, visions and dreams. He tried to give meaning to the otherwise unfathomable forces that worked in human beings and in the natural world. The playwright was his successor: at some unrecorded moment, ritual became transformed into art.

It is impossible for us to know how far the alteration had proceeded before it dawned on those involved that they were doing something radically different from what had gone before. Both onlookers and active participants must have moved a crucial step away from the yoke of scrupulously repeating the same fixed pattern. The onlookers – the audience – must have found themselves able to permit and even to look for something new, a voice for the changes at work around them. At the same time the participants – the performers and the writers – must have found themselves free enough to respond to this need, and to draw on their own creativity to do so, instead of relying on an archaic vocabulary no longer rich enough to respond.

One person, the playwright, became the focus of the transformation. His personal vision crystallized it. In Athens, the power of these creators was great enough to fill the space left vacant by raw belief and compulsive trance. They were so much the voices of their society that the audience was not diminished by being content to observe rather than participate directly. It was their needs and their questions that the playwright addressed; the dramatist, the secular priest, offered a choice of moral directions and created through his art another way of mediating between the individual and the spiritual life.

Aeschylus was the first towering figure of the theatre, the first highly individualized voice. He was born in 525 BC and died at the age of seventy. According to Aristotle, it was he who introduced the second actor, so decisively expanding the possibilities of drama by allowing for interplay between individual characters. Aeschylus apparently inherited a chorus of fifty. In time he divided them into four groups of twelve, and twelve became the standard size of a chorus until later. The introduction of the two actors also marked the declining importance of the chorus. Aeschylus is thought to have written as many as ninety plays, of which only seven survive.

Aeschylus transformed the ancient Greek mythology, as told by Homer, into drama. The old mythology described the struggles of successive dynasties of gods for Olympian supremacy, as the city states were to struggle for the mastery of ancient Greece. The special vision of Aeschylus was to see victorious Athens as the newest cycle of that struggle; his particular genius was to weld the sequence into the cosmic tragedy which unfolds in his mighty trilogy, *The Oresteia*. It is a prototype of epic drama, unimpaired by time. Although Aeschylus deals with public and political life, with great historical or mythological events, and the fates of families, cities and nations, he echoes archaic ritual in recalling a lost golden age, a perfect world poisoned by death.

By dramatizing narrative, Aeschylus pointed the way for all succeeding playwrights. He capitalized on an ancient device which has always captivated human beings: the telling of stories. In their great poet, Homer, the Greeks possessed an oral treasure-house of history, myths, plot and counter-plot, told in epic language, and a style devised for narration to a live audience. These were stories of a long-lost past and a golden age, legends of enormous power which embodied the heroic ideal of what man should be and do and suffer. Aeschylus renewed Greek mythology in the theatre, but more than that, by enacting myth in the person of human individuals, he found a dramatic form and symbolism for society's unconscious.

The human condition, man's apparent inability to escape his fate, was the theme that haunted Sophocles. He was almost an exact contemporary of Pericles, born in 496 BC, when Aeschylus was already in his late twenties. Sophocles' long life – he lived to be ninety – was to span the great period of Athenian history. He refined the theatrical art so that its ritual origins were further submerged. By introducing a third actor, he again extended the potential for interaction between the characters themselves and between them and the chorus, which he increased to fifteen members.

Both as a man and as an artist, Sophocles represented an ideal to the people of his own time. In him they found all the gifts of great dramatic writing: to create a plot with meaning beyond itself, to use the full resources of language, to put character to work, and to move the action relentlessly onwards. Such gifts were not to appear again in one man until the birth of William Shakespeare, two thousand years later. In his youth Sophocles appeared as an actor and was trained in music and gymnastics. As a playwright he seems to have known success early, probably in his late twenties, and he was always a favourite with his audience. Economy and discipline stamp his plays: in *Electra* he reduced to a single play the material which Aeschylus had treated as a trilogy in *The Oresteia*.

One of his works, *Oedipus the King*, Aristotle considered the model drama, and Oedipus the model hero. The play defines its author's vision of man in relation to his inexorable fate. Oedipus is one of the most potent of all Greek myths and has become part of our universal mental landscape. The play stands as an ideal for the discipline of time, place and action that future societies were to admire and imitate as the 'three unities' – a single plot-line, which Aristotle called 'the imitation of one action', a time-span of little more than a day, and a narrow location. (It took a later age to turn these elements of ancient Greek drama into set rules for tragedy. Aristotle never defined them as such.) The subject matter of the play lasts for the duration of the play itself – real time and theatrical time are identical; the action takes place in one location, without a change of scene; and there is but a single plot.

Oedipus the King tells of the dreadful prophecy which is made at the birth of Oedipus: that he will grow up to murder his father and marry his mother. Whatever is done to ward off this fate serves only to make that fate more certain. The taboos against parricide and incest are painfully reinforced through events in which man is depicted as helpless in the face of an unalterable destiny decreed by irrational forces beyond his understanding and

Aeschylus (525–456 BC); Sophocles (496–406 BC); and the philosopher, Aristotle (384–322 BC).

control. In the sequel, *Oedipus at Colonus*, the hero, old and blind, after a long exile from Thebes, finds redemption born of suffering. In these plays man is ennobled by the vengeance and arbitrary injustice of the gods. He is not an innocent victim, but he is somehow sanctified as though by ordeal. Through his tragedies, Sophocles brings to his audience the dual experience of weeping over man's downfall yet at the same time rejoicing over the renewal of his spirit. That is the mysterious function of tragedy, alone of all poetic forms.

The poetic form is important because Sophocles, like Aeschylus, possessed his culture's most commonplace and precious gift, its language. If he was able to write about the most complex emotions with such economy, lyricism and sheer beauty of imagery, it was because those were the qualities of the instrument at his disposal, created by the audience who spoke it, and available to whoever could find them, as the Greek lyric poets also found them. Of that language, we are told that its characteristic qualities are clarity, grace and subtlety. Sophocles heightened, strengthened and dignified the language he found: the relationship was mutual, as between playwright and audience.

The quality of Athenian life and thought was also enriched by the development of drama as an art and of the theatre as an indispensable form of public expression. The plays themselves may seem to have made the connections with religion less overt, but the manner in which the drama was experienced and enjoyed had all the trappings of a communal act of worship.

Archaic religious ritual bequeathed a special legacy to its inheritor, the drama: the theatre was celebrated as an art in Athens at a sacred Festival of Drama, dedicated to Dionysus. Here culture was not private or esoteric but something to be enjoyed, and these concepts of festivity and celebration are important because they do not exclude the materialistic and popular elements in life. The Greeks enjoyed competition, and playwrights, like athletes, competed for prizes in a week-long festival known as the City Dionysia, which took place towards the end of March. Two days before it began, the citizens of Athens made their way at dawn to the Temple of Dionysus on the lower slopes of the Acropolis, a fairly large rectangular building where they pushed and shoved in the hope of playing their part in what amounted to a religious ceremony, presided over by priests, acolytes and attendants. It centred on a statue of Dionysus, which was lifted and placed in a cart, to be taken in procession to a shrine in the outlying village of Eleutherae. At dusk the statue was returned, this time by torchlight. They were celebrating the coming of Dionysus to Athens, and when they returned to the temple of the god and carried his statue a short way up the hill into the theatre named after him, then Dionysus was present in his theatre.

On the first morning of the City Dionysia the people made ready for a great public display of their city's artistic and literary pre-eminence in ancient Greece. All Athenian society was represented; even prisoners had been released on bail to take part in a grandiose street procession. Huge phalluses were carried to symbolize the god's gift of fertility, and a bull was led along the road for sacrifice. At sunrise the people thronged the theatre precinct. It was spring, the crops would grow, the sea was navigable again.

The festival was one of the year's high points, and the competition between the playwrights was itself a popular drama. As many as fourteen or fifteen thousand people probably attended. In the early days of the festival they had to buy their seats, which all cost the same, but when Pericles governed Athens he saw to it that the state paid for the seats of all needy citizens, which gives subsidy of the arts a most honourable ancestry, and shows how much the theatre meant to Greek society. The spectators came with picnics and lunch baskets, for they were to sit out in the spring sunshine all day long, and watch at least three tragedies, followed by the burlesque, and perhaps a comedy to send them home cheerful.

The opening of the City Dionysia was also attended by religious and civic dignitaries, the priests of Dionysus and the Archon, the chief magistrate of Athens. His duties included organizing the complicated system of judging the plays, and appointing a rich citizen to finance the productions. This man, the *choregus*, might be awarded a prize for the best production. The *choregus* was allowed a tax-free year, though the cost of providing properly lavish costumes for actors and chorus was probably far greater than his tax rebate. The sons of men killed in battle occupied seats of honour, and hundreds, perhaps thousands of visitors came from foreign states, but the majority of the audience were ordinary men and women from all sections of Athenian society.

The Athenian amphitheatre represented the egalitarian ideal, just as in future ages different theatrical structures would reflect the structure of the society that built and used them. Here the seating was more or less democratic. The audience sat on wooden benches, because the whole structure was made of wood. Next to nothing remains of those simple theatres of the golden age. The only relics are five stones that formed part of the supporting wall for the *orchestra*, the chorus space, of the Theatre of Dionysus. The theatres of the later period, such as the ones at Epidaurus, Dodona and Delphi, were built of stone but followed the same pattern, so that everybody could be concentrated on the performance. The spectators would look down on the circle of the orchestra, a slightly raised earth platform, and see beyond it a temporary wooden structure with three entrance doors. This was the *skene* (literally 'tent'). The actors changed inside it, and the performance took place in front of it. Painted canvases could be slotted in front of it to indicate the location of a scene. These backdrops are credited to the invention of Sophocles, but Aeschylus used them for his later plays. They were fairly simple but employed perspective.

Two pieces of machinery were called upon to enhance the illusion, cumbersome-sounding conventions, which the audience must have come to take for granted all the same. One was the *ekkuklema*, a sort of platform on wheels which was trundled out at the end of certain tragedies bearing, as you might expect, a great many dead bodies. The other was the *mekhane*, a type of crane which enabled actors to descend from on high as gods – hence the Latin phrase *deus ex machina*, the god from the machine, for a dramatic intervention.

Distance and reputation now incline us to think of Greek plays as lofty literary texts, demanding penetrating intellectual analysis from the director, and from the actors unusual ability to speak and clarify the dense and complex intentions of the playwright, if a performance is to have any life for a modern audience. These may be necessary preconditions, but in their own time the plays would have looked and sounded very different from anything we see today. We know that singing and dancing were major features of Greek tragedy, but we have no idea what sort of music was written and played in those times – although the Oxford Classical Dictionary remarks that 'it is very probable that if we could hear a piece of ancient Greek music properly performed, we should regard it as bizarre, uncouth, and possibly barbaric'! Nor do we have the faintest idea of Greek choreography. It is as if a modern musical were to be revived in the year 4500 AD with neither dancing nor singing, and with the lyrics either spoken or solemnly chanted.

If author or actors failed to please at the City Dionysia, the populace expressed rowdy disapproval. The audience had no inhibitions about pelting the performers with picnic leftovers, and dried fruit, pomegranates and tomatoes would rain down on the Thespians, accompanied by loud hissing and booing, hostile hand-clapping, and the sound of thousands of pairs of heels drumming against the backs of the wooden seats. That combined assault must have scotched the performance and presumably sent the actors fleeing for safety behind the *skene*.

These actors were professionals, paid by the state. Seeing that all of them were men, and that they were required to play many parts in a single play, both male and female, they must have been remarkably versatile. They were called by their contemporaries *hypocrites* which can sometimes mean 'interpreters of dreams and riddles' and the 'answerers of questions'. Behind the *skene* they put on the customary dress for playing tragedy. Each actor wore a mask, a sleeved robe and high-heeled boots, all of which had featured in the worship of Dionysus and were retained as symbols of devotion to the god. The costumes were brightly coloured and covered the player from head to foot, which was an aid to withdrawal from the everyday self.

Much academic controversy surrounds the mask. One school of thought claims that the mask enabled the actor to make quick changes from one role to the next. Theatrical experience and instinct point to what all actors know, that to wear a mask is a way of drastically changing one's persona. Make-up gives a slow transformation, and retains the structure of the face beneath; a mask is an absolute barrier, and by wearing it the actor makes a statement of total surrender to the part he is playing. The mask is a powerful device for the loss of personality: it aids possession. Even so, a further theory is advanced which claims that the mask concealed a small brass trumpet fitted to the mouthpiece, to help the actor in addressing so vast an audience.

This latter notion may have arisen out of yet another controversy, the debate about where the actor stood. Some believe that an altar occupied the centre of the orchestra, robbing the actor of the dominant position, and therefore forcing him to resort to artificial means in order to make himself heard. Here again, theatrical experience questions both propositions. If we know anything about actors, it is that they instinctively occupy the position which gives them the most power over the audience; conversely, the audience forces the actor towards that position because it is likely to be restless if he strays. We are not dealing with a modern theatre, or plays with large casts where the position of the other actors can focus attention on the speaker. In the Greek theatre the point of focus is in the very centre of the *orchestra*.

In any case, one of the most remarkable features of the open-air Greek amphitheatre was its acoustics: masked or unmasked, clear speech requires no aid. There is no evidence for the Greeks possessing any special science of acoustics. It may be that they built theatres in which actors could be heard without strain simply because they were a society that believed in communication. They talked to each other, were keen to exchange ideas, and wanted to listen. The acoustics of a theatre, like its structure, tells us a lot about the society which built it. The Greeks heard because they wanted to listen.

On the final day of the great Festival of Drama, there were two main events: the prizes were awarded to the poets and actors chosen by the judges, and the punishments were handed out to those who had misbehaved. These penalties could be extremely severe, for the City Dionysia was a sacred event, and the public were expected to behave with proper decorum. We are not told how those who showed such vigorous disapproval of the performances were dealt with, but violence during the festival was punishable by death.

Both Aeschylus and Sophocles were frequent prize winners. Between them they had created the dramatic form of tragedy, and their genius had helped to shape the art of theatre out of the raw material of ritual and cult-worship and the needs and changes of a new age. But even their achievements were to be questioned, rebelled against, transformed. A third dramatist of towering gifts appeared to purge any complacency that may have set in, to vex the public order, and, like all rebels, to suffer for his pains. In the words of the theatrical historian Margarete Bieber: 'When Euripides (c. 484–406) appeared, the external and internal structure of tragedy had been completed. It would ... never have attained the significance for the world's history, literature and civilization had not this philosopher among the poets altered it again.'

The portrait of Euripides, a bust made in old age, bears witness to a character formed by determination, struggle and disappointment. He has retained something of his youthful arrogance, but there is a hint of aggression that makes him seem all the more dangerous. Given the hardship he endured, and the lack of early success, it is no wonder that by the end of his life he had learned to put up defences. Euripides turned to the theatre comparatively late,

Left Euripides (484–*c*.406 BC), and *right*, a frieze depicting actors assembled before Dionysus.

when he was almost thirty. His early training had been in painting, and then philosophy. He did not win a prize in the City Dionysia until he was forty, and had to wait fourteen years before he won another. His masterpiece, *The Bacchae*, was not performed until after his death, when it was awarded a posthumous prize.

Contemporary recognition came hard. Comedians satirized him, and we are told that he often appeared as a figure of fun in works by other dramatists. He was often defeated by lesser poets, but long before he died he had won a great reputation throughout the Greek world. Plutarch, in his *Life of Nicias*, says that Athenian prisoners held captive in Syracuse during the cruelly fought Peloponnesian War could escape death and even received their freedom if they could recite passages from the work of Euripides. Aristotle called him 'the most tragic' of the poets. In the popular imagination he was thought of as a gloomy recluse who never laughed.

Of the three great dramatists, he was the closest to the modern mind. He was interested in politics, addressed himself to the younger intellectuals, and was sceptical of established values and beliefs. The awesome gods who peopled Aeschylus' imagination held no terrors for him. He seems to have wanted to reduce the legendary heroic past to a human scale. The fictional characters he created were to be recognizable mortals. The dramatic interplay of the protagonists interested him more than the chorus, whom he reduced to chanting commentators on the main action. He also introduced a prologue which spoke for the dramatist himself.

Towards the end of his life, Euripides was living in self-imposed exile in Macedonia, and there he wrote a play in brutal contrast to his earlier work. For a man who had placed himself against the mainstream of Athenian life, a theatrical revolutionary, regarded as an atheist, his great work, *The Bacchae*, must seem all the more extraordinary. Euripides had preached the doctrine of

Heraclitus, who asserted that the basic condition of life was change, and the basic element fire; he attacked the gods, denounced the seers and oracles, and proclaimed that dreams and divination were meaningless. He was the personification of the new order, the move towards reason. Yet the paradox is that this man's last complete play, possibly written in the year before his death, has an impact more religious than almost any other play of the century before it.

In *The Bacchae*, Euripides sees the gods – Dionysus in particular – as an overwhelming force against which there is no resistance. The work is composed in an archaic form, untypical of his style, using ancient cult hymns in the choruses. At the close of the great period of Athenian drama comes a play which centres upon the god of the theatre and is steeped in religious mystery. In no other work is the cult of Dionysus so rapturously described. Through a savage exposure of suppressed inclinations, the human being becomes the sacrifice, the sacred means of communion with the god. It is a work which burns with the power of the theatre and gives insights into the reasons why the drama was needed by the Greeks, as it has been by the civilizations that followed. In *The Bacchae*, the expression of the irrational is uncompromising and defiant.

The story of the play brings Dionysus, an invader from the east, to Thebes, which has rejected him. The king, Pentheus, is particularly sceptical because he shares the belief of the rest of his family – his mother Agave included – that Dionysus' mother, Semele, had pretended to have slept with a god in order to cover up her own immorality. Dionysus retaliates against finding himself opposed by driving the Theban women mad, and once possessed they go up into the mountains of Cythaeron and live as Bacchae, followers of the god. Pentheus has Dionysus arrested and brought before him for interrogation. In this early scene he appears the more dominant figure – a king, a traditional Greek aristocrat, arrogant but no fool, he knows that Dionysus is a threat to the continuance of the society he rules. Dionysus contains the duality of the male and female instincts in perfect balance. To Pentheus this means effeminacy; he mocks and despises Dionysus, and has him thrown into prison. There is a great cry, a thunderbolt, an earthquake, and the palace of Pentheus falls. Dionysus is free again. Pentheus searches for him, only to find his own power is waning.

Slowly, craftily, Dionysus tempts the king with the idea of seeing the Bacchic revels in the mountains. The imbalance between god and king grows clearer. Pentheus is all masculinity; Dionysus is androgynous. Pentheus has suppressed the feminine in his own nature, and Dionysus plays on the weakness. In a powerful scene of enticement, he tempts Pentheus to dress as a bacchante and set out for Mount Cythaeron. When Pentheus emerges in female dress, carrying the thyrsus, the sacred wand of the Bacchae, wreathed with ivy and vine leaves, he is a comically macabre figure. The masculine ruler of Thebes has been reduced to a gulled grotesque. The balance of the play has tipped: Dionysus is now the superior figure, with Pentheus subservient to his will.

Dionysus leads Pentheus up the mountain and there uses the strength of a god to bend a pine tree to the ground and bind the king to it. Then he lets it spring back, and shouts to his followers, the Bacchae, that there is a man spying on them. The women pull down the tree by sheer weight of numbers, and Pentheus falls into the arms of his mother Agave, lost in frenzy. He tries to tell her who he really is, and pleads for his life, but she is possessed by the power of the god. Unable to hear or see her son, she wrenches off his head. The other Bacchic women tear Pentheus apart and play with bits of his flesh as though with a ball.

The Bacchae ends with Agave coming down into Thebes holding a head which she deludedly sees as a lion's, but which is, of course, the head of her son. The moment of her realization is one of the most agonizing in all Greek tragedy, as she gives a howl of horror and anguish. The body of Pentheus, what remains of it, is brought on stage and Agave mourns over each dismembered piece. Finally, enter the *deus ex machina*: Dionysus reappears to deal out punishment to each character. The god is without mercy, the sentence beyond justice. All must pay the price of exile or worse. There is no hero. We are left with the unburied body in an otherwise empty city.

Man and the god cannot be reconciled, but his terrible power may not be mocked. Euripides gave a form to the dilemma faced by himself and perhaps many others in his time: the struggle of the man of conscious intellect to acknowledge forces beyond his control and immune to rational understanding. They will not be ignored, and yet cannot be fought. The impression is of reason and passion, earth and heaven, perpetually at war.

Like us, not all of Euripides' audience would have grasped every word of his stylized poetry. Nevertheless the Greeks believed that tragedy caused something profound to take place, a sort of mystery. Aristotle called it catharsis, which can be taken to mean purification, as from pollution, or flushing out, as by a purgative. The assumption is that the emotional stresses within us, often subconscious, and the moral contradictions too, likely to be equally deeply buried, need to be relieved and resolved. By losing our everyday awareness of ourselves and by identifying with the actors – themselves divested of self in the drama's heightened world – we expose ourselves to the full force of their sufferings and sins as we may never be able to admit our own, and the effect is relief. We license what we repress, the spirit of Dionysus again, possession by the god. Aristotle thought that to witness tragedy in a theatre is one of the ways by which human beings can be purged of stress and inner conflict. Our own pity and fear draw us towards a point of balance, he believed, and from this comes a sense of health, and therefore of pleasure.

The Greeks believed that life was to be enjoyed, but they also knew its pains and terrors, and their own vulnerability to its dark and irrational forces. Tragedy was a means to contain and express the paradox, but it was also an end in itself, the creation of something for the living even out of death. At the same time the Greeks also understood that laughter too could possess and purge an audience – after all, what could be more irrational, less subject to conscious control, than laughter? Nothing was too sacred for the Greeks to laugh at, not even Dionysus himself, and the same century that heard the tragic howl of Agave returning to her senses could laugh at the comic spirit that was to power the next great explosion of theatrical life.

NOW COMES
MY COMEDY

Why an audience should submit itself to the harrowing of tragedy it is hard to say, and the challenge has produced volumes of critical definition and analysis. With comedy, there is no such problem. It makes us laugh. There is a story in Plato's *Symposium* about the contribution of the great comic writer Aristophanes to a discussion of the nature of comedy. According to Plato, Aristophanes fell asleep. In an age when comedians and writers of comedy are at pains to stress the serious social content of their work, one can only sympathize with him. So anyone who wants to question the need for laughter has to listen for the sound of Aristophanes snoring.

It seems that there has always been a need for comic writers and actors, and what we know of the history of comedy suggests that its concerns in ancient times were much the same as they are today. The nature of tragedy has changed, but not the nature of comedy. Contemporary dramatists no longer ask us to weep for a deposed king, but they continue to invite our laughter at cuckolds and hypocrites. The comic spirit is eternal, and has never been far away from the genuinely popular forms of theatrical experience. Although it is bound to have serious implications – not least for the lethal hostility that laughter can contain – comedy is more immediately perceived as entertainment. The word itself is derived from the Greek *komos*, meaning a revel, an occasion for merrymaking, which suggests that drama has more than one way of embodying the licence and riot of Dionysus.

Comedy expresses the recognition that life will not be denied and had better be enjoyed. In its relation to the life of ancient man in particular, these ideas are present in rituals encouraging living things to reproduce themselves, and asking the gods to assist the process. Early comedy instinctively admitted what later ages edged away from as obscene and salacious, because human sexual energy too was understood to be part of the fruitfulness of life – so that in much of early comedy, the phallus is a familiar symbol. Comedy is a celebration of life, and just as the death of the hero was obligatory in tragedy, so the happy ending was the gift of comedy.

According to Aristotle, another important element of the *komos*, the revel, was that it originally contained songs abusing unpopular people. Society seems to have been ready to license satire on its kill-joys and repressers, and on aspects of its own behaviour which worked against the forces of life. Man had discovered that one of the healthiest ways of dealing with the intolerable was to make fun of it. In this respect, that it works as a psychological release, an arena for the full expression of powerful forces, comedy can be compared with tragedy. And to find the roots of the comic tradition, we have to return again to the theatrical forms of ancient Greece.

As in Greek tragedy, comedy made use of a chorus wearing masks, often animal masks. Margarete Bieber suggests that the reason was the reluctance to be recognized when delivering criticism and abuse of fellow citizens, though the loss of self which the mask engendered would presumably have been found to favour comic invention. According to Aristotle improvisation was an early feature of comedy, when the leaders of the phallic ceremonies and reciters of phallic songs would step forward to deliver their spontaneous orations. In time, the leader of the chorus came to represent the author's voice, directly addressing the audience like a modern stand-up comic. This figure was to become the Prologue who set the mood of the play, anticipated the plot, and in general took the spectators into his confidence. Comedy talked about itself; theatrically, it was allowed to be self-conscious. The following lines were written by Aristophanes for *The Clouds*, which had its première in Athens in 423 BC:

Now comes my comedy – just like Electra in the play, finding her
   brother's lock of hair, and knowing she'll be saved;
My play's the same, praying to find an audience as appreciative as those
we had before!
This is a *decent* piece, mind! For a start, you won't get actors waving
   damn great red-tipped tools to give the kids a giggle, poking fun at bald
   old men, or going through a filthy bump-and-grind routine!
No old boy in *this* comedy's going to play at slapstick just to cover up a lot
   of corny gags!
No torch-lit spectacles, shouting about, no song and dance; this play relies
   entirely on its own merits.
You know me: I'm a poet, but not one of the long-haired, the hairy-fairy
   types! I'm not the sort to give you a repeat and put it over as a new idea!
Not me!
Mine are original, they're always new!
And everyone's a winner!

Aristophanes was a brilliantly inventive dramatist, and loved to be bawdy and scurrilous, yet his comedy had an important purpose. He was a devastating satirist who attacked and lampooned leading politicians, soldiers, philosophers, poets, anyone who seemed to him to be acting against the interests of the people. Among others, Pericles, Demosthenes, Nicias and Euripides appear as characters in his plays. Socrates too is parodied in *The Clouds*, and it is said that he stood up during one performance to let the audience acknowledge the accuracy of the portrait. Not all the playwright's victims were quite so secure in themselves. Aristophanes received no honorary statue, as the tragic writers did.

'Captive Greece captivated its captors.'

The Romans, obliged to look back on a golden age of drama, were nevertheless inspired by its example, and encouraged to adapt it to their own use.
Above a kylix from Ferrara depicts the murder of Clytemnestra, an ancient myth elemental to the Greek classical theatre.

Left a vase fragment at Syracuse depicts a performer of phlyakes, the ribald farces which were precursors of Roman comedy.
Right for tragedy, the later Greek elaborations – the high onkos, or headdress, and cothurni, or boots – set the grandiose style for Roman performance, as is seen in this ivory statuette.
Below a tomb mural of 470 BC gives an idea of the musical accompaniment of the time.

From a tomb painting of the 5th century BC,
a funeral chorus. Out of the rhythms and
patterns of ritual, the drama was emerging
(Museo Nazionale, Naples).

Above and *right* Roman actors of the 3rd
century BC, preparing with their dressers.
From frescoes now in the Museo Archeologico Nazionale, Naples.

Left a scene from a phlyakes farce: Zeus is about to mount the ladder to the chamber of his mistress, Alcmene.
Below a green room study of actors, dressers and musicians, from a mosaic at Naples.

From Milan, a vase depicting a scene from an early Italian comedy.

Aristophanes took politics very seriously. Born around 450 BC, he was a young man at the outbreak of the Peloponnesian War, the conflict between Athens and Sparta which lasted more than a quarter of a century and spanned the better part of the playwright's maturity. Aristophanes opposed the war and the bellicose Athenian statesmen, from Pericles to Cleophon, who backed it. One such leader, the demagogue Cleon, was his target in *The Babylonians*; Aristophanes was impeached for that, but got off lightly. He called himself 'the poet who risked his life to tell Athens the truth'. Even in the twentieth century, he risked becoming a non-person: when the Colonels seized power in Greece, they banned his plays. He died in his early sixties, having written some forty plays of which eleven survive.

Greek comedy drew on the rituals and revels of the archaic past to celebrate procreation and continuity. Another, if unlikely, contribution to the comic tradition was made by the philosopher Theophrastus, a pupil of Aristotle, born *c.* 372 BC, whose most lasting work, *Characters*, consisted of thirty brief and vigorous sketches identifying moral types. To give a taste of his style and thinking, here is his definition of *The Lout:*

The lout is the type who, when he meets womenfolk, lifts up his clothes and displays his private parts; who claps in the theatre when everyone else has stopped and hisses at actors the rest of the audience are enjoying, and when you could hear a pin drop, he lifts up his head and belches to make people turn round. In company he calls complete strangers by name as if he were a life-long friend. If he sees people in a hurry somewhere he calls out 'Wait a moment!' When his mother comes back from consulting some fortune teller, he goes out of his way to use ill-omened words. If he wants to spit, he does it over the table at the slave who is serving wine.

The theatre quickly absorbed the possibilities of this kind of character delineation, and was to develop the notion of 'stock characters' as a helpful way of observing and possibly identifying one's fellow men. If clichés are truths found worth repeating, these stereotypes, strong and well defined, are rooted in familiar recognition. They tend to divide into the two opposing camps of those who assist and who interfere with the enjoyment of life. The tension between the two often causes the laughter. The lover, the courtesan, the slave, the stern father, the miser, the money-grubbing pimp – we laugh *with* those who champion life and we laugh *at* those who don't. The playwright Menander, more than any other, was to create a comic tradition, drawing on a gallery of stock characters, which survives in our own time, still fuelled by the longevity of its subjects – one ancient critic asked of his work: 'O Menander, O Life, which of you imitated the other?'

At the time of Menander's birth, in 342 BC, Athens was weakened by war and in decline. Comedy no longer concerned itself with public affairs, not for reasons of indifference, but because the political situation had radically altered. Athens was no longer an independent city state, but a province under the rule of Macedonia. The freedom of speech which had spurred Aristophanes no longer existed, and Athens itself was displaced from the centre of affairs. As a university town, it retained some of its old philosophical and scientific distinction, but now it was a provincial place. Satire was no longer possible: it was not just that it had become politically dangerous, but that society now lacked the confidence and energy to undertake merciless probes of its own shortcomings. Menander and others therefore turned their attention to the events of everyday life, to sexual intrigue, adultery, money – the perpetual themes.

We know that Menander was influenced by the great tragedians, especially Euripides, and that he attended the lectures of Theophrastus. He was also a friend of his immediate contemporary Epicurus, whose philosophy came to influence his work. It is a reminder of the distance the theatre had travelled from its ritual origins that already it could find room for the intellectual cross-currents of its own time, as the comedy of manners has done ever since. In Menander this is particularly striking because his Epicureanism was not the hedonistic doctrine of its later reputation, preaching pleasure or happiness as the chief good: the ideal of Epicurus was of freedom from pain, and imperturbable serenity and tranquillity in suffering.

Menander's tone could be austere and moral – crime never pays, greed is always ugly – his language clear and simple. His characters may dictate the action of the play, or at least remain true to their own individuality, but always as the pawns of chance. They are neither caricatures nor cardboard cutouts, but are free to strike a variety of attitudes, liable to make mistakes, and frequently weak. Menander is often sympathetic towards women while he ridicules men, whom he accepts all the same for their failings as well as their virtues. In the main he is tolerant, but he does not hide his approval for those who are kind and understanding, or stifle his scorn for the avaricious, the pompous, the phony or the hidebound – for instance the older generation unsympathetic towards the young.

For centuries Menander was known to posterity only indirectly, through fragments of his work quoted by contemporaries or by later writers, and by imitation and reputation. But in 1905 a papyrus, now in Cairo, was discovered which contains substantial portions of four plays and gives insights into the style and content of his work. A complete play, *The Curmudgeon*, was discovered in Cairo as late as 1957, one out of the hundred or more which he is thought to have written. Little is known of his personal life, and he is supposed to have died by drowning while swimming in the Piraeus, the port of Athens.

From the little that has been salvaged we know that love was a constant theme in Menander. He was the first playwright to present ordinary situations taken from life, especially from the life of the rich Athenian middle class. A favourite motif was of the love of a rich youth for a poor girl who had been abandoned as a baby (this is a borrowing from tragedy) but who remained a decent girl; at the end of the play she is reunited with her long-lost parents and marries her lover. Remember that in ancient Athens the abandonment of babies was permitted, so there would be nothing shocking about this plot. A distinctive feature is the way the fate which governs the characters in tragedy is replaced in the comedies of Menander by chance, accident and coincidence, artificial conventions to propel the plot.

The reasonableness of Menander comes across in the brief philosophical sayings for which he was especially admired. Some of them are not unfamiliar:

He whom the gods love dies young.
We live not as we wish but as we can.
Evil communications corrupt good manners.
If one faces the truth, marriage is an evil, but a necessary evil.
It is impossible to find anyone whose life is free from trouble.

There is one passage in particular which expresses his attitude to life and reveals a mind that is lively, elegant and civilized:

I count it happiness,
Ere we go quickly thither whence we came,
To gaze ungrieving on these majesties,
The world-wide sun, the stars, water and clouds,
and fire. Live, Parmeno, a hundred years
Or a few months, these you will always see
and never, never, any greater things.

Think of this life-time as a festival
Or visit to a strange city, full of noise,
Buying and selling, thieving, dicing stalls
And joy parks. If you leave it early, friend,
Why, think you have gone to find a better inn:
You have paid your fare and leave no enemies.

The bawdy vigour of Aristophanes and the bitter-sweet genius of Menander, separated by more than a hundred years, are the polar limits of ancient Greek comedy, and the latter represents the final echoes of the great explosion of Athenian drama. By the third century BC the simplicity and purity of the golden age were gone. Theatres were no longer built of wood, but solid stone. The position of the playwright had been usurped by the actor who did not surrender his personality to the part, and was beyond allowing himself to be possessed in the Dionysiac sense, but stood on a raised platform the better to exhibit his individual personality. In time he would remove his mask so that he could be more easily recognized for the celebrity he was; he would rewrite the old tragedies in order to improve his role, although a fourth-century edict imposed severe penalties for such deviations.

After that time, the individual, both in society and in the theatre, became increasingly important and increasingly self-absorbed. Thus was lost all connection with the divine, and the kind of comedy that survived concerned itself with man at his most human, fallible and earth-bound. What the theatre gained was the human being on a stage, speaking in a recognizably human voice,

Left a moment from Menandrian new comedy – a mosaic now in Naples. *Right* a terracotta figurine of an early comic actor.

with a face laid bare to the audience. The theatre had relinquished the dimension of mystery, but gods and masks were not the key to that dimension, even if they were its most imposing gateway. The separation was not permanent.

The glorious achievements of the ancient Greeks have come to be seen as a pinnacle in the history of civilization. The art of the drama, like other expressions of their culture, set a standard for later ages, and most immediately for the Romans, who learned from the Greeks and recognized a debt to them. Although they were obliged to look back on a golden age of drama, they were nevertheless inspired by its example, and encouraged to adapt it to their own use. They were a practical people, and one of their surprising virtues was the ability to learn from the people they conquered. What they took from the Greeks was the model of their art and literature: as Horace pointed out, captive Greece captivated its captors.

Not that the theatrical tradition of ancient Rome was altogether without its own individuality. According to the historian Livy, actors – some of them slaves – first appeared in the city in 364 BC, in rituals intended to appease the gods in time of plague. Once again we find the element of religion and magic catalysing the beginnings of drama. But the earliest signs of Greek influence can be identified in the Greek settlements of southern Italy, where the theatre played an important role. The theatre of Syracuse, dedicated in about 460 BC, was known as the oldest and most beautiful in Sicily, and it was the south which brought its own dramatic form to the shaping of comedy.

There a kind of farce was acted by performers known as the *phlyakes*, which means 'gossips'. An impression of their style is vividly preserved on many vases of the period. The actors wore ill-fitting tights, padding, a grotesque mask and, inevitably, a huge leather phallus. They parodied the gods, tragic drama and everyday life. Stock characters were used, but more importantly their coarse humour was improvised, for in the beginning improvisation was common to all drama, but fell into disrepute with the rise of the individual playwright. In comedy, it persisted, and has continued to do so. It is a means of discovering the sudden insight, letting in the new and unexpected, and introducing the exciting dramatic ingredient of danger by creating fast tempos or spiralling flights of fancy which may die if not developed from one split second to the next, and bring the performance down with them.

In the city of Rome and round about it there also existed another strong comic tradition, a particularly Italian type of farce from Atella, a town between Naples and Capua. As a form it was rustic, and probably obscene, and its themes were cheating, trickery and general tomfoolery. But as with the *phlyakes*, its most interesting feature from our point of view was the use of stock characters: Bucco, the glutton or braggart; Pappus, the foolish old man; Dossenus, the cunning swindler; Maccus, the fool, the half-witted clown. The story goes that it was one of the actors renowned for playing Maccus who became the focus and expression of all the streams of comedy, under the name of Titus Maccius (or Maccus, probably because of his expert clowning) Plautus.

He is thought to have been born some time in the 250s BC, and died in 184 BC.

Legend has it that Plautus made a fortune as an actor, invested the money in commerce, lost every penny, and began to write comedies while working as a labourer in a flour mill. Although the tale is doubted by scholars, it has to me the ring of theatrical truth, for it seems likely that the greatest Roman comedian was in that splendid tradition of actor turned dramatist. He based all his plays on Greek models, and on the comic inventions and improvisations of his native land, using the Prologue to great effect, more often than not as a means of getting the audience to laugh as soon as possible. He is the author of the shortest Prologue on record:

> If you want to get up and stretch your legs, best do it now. We've a play by Plautus next – and it's a long one!

Plautus, like Menander, also used the Prologue to prepare the audience for the most excruciatingly complicated plots, whose convolutions were all part of the fun. A good example is the Prologue to *The Pot of Gold*:

> In case you're wondering who I am, I'll tell you briefly: I am the *Lar* – the god of this household here. I've been in charge of the place for years now – yes, I looked after it for the father and grandfather of the man who owns it today.
> (confidentially)
> Now, long ago, in great secrecy, the grandfather of the present owner entrusted to my care a hoard of gold. He buried it under the fireplace in the centre of the house and begged me to keep it safe for him. Well, he was a miser; he had no intention of telling his son about the treasure; he preferred to leave him without a penny! When he died, I began to wonder if the son would show me any more regard than the father had. Huh! He cared even less than his father, showed me less and less respect, so I did the same for him, and he died a poor man, leaving the son who owns the place today. Now – he's a miser, the same as his father and grandfather before him – *but* he has this daughter, and she's always praying to me, every day she brings me offerings of incense and wine or something, gives me garlands of flowers. Out of regard for her, then, I saw to it that Euclio, her father, found the gold –
> (out of character; to the audience)
> the treasure, that entrusted to me by her father's father's father. Have you got all that? I'm so glad ... eh? Oh dear, there's a man at the back says he can't hear ... well, come a little closer then! Can't find a seat? Well, go and perambulate yourself outside, then! Want me to lose my job? If you think I'm going to bust a gut to suit you, you can think again! Now then, where was I?
> (serious again)

Ah, yes. I've seen to it that old Euclio – that's the girl's father – has discovered the treasure (remember? good!) so he'll be able to find a decent husband for her.

(confidential)

Now listen, this is no hackneyed version of another play. This play's different! There aren't any filthy lines you can't repeat, and there's no double-dealing pimp, or loose women, and no wind-bag military types either ... But you see, a young man of excellent family has had his way with Euclio's daughter. *He* knows who *she* is, all right, but *she* doesn't know who *he* is (it *was* dark!) and her father doesn't know anything at all. Here's what I'm going to do: I'll get the old man who lives next door to ask for her hand in marriage. That way it'll make it easier for the young man to marry her himself...

What strikes the listener straight away is the directness of approach: it eliminates the two thousand years between, and makes one aware how little the comic spirit has changed. The devices used in Plautus' time are still working today, especially the actor's banter with his audience, and easy relationship with them, as between old friends. Plautus was a veteran actor with fine theatrical instincts. He used his inheritance from the Greeks and grafted on to it the wealth of native farce and the vitality of his own genius. He was not interested only in plot, but in character too, so when he took in the Atellan stock types he fleshed them out and made human beings of them. His favourite theme was the love of an extravagant or innocent youth for a courtesan or daughter of a worthy citizen, and the way he is helped by the cunning and trickery of a slave. This impudent, scheming figure was an inspired creation, and immensely popular: he is illustrated by any number of masks and statuettes unearthed in Italy.

With Plautus we are a long way, in every sense, from the fine stone theatres of Greece and the dignity of Greek drama. The tradition of farce and comedy they worked in dictated that he and his actors performed in temporary stage buildings, touring the country, travelling from town to town as Thespis is supposed to have done, and many a long-forgotten company after him. They played at public games and festivals, five or six men and a flute player, setting up their makeshift stage and giving the public what they wanted: comedies, and especially comedies by Plautus. With Plautus, the actors could rely on belly-laughs and popularity, and the audience looked forward not just to his ribald humour but also to his wit, songs and charm. Many of his plot devices are part of the playwright's armoury to this day – confusion of identity, overheard conversations, recognition, frustrated lovers united, the world restored to order and wholeness. Although his plays are seldom revived in English, their influence has been enormous.

In particular, his plots have been borrowed by dramatists ever since. An interesting case is *The Brothers Menaechmi*, with a plot as complicated as any he ever wrote. The machinations revolve around a set of twins and the consequent misunderstandings. Shakespeare used the device, but doubled the number of twins and quadrupled the misunderstandings in *The Comedy of Errors*. In 1938, Rodgers and Hart used *The Comedy of Errors* as a basis for their musical *The Boys from Syracuse*, and as recently as 1962, *A Funny Thing Happened on the Way to the Forum* was a successful stage show and later a popular film. In England, a television series called *Up Pompeii* attracted huge audiences in the eary 1970s with scripts that were closely based on dialogue and plots by Plautus.

In comedy, the continuity of tradition and content is possibly clearer than in any other theatrical form, for it can be demonstrated not only in terms of plot and literary influence, but also in theatrical practice. The Prologues which Plautus wrote require a special kind of performer: no lines, however funny they may be to read, will evoke so much as a titter if the actor delivering them does not possess a comic gift. Nowadays there is a great deal of stress laid on 'timing', which might be defined as an instinct to deliver the lines at exactly the right moment – to know how long an audience can be kept waiting. While this talent is certainly useful, I believe that the very finest comedians and comic actors possess a gift of greater importance, and which is a part of their personality: a highly individual tension within the performer which causes the audience to anticipate laughter. The words of Plautus imply this kind of actor, and depend on him, as do the words of all writers of comedy.

The dénouement of Shakespeare's *The Comedy of Errors*: after a painting by John Francis Rigaud (1742–1810).

In a more formal sense, the tradition of improvisation, stock characters, and knockabout situations with obscene overtones has infected the writing of farce whenever and wherever there has been farce at all. Georges Feydeau, Arthur Pinero, Brandon Thomas (the author of one of the genre's classics, *Charley's Aunt*) and Ben Travers all have relied on the devices first made workable by Aristophanes, Menander and Plautus. And we shall meet them again later in this narrative, in the form of the Italian *Commedia dell'Arte*; although no one can prove that this is directly descended from Roman comedy, it plays to the same audience and calls on the same techniques.

The farcical knockabout tradition is one side of the development of comedy, but Rome produced a subtler influence and a mind more in key with the best of Roman culture. It belonged to the author of the famous saying: '*Homo sum: humani nil a me alienum puto. Vel me monere hoc vel percontari puta; rectumst ego ut faciam; non est te ut deterream.*' 'I'm a human being: nothing that concerns a man is a matter of indifference to me. Call it solicitude or curiosity. If you're right, I can do the same; if you're wrong, I can try and stop you.' It is hard luck on Terence to have been translated into the gloomy half-world of the dictionaries of quotations; many of his successors among the comic dramatists would have been pleased to take these words as their motto.

Terence is said to have been born a slave in North Africa in about 195 BC, and would have been eleven years old when Plautus died. He was brought to Rome by his master, who educated and then freed him. His fine looks and intelligence took him into the aristocratic literary circles where he liked to move. Unlike Plautus, he generally made little appeal to popular taste, and consequently most of his six plays were failures. Four of them were based on plays by Menander, whom he idolized. His humour was subtle, and in general he did not favour farce or exaggerated characterization. Terence died young, and one account of his death is tinged with tragi-comedy: he is said to have gone to Greece in search of plays by Menander suitable for adaptation, and there to have died from grief because the baggage containing the new plays he had written had been lost. Even if the story is not true it symbolizes what Aristophanes discovered, and the biographies of many later comic and humorous writers confirm, namely that making people laugh is no joke.

In his last years, Terence realized that times were changing. He sensed that the theatre as he knew it was in decline, and put these words into the mouth of his actor-manager, Lucius Ambivius Turpio:

This play is *The Mother-in-Law*, a repeat performance, since we were never given a decent hearing before. There has been a jinx on this production! Something has always gone wrong. You can make up for that if you give me your sympathetic support this time.

At the first performance, people got wind of some boxers, and a tight-rope walker appearing, and the crowd of their supporters, all the commotion, and the cries of the womenfolk, forced me to abandon the play prematurely. Then I decided to revive an old practice of mine and try a second time. I put it on again. The first act was going down well when suddenly news came that there was to be a gladiators' show. The people swarmed together, there was confusion, pandemonium, they were fighting for a place! Well, I stood no chance: I just left. Today, however, there is no disturbance; it is peaceful and quiet. This is just my chance to present the play, and your chance to pay the theatre some respect.

That plea for the theatre fell on deaf ears, and the speech itself contains the explanation: the majority of people wanted spectacle, gladiators, jugglers, boxers and acrobats. The traditional Roman virtues of gravity, severity and dignity were soon to count for nothing. By the time of Christ's birth, Augustus Caesar, the first emperor of Rome, had been in power for more than twenty years, dominating an area which included Europe, North Africa, Asia Minor and beyond. He and his successors were among the most powerful men who have ever lived, and it was a material power, enforced by armies and expressed by stone and gold. Materialism flourished in all its varieties, wealth flooded into the city, and a mad race for money, luxury and enjoyment developed. Religion, the pagan religion of Rome, lost its hold.

For the theatre, it is a sad paradox that the great age of Roman drama did not coincide with the great age of theatre building: they were out of tune with one another. In the heyday of Plautus and Terence there were no permanent theatres in Rome, and for a curiously puritanical reason. It was believed that a permanent theatre with seats would be harmful to public morals. Each time an attempt was made to build a theatre, it was prevented. The Roman general Pompey was to find a cunning way around these restrictions: he placed a shrine to an important goddess behind the seats on the top of what is called the *cavea*, the auditorium. The result was that the seats became steps to the shrine. It was one thing to pull down theatres, another to desecrate temples: the breach had been made. Theatre construction became more and more elaborate, with linen awnings to protect the audience from the sun, and extravagant seating and stage buildings. Soon they became temples to spectacle.

The Colosseum, for example, could seat nearly 50,000 people. There Romans could watch gladiators fight against each other, or against exotic wild beasts; the place could even be flooded for mock naval battles. The theatre was necessary to Imperial Roman society, but not for drama, and not for the quasi sacred purposes of the Greeks. The satirist Juvenal said that only two things interested the masses – bread and circuses – and the more spectacular the circus the better it pleased. Rome was very wealthy, but its population was very large, and generally uneducated and illiterate, in a free-for-all economy where the unemployed could number as many as 150,000. At one period there were nearly six months of public holidays. The masses had to be kept diverted, pinned down to the passing moment. That meant cramming their senses and dulling their minds; the theatres were filled with spectacles unequalled for gaudiness, lavishness and brutality. The most popular of all events was spilling human blood.

Spectacle was not the only form of entertainment, however, and all over the empire the Romans built new theatres or adapted Greek ones, making them more grandiose and less democratic, with special seats for the favoured few. The Roman theatre echoed the class structure of society, each class seated in a different gallery separated by barriers. One factor worth noting here for its influence on a later age is that during the period of all this building, an architect called Vitruvius was at work on a massive ten-volume treatise on his subject, *De architectura*. Book V dealt with theatre construction and was illustrated by diagrams. Vitruvius did not concern himself with what was performed in the theatres which he went to such pains to systematize, with their decorated niches, sumptuous architectural scene fronts, and boxes for the privileged. For the most part it was comedy, either revivals of Plautus and Terence, or contemporary pieces none of which survive.

Dramatic art had become decadent too, and perhaps the most revealing dramas written in the Imperial age were the tragedies of Lucius Annaeus Seneca, which were not performed in theatres, if they were performed at all – they seem to have been written in order to be read or recited. These were dramas of blood and horror, reflecting the violence at the courts of the emperors Caligula and Nero, where human life was a cheap commodity. Seneca was born in Cordoba, in Spain, in 4 BC, and enjoyed a successful career in politics and the law before being exiled by Claudius in AD 41, allegedly for adultery with the emperor's niece. Later he tutored the young Nero, and exercised considerable power for a time before being ousted from the emperor's favour and strategically retiring. Eventually he was accused of involvement in a plot to assassinate Nero, who ordered him to commit suicide. He too was to have his strongest influence on later times, in the formation of Renaissance tragedy, and on the blood and rhetoric plentiful in plays like Thomas Kyd's *The Spanish Tragedy*.

Seneca's work was never appreciated outside court circles. During his lifetime and in the years following his death, the populace preferred another type of entertainment which was Greek in origin, secular, and not restricted to religious festivals. Actors were seen unmasked and in contemporary dress. Although it was in essence improvised farce, in time it came to be written down. Women, often prostitutes, appeared naked on stage. Adultery was a popular theme, and the emperor Heliogabalus ordered its actual performance in front of him. It is hardly surprising that actors should have been thought immoral and socially inferior. Another plot called for an execution, and some unlucky criminals were crucified on stage.

This form had the confusing name of mime, imitation, though it was not what we call mime today, because in the Roman version the actors spoke. It was Rome's most popular theatrical genre, and as late as the sixth century AD a mime actress, Theodora, became empress at Constantinople. The Romans once expressed the importance of mime by rioting over who was the greatest mime artist of the day.

Mime in the sense of dumb-show did exist, though. A story has it that an early actor and playwright, Livius Andronicus, strained his voice and had to confine himself to making the proper gestures while a singer sang the words. The first-century AD teacher and rhetorician, Quintilian, gave this account of the performers:

> Their hands demand and promise, they summon and dismiss; they translate horror, fear, joy, sorrow, hesitation, confession, repentance, restraint, abandonment, time and number. They excite and they calm. They implore and they approve. They possess a power of imitation which replaces words. To suggest illness, they imitate the doctor feeling the patient's pulse; to indicate music they spread their fingers in the fashion of a lyre.

The participants in spectacle, circus performers, comedy and dumb-show artists and mimes were the purveyors of entertainment throughout the Roman Empire, and they reflected the values of that Empire. When Rome persecuted the Christians, the mimes parodied their ritual and made fun of practices such as baptism. In return, the early Christian Church branded mime as immoral. Yet the encounter between the theatre and the new religion was not altogether antagonistic, and the Church remembered one story in particular.

In 287 AD, when Diocletian ruled Rome, a persecution of the Christians was ordered by Arianus, prefect of the Egyptian city of Antinoe. One man, a deacon, accused of having embraced the new faith was evidently not cut out for martyrdom, and he hit upon a plan to save his skin by persuading a famous mime called Philemon to take his place in a ceremony in which he would wear the deacon's robes and make the customary offerings to the pagan gods. That would absolve the wretched deacon. Philemon agreed to the masquerade, but when he came to stand before Arianus, with his head bowed and hooded, he was possessed by the spirit that should have been the deacon's. Instead of making the pagan offering, Philemon said: 'I am a Christian and will make no sacrifice.' He let fall the hood so that all could see that he was not the timid deacon but their popular favourite. Arianus and the mob pleaded with him to recant, but he refused. He went joyously to his death, and for his constancy was canonized by the Church.

True or not, the story of St Philemon is significant for what it foreshadows. All the forces are represented: the pagan past, the Christian future, the theatre and the Church. No matter how great the apparent antagonism, religion and drama were inevitably to be drawn together once again. In the meantime, in the fifth century all mimes were excommunicated, and in the sixth, the Christian emperor Justinian closed all the theatres in the Empire. The theatre went into the streets.

MYSTERIES

At first glance the contention that the drama is necessary to man's existence appears to be refuted by almost a thousand years of European history. With the disintegration of the Western Roman Empire all vestiges of official, organized theatrical life vanished. In the early Christian centuries no major playwright was at work. The drama was dead, it seemed, or at best in a state of suspended animation. Yet it might also be argued that man requires an ordered world and a relatively open society, and that his ability to destroy both these necessities is another of the theatre's great themes, which only a flourishing communal life can resurrect.

Most scholars agree that while no formal theatre existed, a number of its necessary elements lived on. For instance, the skills of the Roman professional actor were somehow maintained, though the means of their preservation are not recorded. Perhaps they just sank back into the lives of the common people, where custom and folklore were too stubbornly rooted to be swept away by the history made by generals, kings and popes. Their need may have ensured that the popular traditions of song, dance, mimicry and farce were bequeathed to succeeding generations of performers. What is certain is that the burgeoning power of the early Christian Church was used to crush the art of the drama, and since it was the victors who wrote that history too, any surviving familiar manifestations are impossible to detect.

From the beginning, the new religion set its face sternly against the theatre, to which it would take an ambivalent attitude throughout its history. After all, Imperial Rome had used the theatre as a propaganda weapon against the early Church, and made a spectacle of its persecution. Furthermore, the Roman theatre had been lewd and obscene, the voice of paganism: if that was the typical function of theatre, it was an enemy of the new moral order. Yet if this moral order was going to express the full range of man's needs, it was going to have to give voice to the drama. No matter how primitive or sophisticated, human beings seem to demand that the mysteries of their existence should be demonstrated in art, whether these take the form of human conflict itself, or the struggle with forces beyond our control, or the urge to understand our place in the scheme of things. In time, the Church itself came unintentionally to accommodate the need for drama through its resolve to demonstrate the mystery of Holy Communion.

The most sacred rite of the Church was described by St Gregory as 'the one thing made visible and invisible'. From the secular point of view, tragedy could be similarly described. In fact the Mass itself has been interpreted as a dramatic performance with a plot and definite roles assigned. This is an account given by Honorius of Autun in the year 1100:

It is known that those who recited tragedies in the theatres presented the actions of opponents by gestures before the people. In the same way our tragic author – that is, the celebrant – represents by his gestures in the theatre of the church before the Christian people the struggle of Christ and teaches them the victory of His redemption.

Honorius' analysis interprets the Mass as ritual drama and presents certain compelling parallels with Greek tragedy: a fall from grace, suffering, the renewal of life. Christ may even be regarded as a tragic hero in whom the congregation, the people, place their faith. The priest consecrates the bread and the wine; they become the body and blood of Jesus Christ. That is the most profound belief of Roman Catholics. It is a doctrine that demands absolute faith. The transformation of matter by means of a priestly mystery is in itself an act of great drama, requiring the audience, the congregation, to submit to what reason will not explain. The supplicants take into their mouths the consecrated wafer and are in communion with their god. In so doing they are echoing the rituals of a pagan past. Dionysus too was eaten by his followers.

Holy Communion is the celebration of God made man, and in order to communicate its meaning the early Church fathers succumbed to the need for theatre as the vehicle of mystery. The uneducated had to be made to grasp the miracle. In our terms, both celebrants and congregation had temporarily to abandon the self of their rational beliefs and practical behaviour in the conscious world, and this can happen most powerfully when we enter the dimension of drama, a heightened state of awareness in which our spirit and imagination are free to explore what lies behind the everyday surface. In that extended awareness, the irrational in man can be contained, and his acceptance of the mysteries enhanced.

So the Church admitted theatre in order to express its mysteries. But it also had a more straightforward kind of information to impart to its generally illiterate congregations, in the shape of the story of Christ's life. Painting and sculpture created symbolic figures which were instantly recognizable and which made the life and Passion of Christ a vivid and familiar story. In the words of an unknown author of 1493, these images served three purposes:

For they be ordained to stir man's mind to think on Christ's incarnation, and on his passion, and on his living, and on other saints' living. Also, they be ordained to stir man's affection and his heart to devotion. For, often man is more stirred by sight than by hearing or reading. Also, they be ordained to be a token and a book to the lewd people.

The Church well understood the need to make the invisible visible. It made drama and symbolism work as part of the theatre of worship, and it gave form and shape to many biblical figures. In this way it was to become the midwife to a new secular drama whose birth lay in the future but whose cradle was, ironically, the pagan and pre-Christian past.

In the first centuries after Christ's death, the Church had to find a policy for absorbing the religious impulses of the pre-Christian past while smothering the old religions themselves. The solution was the bold gamble of growing right around them. For instance, the building of churches on the sites of pagan temples was a deliberate, rational policy clearly expressed by Pope Gregory the Great in the instructions he issued to St Augustine at Canterbury:

> Destroy the idols; purify the buildings with holy water; set relics there; and let them become the temples of the true god. So the people will have no need to change their places of concourse and where of old they were wont to sacrifice cattle to demons, thither let them continue to resort on the day of the Saint to whom the church is dedicated and slay their beasts no longer as a sacrifice, but for a social meal in honour of him whom they now worship.

Not only were the pagan sites to be used, but also pagan celebrations, so saints' days, Christian feasts and festivals were timed to take place on days which custom had always identified as important. The marriage of the Christian and pagan calendars now becomes central to this story, because the festivals of Christianity, like those of ancient Greece and Rome, were to play a vital part in the development of the new theatre.

Masquerading mummers of the reign of Edward III. Their costumes and dances originated in a pre-Christian past.

Spring, which in any case had always been the season for rejoicing, naturally became the season of the Resurrection. English Christians even called their spring festival after its Anglo-Saxon goddess, Eostre, and Easter was the name given to the festival that proclaims a Christian mystery, Christ's rising from the dead, as it proclaimed the pagan mystery of the seed rising from the cold ground. In the spring, performers acted out a rite, a sort of play or dance, such as mummers perform at Abbots Bromley, in England, to this day, although for some unexplained reason the event now takes place in autumn. All over Europe similar rites were once performed, centred upon the theme of the resurrection of life.

The Resurrection of Christ must also be proclaimed, the mystery enacted and made memorable. At first the priests felt this need for themselves, as celebrants, but later it became a question of communicating it to the illiterate peasants who formed the great majority of their congregations. The tenth century provides the earliest unequivocal evidence of what may be called a simple dramatization of the Easter liturgy. An English manuscript, *Regularis Concordia*, dated *c.* 965–75, contains a passage setting out a ceremony known as *Visitatio Sepulchri*, the visit to the tomb, in a clear dramatic form:

> ...four brothers robe themselves, one of whom dressed in an alb enters as if for another purpose and discreetly goes to the place where the sepulchre is, and sits there quietly with a palm in his hand ... the remaining three come forward, everyone dressed in a cope, carrying thuribles with incense in their hands, and hesitantly like people seeking something, come to the site of the sepulchre. For these things are performed in imitation of the angel sitting in the tomb, and of the women coming with spices to anoint Jesus' body. Consequently when the one sitting there sees the three nearing him ... he begins to sing sweetly in a moderate voice:
> *Quem quaeritis in sepulchro, o Christicolae?*
> When this has been sung all through, the three reply in unison:
> *Ihesum Nazarenum crucifixum, o coelicola.*

'Whom do ye seek in the tomb, O lovers of Christ?' asks the angel. 'Jesus of Nazareth, He that was crucified, O heavenly one,' the three representing the women reply. And the angel continues: 'He is not here. He has risen as he had prophesied. Go, announce that he has risen from the dead.'

That ceremony, which has come to be known because of the first question as the *Quem Quaeritis*, argues that as early as about 970 a piece of liturgy has been transformed into ritual drama. The clergy represented characters other than themselves, and the three Marys wore head adornments to signify womanhood, but the dramatic heart of the *Quem Quaeritis* is symbolized by the angel revealing the empty tomb. From the *Regularis Concordia*:

> ...he rises and lifts the curtain, and shows them the place with the cross gone but with the linen cloths in which the cross was wrapped lying

there. Having seen this, they put down the thuribles which they carried to the sepulchre, and take up the linen, and spread it out in the sight of the clergy, as if making it plain that the Lord has arisen and is not wrapped in the grave clothes now . . .

So effective and compelling did the *Quem Quaeritis* prove, that today we have over 400 different versions from monasteries all over Europe, many containing lively dramatic invention. For example, in some later versions the Three Marys go to buy spices before they visit the tomb. The spice merchant is portrayed as a sort of pagan quack doctor, a figure probably borrowed from the early Mumming plays, who indulges in comic business with his wife and assistant. These additions and embellishments are important because they introduce the human element, the profane side by side with the sacred, a part of that impulse to embrace all human experience which is best summed up by the great medieval cathedrals, where carved stone demons and the peasant figures on wooden pew-ends people the same world as the radiant stained glass and towering spires which reached up to the heaven of the Roman Catholic faith of the Middle Ages.

That sense that all human experience might be brought together was one of the powerful unifying forces of the medieval world, and it would mould the shape of theatrical things to come. The explosion of drama in the Middle Ages differs from others in two important respects: first, that it was not confined to a single country; second, that it was in no way exclusive. On the contrary, the theatre of the period stretching roughly from the twelfth to the fifteenth century was the most truly popular in history, speaking directly to people of all classes, for it conformed faithfully to the rhythm and motor of the age.

Medieval man needed to fit within a frame all he knew and understood. The cathedral best symbolizes that impulse because its structure contained the entire moral universe as a real dimension: enter it and you faced the creation and the last judgment, good and evil, the profane as well as the sacred, life, death – and resurrection. Medieval man could acknowledge even the horrible, the grotesque and the irreligious because his acceptance, call it of God's universe or of the variety of life, was unshakeable. He had as little sense of chronological as of spatial perspective: what mattered a lot figured large, and what mattered less was made to appear smaller. The historical, which included the biblical, past was one with the present. It was perfectly natural that the chief episodes of Christ's life on earth should be translated straight into contemporary medieval images without the slightest sense of strain. Herod becomes a ducal tyrant, Noah a shipwright of some North Sea port, and the shepherds of Bethlehem tend their sheep on the Yorkshire fells.

The Resurrection was one of the two great events in the Christian calendar; the other was the Nativity. Both were embraced by cathedral architecture. The West represented the world in darkness; the East, where the High Altar is placed, the Star of Bethlehem, the light of Christ's incarnation. And since the

A 16th-century misericord at Beverley minster, Yorkshire, England, from which a medieval jester grins.

dramatization of the Easter mystery had proved so effective, it was natural for the Nativity to be similarly treated. But it was in dramatizing the Nativity that the Church encountered a disturbing moral dilemma, in the person of Herod.

Herod was an evil man, and the question arose, should evil be perpetrated in the house of God? Furthermore, was it right that a priest should impersonate such a figure? Was it blasphemy? For the time being, the solution was both theatrical and human: the character of Herod took over the Nativity plays – the villain proved irresistible. Yet the central question remained, and the Church fathers asked it for the first time: should evil be dramatized at all? They were concerned about blasphemy and immorality inside the drama, and the antipathy to theatrical spectacle surfaced once more. Of course this problem of fiction enacting but not being the same as what it shows continues to baffle moralists and to fuel the perennial debate on censorship. It is inherent in my own argument that the imaginative truth of drama is not merely an 'aesthetic' experience, but that it matters to people.

The Church's dilemma is illustrated by the work of an extraordinary woman, a nun called Hroswitha, who lived in the convent of Gandersheim in Saxony in the tenth century. As a student of Latin, the language both of worship and of pagan Rome, she had read and admired the comedies of Terence, and was inspired to write six plays modelled on his. Her approach to the task conveys the prevailing mood. Here is an extract from a preface to what are described as 'the plays of Hroswitha, German religious and virgin of the Saxon race', who may be counted as the first woman dramatist:

I ... have not hesitated to imitate in my writings the poet Terence, whose works are so widely read, my object being to glorify, within the limits of my poor talent, the laudable chastity of Christian virgins in that self-same form of composition which has been used to describe the shameless acts of licentious women. One thing has all the same embarrassed me and often brought a blush to my cheek. It is that I have been compelled through the nature of this work to apply my mind and pen to depicting the dreadful frenzy of those possessed by unlawful love, and the insidious sweetness of passion – things which should not even be named among us. Yet if from modesty I had refrained from treating these subjects I should not have been able to attain my object – to glorify the innocent to the best of my ability ... In the humbler works of my salad days I gathered up my poor researches in heroic strophes, but here I have sifted them into a series of dramatic scenes and avoided through omission the pernicious voluptuousness of pagan writers.

Sin recreated and evil 'performed' reinforced the belief that theatrical presentation was an immoral influence. The Church's predicament was redoubled because the drama worked. With no organized theatrical companies to act them, Hroswitha's decorous versions of Terence would remain private exercises. The problem for the clergy was dramatizations performed inside a church. Of the various solutions, one was for the controversial part of Herod to be played by a layman instead of a priest. That must have come as a relief to the clergy of Padua, where a version of the Nativity was played in which Herod was obliged to beat the local bishop with an inflated bladder. But now the immortal soul of the layman was at risk: would *he* not incur everlasting damnation by portraying wickedness? To this day, in Oberammergau, where the famous Passion Play is given, the actors receive a special pardon, the *Ablass*, before the performance, just in case ...

In a sense, the conflict could never be resolved. Organized religion persisted in viewing the drama with suspicion, and now and then would actively oppose it. In 1210 Pope Innocent III issued an edict forbidding the clergy to act on a public stage. But it was the Church itself which gave the theatre its next push forward, and an impetus which was eventually to take it altogether beyond the Church's control.

The Church already held festivals to commemorate the birth and crucifixion of Christ and the foundation of the Church itself. These were celebrated as Christmas, Easter and Pentecost, and had their own special dramas. The doctrine of Transubstantiation, which declares the Real Presence of Christ in the consecrated bread and wine, gives to the Eucharist, the sacrament which recalls the Last Supper, the status of a miracle to stand beside the Virgin Birth and the Resurrection. The idea that the Church should institute a feast to celebrate the miracle is attributed to St Juliana, a Belgian prioress from near Liège. Her archdeacon was Jacques Pantaléon, who became Pope Urban IV in

1261. Three years later he ordered the whole Church to celebrate the new festival of Corpus Christi, and asked St Thomas Aquinas to compose the liturgical office.

Because Pope Urban IV died in that same year of 1264, his decree was not ratified until the Council of Vienne, in 1311–12. By the fifteenth century it was a major feast of the Church in western Europe. Until 1311, the Sacrament had been celebrated on the eve of Good Friday, a period when the Church's calendar was crowded and the mood sorrowful. The vital decision from our point of view was to move the date on to the first Thursday after Trinity Sunday, in summertime: The consecrated Host was carried from the Church for display before the people, brought out of darkness into sunlight. It was as if the feast of Corpus Christi emphasized Christ's humanity rather than his divinity.

Church hierarchy, city corporation and craft guilds, each in their own right accustomed to mounting processions, collaborated to present a magnificent spectacle. The clergy in their ornately embroidered vestments, the mayor and corporation in their ceremonial robes, and the craft guilds in distinctive costume, carrying banners emblazoned with their insignia, processed through narrow streets jammed with people ready to marvel and enjoy. In England, records show that the countryside flooded into cities like York and Norwich to share the festive spirit. So great was the holiday atmosphere that affairs of state, even those involving acts of war, were broken off in order to allow royal personages and high-ranking officials to attend.

In time, though no one is certain when, tableaux on floats appeared, carrying participants who performed dumb-show presenting Adam and Eve, 'Noyes ship', the Nativity and so on, and who even exchanged snatches of dialogue (in the vernacular, not Latin) which had to be kept brief so as not to hold up the rest of the parade. Out of such exchanges developed a drama known as *The Play of Corpus Christi*, which became very popular in Britain. Similar festivities took place throughout Europe, and so the stage was set for a new form of theatrical presentation: a festival, drama, the celebration of man's salvation. These plays were known variously as Mystery and as Miracle plays, and although the Middle Ages made no sharp distinction between them, these terms have come to be applied to those which dealt respectively with biblical stories and with the lives of the saints. France had the *mystère*, Germany the *Mysterienspiel*, Spain the *auto sacramental*, Italy the *sacra rappresentazione*. But whereas in Spain, Italy and Germany it was the Passion play that dominated religious drama, in France, as we shall see, a secular theatre evolved, as it did in England, where the plays were administered by town and city corporations, and financed and performed by the trade guilds.

The clergy's exclusion from the list of participants marks no deep split, because the Church permeated medieval society and the plays were rooted in it. They moved out into the streets not only because of the clergy's discomfort with drama but also because of a natural evolution: in a society of public religious celebration and street processions, the plays were *drawn* outside the churches.

In keeping with the familiar longing to embrace all of human experience pell-mell, the Mystery plays set out to display the entire history of the universe, from creation to the end of the world. This was not too overwhelming a project, given the simplicity of the medieval world-picture, but it still left a great many events to string together, to say the least. The Mystery plays contained them in a cyclical form made up of a series of short pieces which began with God in Heaven, victorious over Satan and banishing him to rule over Hell, and ending with the Last Judgment. In between came dramatizations of Old and New Testament stories, together with legends based on the Apocrypha. The Mystery cycles all seem to have followed a similar course:

1 The Fall of Lucifer.
2 The Creation of the World.
3 The Creation and Fall of Man.
4 Noah and the Flood.
5 Cain and Abel.
6 Moses receiving the Ten Commandments.
7 The Annunciation: Mary receiving the news that she is carrying Jesus, and Joseph's doubts concerning his wife's fidelity.
8 The Nativity.
9 Incidents from the life of Jesus.
10 Judas betraying Jesus.
11 The trial of Jesus.
12 The Passion, including the Crucifixion.
13 The Resurrection and the reappearance of Jesus to his disciples.
14 The Ascension of Jesus into Heaven.
15 The destruction of the world.
16 The Last Judgment.

There were two forms of staging this vast dramatic narrative. The first, which grew out of the Corpus Christi processions, used 'pageants', movable stage wagons, which were pulled through the streets to stop at chosen places along the route and give their particular play. Although it is generally accepted that a procession of some sort took place, the details are a scholastic battlefield. Given the number of pageants required, it is argued that it would have been impossible to fit the entire cycle into the available daylight hours. Perhaps the performances continued after dark then, by torchlight, or perhaps the moving wagons only presented tableaux and mimed versions of their plays along the way, before coming together to act out the spoken texts in some central place. What can be said for certain is that wagons carried a set built to represent a given background against which actors performed, and that the Mystery plays were a form of genuine street theatre.

The second method of staging the Mystery plays, more popular on the Continent than in England, was static. The French example is typical, and worth dwelling on before we return to medieval England because it demonstrates how much the Mysteries began to diverge according to the ground they grew in, and because it became the prologue to French drama as its cross-Channel counterpart did to the English golden age.

The French adopted a series of static stages which were arranged in front of the church or round a town square or the courtyard of a noble house. They were called *compartements*, and the audience must have circulated from one to another. The design can be seen in a famous medieval illustration, the only one to show a *mystère* in performance; it was painted around 1460 by Jean Fouquet, and shows the martyrdom of St Apollonia. The whole of creation from Heaven on the left to Hell's Mouth on the right is arranged in a semicircle, a single ordered sweep.

Some time during the late twelfth and early thirteenth centuries, the French Mystery and Miracle plays had moved out of the Church and come to be performed in the vernacular instead of in Latin. Responsibility for the productions belonged not to the trade guilds, as in England, but to specially constituted bodies. They tended to revolve around the lives of the saints, but their tone was perhaps more ribald than in the English Mysteries: farce and buffoonery were popular elements, often provided by the antics of the devils, and the contemporary world was portrayed, sometimes through critical accounts of great lords or clerics.

In time, the production of religious plays became an accepted part of French urban life, and spectacular presentations were regularly staged by several cities. They were supported by the Church, which still saw them as encouraging popular faith, and merchants and other commercial interests helped to pay the costs because the performances attracted visitors from far and near. The citizenry who watched or performed in the plays looked forward to them as a respite from the severity of everyday life. In trying to please all interests, the productions grew more and more to distort the content in favour of glittering and complex staging. Spectacular effects were introduced, using intricate machinery. Stage and Church were ready to part.

But it was a long time from the flowering of the Mystery plays all over Europe to their eventual decline, and that had to wait until the Middle Ages themselves had passed. Their heyday had expressed a social and religious unity whose strength of belief is unmistakable in the surviving English texts, as well as in what we know about the way they were performed. Performances took place all over Britain; the cycles that survive more or less intact are those of Chester, Coventry, Wakefield and York, and the Cornish plays.

It is the comprehensive quality of the Mystery plays that is most striking to later ages. Bells would have rung all over England. The presentation of the plays involved men and women from all walks of life, all major cities and centres of influence. In York, for example, out of a population of five thousand, two thousand took part. There is much evidence to support the view that participation and enjoyment were classless: the drama became part of the mental world of performers and spectators alike, planting the seeds of the vibrant English theatrical tradition. Once a year, the cities of England were converted into theatres and the populace absorbed in a total dramatic experience.

York was one of many northern towns which prospered in the Middle Ages largely because of the wool trade. A thrusting, aggressive mercantile class had sprung up, imbued with civic pride. York shared with most cities of its time the medieval love of pageantry, the public symbol of disciplined vitality. Underpinning the city's prosperity were the trade guilds, secular organizations which regulated the plays and shared them out among themselves. Each guild presented its own play, often related to its own activities. A professional director was sometimes employed: at Coventry, Thomas Calcow supervised the Skinners' play on a twelve-year contract of 48 shillings and 8 pence per annum.

High standards were required: the guilds must cast 'good players, well arrayed and openly speaking'. An order issued on 3 April 1476 demanded four of the most 'cunning, discreet and able players'. Although they were amateurs, these actors were paid according to the importance of their roles. At Coventry, God earned 3 shillings and 4 pence, Souls (saved or damned) 1 shilling and 8 pence, and the Worme of Conscience a shilling less. In return, the actors must not only perform well, but also conform to strict rules of behaviour. In France, at Valenciennes, fifteen articles governed a performer's contract, and included the following obligations: to perform on prescribed days, with illness the sole excuse for absence; to accept the part or parts assigned without complaint; to be on time for rehearsals, or else pay a fine; not to argue with the producer; never to get drunk. (It is the voice of managements through the ages, a triumph of hope.) In England, actors were enjoined to learn their lines by heart but were followed by one called an Ordinary, holding a prompting script and telling them 'softly what they must pronounce aloud'.

These performances must have taken a good deal of organizing, and there would have been great activity behind the scenes. As soon as one cycle was completed, planning began for the following year. Sets had to be built and painted, the pageant wagons decorated, sometimes at enormous expense. Costumes too were sumptuous and costly, and were made by the townspeople themselves. Accounts from Coventry and Worcester record that silk was required for a crown, gold and silver foil for mitres, scarlet cloth for a bishop's tabard, and white leather purchased for God.

A seventeenth-century description from Chester, generally accepted as authentic, tells us a lot about the way the event was managed and performed. A proclamation read by a herald announced the time and content of the plays and gave a stern warning against any breach of the peace and against carrying offensive weapons. Acts of violence were severely punished. At York, the players were ordered to assemble with their wagons 'midway between three and four o'clock in the morning'. Performers were punished for any shortcomings. At Beverley, the Butchers were fined for arriving late, the Smiths for failing to present their play. The Painters were penalized because their production of 'The 3 Kings of Colleyn was badly and confusedly played, in contempt of the whole community and before many strangers'.

The Miracle and Mystery plays represent a truly popular theatre, naive because it addressed a broadly illiterate audience and because theatre had lain fallow for so long, but naive also because it expressed the plainest simplicities of the medieval view. Scholars argued and scientists speculated about the movements of the planets in medieval times, but none of this came near the Mystery plays; nor do they display any great subtlety as texts, and reading them it would be impossible to deduce that a literary artist of the quality of Geoffrey Chaucer was their contemporary. Such simplicity carried great advantages too. The Mystery plays perceive no difference between fourteenth-century man and the people who lived at the time of the Exodus from Egypt or the time of Christ's Nativity. The carpenters who built the ark had brothers in the local workshops; the shepherds who attended Christ's birth could be seen tending sheep on the outskirts of town; the high priest of Solomon's temple was robed identically to the bishop of an English diocese. The figures of biblical legend lived and breathed in the city streets of medieval Europe.

The cycles were not conceived as a unity, and playlets were arbitrarily added or removed. Each country stressed different elements. The Germans favoured nightmarish devils, Jew-baiting and satire in which recognizable contemporary personalities played scenes with historic figures. We have seen that the French favoured both the satanic and the ribald too, but the *mystères* also make room for long lyrical passages with real emotional content. In England the devils appeared, but as rather restrained figures of fun; comedy and farce had a place, not as set-pieces in themselves, but as relief from the more harrowing episodes. The text itself was not yet informed with emotion or passion, and the writing often lacks insight – as when Abraham, on the point of sacrificing Isaac, intones:

Oh, comely creature, but I thee kill,
I grieve my God, and that full ill:
I may not work against his will
But ever obedient be.

Yet for a modern reader perhaps there is after all a poignancy in the dumb obedience that grieved but could not express its grief. A medieval audience might have recognized the sense of docile helplessness these words project.

One of the more spectacular items to enthral a populace that feared damnation and hoped for Heaven was The Harrowing of Hell, presented in York by the Saddlers. Jesus, Adam, Eve, Isaiah, John Baptist, Moyses, Belzabub, Satan and an assortment of devils all appear. The play is based on the apocryphal Gospel of Nicodemus, and tells how Christ, between the Crucifixion and the Resurrection, descended into Hell, released the prophets and

'While no formal theatre existed, a number of
its necessary elements lived on.'

Above in an illuminated medieval manuscript
from Montecassino, minstrels and dancers are
seen performing.

Christian hagiography, like Greek mythology, provided material for dramatic treatment. *Left* a decapitation scene from Montecassino. Educated churchmen were fascinated by the theatrical past: from the Vatican library, the characters of Terence's *Andria* are depicted below.
Right the *Martyrdom of S. Apollonia* was enthusiastically staged, and directed, before a medieval French audience: the painting, by Fouquet, is from the *Heures d'Étienne Chevalier*.

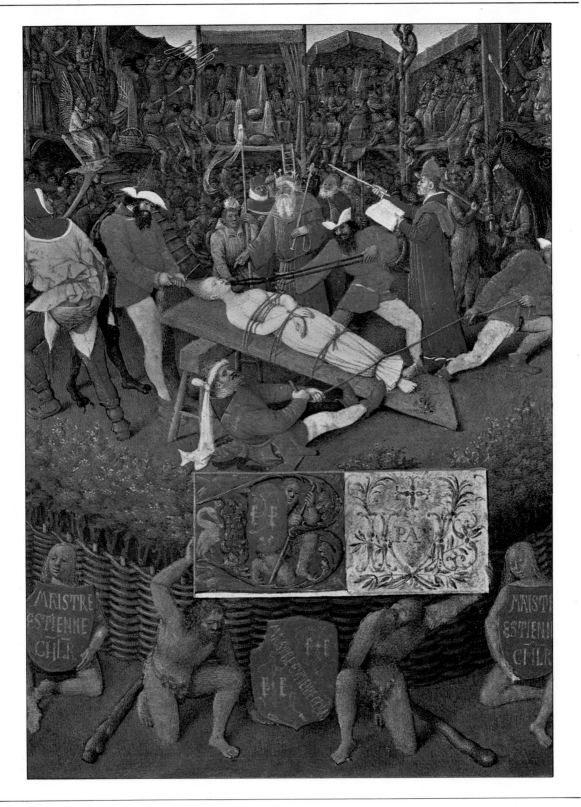

The elaborate *décor simultané* of France is
well illustrated in the 16th-century setting
for the Mystère de la Passion at Valenciennes. From Paradise, we range through
Nazareth, The Temple, Jerusalem, the
palace, the bishop's palace, the golden gate,
the sea, Limbo and Hell.

Left Christ releases the souls from Hell's Mouth in the *All the World's a Stage* production of *The Harrowing of Hell*.

le mistere de

Le limbe des peres

Lenfer

La porte doret

Maison des enseignes

La mer

The medieval secular tradition was to flower all over Europe in the Italian *Commedia dell'Arte*. Its origin is uncertain, but its roots are older than the millennium. This French engraving of 1634 depicts Gandolin: *right* the perennial figure of Arlecchino.

Das Comedien Haus.

Die zwey *Acteurs*.
Ach liebster Printz/ Wenn meine Schmertzen,
Euch gar nicht gehen mehr zu Hertzen,
so bin ich auch im Leben todt.
Prinzeßin schweigt von eürer Liebe,
Ihr setzet mich durch solche Triebe,
und Euch zugleich, in große Noth.

Die Vier Narren.
Wer uns nur sieht, der muß gleich lachen,
bloß weil wir das vorstellig machen,
wofür man uns doch selbst nicht hält.
Am Ende: Wenn man es betrachtet,
so ist diß Spiel, zwar ohnweracht et,
mit Narrheit meistentheils bestellt.

23

Above Commedia dell'Arte in Germany in the 17th century and (*left*) today: Arlecchino and Colombina as performed by the Cooperative Autori Citet, Venice.

patriarchs from Purgatory, and then commanded Satan down into the flames. 'Alas, for dole and care!' Satan cries. 'I sink into hell pit.' This would have been the cue for formidable stage effects: possibly thunder, certainly fire, which was frequently employed, and perhaps even a device for lowering Satan into the underworld. Hell was represented by a terrifying dragon's mouth.

The Mystery plays kindled a theatrical flame which has continued to burn all over Europe, though nowhere more strongly than in England. As literature on the printed page, their language tends to be often flat, and their rhythms sing-song: it is easy to imagine them being composed as Bottom and Flute compose Pyramus and Thisbe. Yet there are also many passages of remarkable beauty, the dramatic invention is often startling and powerful, and the sense of irreverence infectious. Furthermore, it cannot be stressed too strongly that these are *plays*, written for performance in a very special theatre, on a day of religious exultation, in front of an audience which brought all its own feeling and imagination to the performance. For our present purpose, the strength of the medieval theatre was its blazing theatricality, its universal embrace, and the place it won in the hearts of people.

Having used the word 'theatricality', I will not be allowed to beg the obvious question. After all, the Shorter *OED* traces the word theatrical in the sense of 'artificial, affected, assumed' back to 1649, and in the sense of 'extravagantly or irrelevantly histrionic' to 1709. Chambers bluntly defines theatricality as 'staginess, artificiality'. I use the word here (and elsewhere in this book) to express the unembarrassed art and verve of the theatre triumphant.

Even in the great age of the city as theatre, with its themes provided by scripture and the saints, Europe had other forms of presentation, and other dramatic themes. At Perranporth, in Cornwall, for example, the plays of the great Cornish Mystery Cycle are still performed, in the round, in the only medieval *theatre* to be found in Britain. Nor were the Miracle and Mystery plays to hold the stage alone. There exists a medieval manuscript of a play which has production notes attached, and a stage plan for performance. The piece is called *The Castell of Perseverance*, and it is a Morality play, dating from about 1425. It is the earliest complete extant example of the genre, and it too was performed in the round.

Morality plays reached their height of popularity in the last fifty years of the fourteenth century. If I call them a kind of dramatized sermon I do not mean to convey the yawning dullness of a modern pulpit. The medieval preacher was, or was capable of being, an allegorical poet, seizing vivid images to capture the minds of his congregation. Symbol and metaphor were not just literary devices to the medieval mind: the longing to embrace the whole of life stemmed from a deep sense that it was all one, that there were real connections for instance between things and ideas, or between one set of hierarchies and another. The preacher's aim was both to enlighten and to entertain: the one involved the other. Likewise, the Morality play was intended to make a moral point as in a parable or fable, rather than narrate biblical history or drive home the more complex notions of doctrinal theology. A lonely hero, like a lost soul, moves through a timeless landscape and is accosted by personifications of vice, virtue, evil, repentance, wisdom, folly. The Seven Deadly Sins often appear as characters, or rather as the mouthpieces of the force they represent. Like the heroes of these plays – Mankind, Everyman – they are named for their quality: Pride, Envy, Lust and so on. They are abstractions, symbols in the allegorical tale, as are their opponents, the Seven Graces.

The Castell of Perseverance is very long, and some passages seem never-ending. The hero is Mankind making his journey through life, besieged by evils and protected by the virtues. Great claims have been made for the play's epic quality, social message and morality. The wonder is, then, why it is seldom revived. Any play which requires intense study of text and subtext, motive and intention, before it can be appreciated undermines the very function of theatrical presentation, which is to create a shared consciousness between actor and playgoer, formed by the heat of a live performance and a live involvement.

Even so, there are two points of special interest in *The Castell of Perseverance*. First there are the production notes and stage plan. Though both are hard to interpret, they tell us that the piece was performed in the round. In Richard Southern's brilliant study, *The Medieval Theatre in the Round*, he makes a case for seeing the circular plan as the blueprint of a theatre, and comes to the startling conclusion that spectators might watch the play from inside the circular arena itself. Nathalie Crohn Schmitt challenges this view, and argues that the circular plan is for a set, not a theatre. But the circle remains, in either interpretation, and was in use at a time when another method of staging was infinitely more popular. It provides us with a link to the past, and perhaps even an influence on the future, which was to revive the familiar circle on the bank of the River Thames.

The second point of interest is a vital one for English drama. It concerns the attitude of the unknown author of *The Castell of Perseverance*, and the equally anonymous authors of other Morality plays of the fifteenth century. In spite of the sermonizing, they contain the first tentative steps towards the psychological observation of character. The hero's feelings are examined and analysed through dramatic dialogue. At the same time the playwright reveals a critical approach to man and the world he lives in. This is Folly and Lust introducing Mankind to the World, their master:

> Of worldly good is all his thought;
> He would be great of name;
> He would be a great honour
> For to rule town and tower
> He would have as his paramour
> Some lovely high-born dame.

In the finest of the Morality plays, *Everyman*, the playwright is starting to emerge from behind the message. The hero and protagonists are still generalized, but they are developing voices and traits of their own. The story of *Everyman*, which has a Dutch analogue, *Elckerlijk*, and may be a translation from the Dutch, tells how God, enraged by man's materialism, orders Death to summon the hero. Everyman prevaricates, stalls, and then looks for anyone who may keep him company on the dread journey. He appeals to Fellowship, then to Kindred and to Cousin to join him; all refuse. He turns to Goods – worldly wealth – and then to Good Deeds, and they too decline the invitation, but Good Deeds recommends his sister, Knowledge, who answers with the famous line:

Everyman, I will go with thee, and be thy guide.

The play proceeds on orthodox religious lines. Knowledge leads Everyman to Confession, Discretion, Strength, Five Wits and Beauty. In the end Everyman, facing Death, is deserted by all except his Good Deeds.

The drama has a universal quality, and has proved popular ever since. Its strength lies in the author's gift for lightening the characters of their symbolism and instead allowing their vivid individuality to express itself:

Fellowship: Sir, I must needs know your heaviness;
I have pity to see you in any distress;
If any have ye wronged ye shall revenged be,
Though I on the ground be slain for thee –
Though that I know before that I should die.
Everyman: Verily, Fellowship, grammercy.
Fellowship: Tush! by thy thanks I set not a straw.
Show me your grief, and say no more.

The moral substance is enhanced by bringing a speaking human tone into the broader allegory.

Everyman, afraid of Death and of everlasting damnation, is a figure who, in other Morality plays, is victimized by his own vices. His moral welfare is the castle against which these vices, sometimes comic, sometimes sinister, make their attacks. The figure of Vice was to prove the most compelling image of the Middle Ages. He is an amalgam of Herod in his pride and vanity, and of Lucifer in his cunning and two-faced nature. Vice deceives by pleasing. He had to be amusing, of course, but with a cynical and vicious cutting edge not far beneath the surface. Devil or clown, with his gleeful henchmen he breathed life into the Morality play, appearing again and again, until at the end of the sixteenth century he enters his most famous incarnation in the person of Christopher Marlowe's Mephistopheles, in *Doctor Faustus*. Marlowe drew on all the usual trappings of religious drama – vices, devils, temptation, sin, damnation. *Doctor Faustus* stands at the end of one tradition and the dawn of another.

The Middle Ages had revived the theatre and brought it back into the life of the community. In England and elsewhere, there are grounds for believing that the folk imagery and traditional figures of quite a different tradition, the ritual culture of the Teutonic north of Europe, managed to creep into the form, and enliven it. In the early sixteenth century, the names of individual authors began to be attached to Morality plays – John Skelton in England, Sir David Lindsay in Scotland (the latter's *Satyre of the Three Estaits* introduces the theme of politics). At the same time the religion which had once underpinned the medieval theatre was no longer common ground. In 1517 Martin Luther drew up his Ninety-five Theses 'for the purpose of eliciting truth' and fastened them on the door of All Saints Church, in Wittenberg. Sixteen years later the English Church broke from Rome and became, in effect, a spiritual department of state, ruled by the king, Henry VIII, as God's deputy on earth. The Catholic doctrines embodied in the Mystery and Morality plays were questioned, censored, and finally suppressed.

The ferments of the new century cracked the old forms apart. They had expressed a civic and communal consensus, and a timeless sense of human kind. The sixteenth century had controversies to explore, together with all the individual strains and energies released with the shift of religion and morality towards the arena of each person's conscience. It would be a very different kind of theatre that could tackle this changed condition, but its predecessor had left a store of useful props.

These facts display a rare chronological symmetry. In 1576 the Diocesan Court of High Commission for York banned the Mystery play performed at Corpus Christi in Wakefield. No more pageants, no more counterfeiting the Lord's Last Supper. The Protestants were attacking Catholic superstition and idolatory. That same year, a carpenter turned actor, James Burbage, combined his two skills and built a playhouse in London which he called The Theatre. He built it in the shape of a circle, a wooden O.

The Gregorian Mass, in a 14th-century manuscript illumination

A MUSE OF FIRE

Between 1580 and 1635 a Londoner could have seen plays by Francis Beaumont, George Chapman, Thomas Dekker, John Fletcher, John Ford, Robert Greene, Thomas Heywood, Ben Jonson, Thomas Kyd, John Lyly, Christopher Marlowe, John Marston, Philip Massinger, Thomas Middleton, George Peele, William Shakespeare, Cyril Tourneur and John Webster. Some of these are probably lucky if they are revived once a decade; one of them is the most universally performed of all the world's playwrights. They all belong to the great theatrical explosion which was Elizabethan and Jacobean drama, and since Margarete Bieber described as 'miraculous' the set of conditions which converged to give rise to the emergence of drama as an art in ancient Greece, it is no use avoiding the same word to describe its rebirth and transformation at the other end of Europe two thousand years later.

Since the decline of Rome, the drama had survived ordeals which might have obliterated a less essential tradition. As a pagan form, it might have been rooted out by the Christian Church. As literature, it might never have survived its hundreds of years of suspended animation. Even as a performing art, its practitioners had been elbowed onto the fringes of social life and acceptance. In the fifth century, halfway between the worlds of ancient Greece and Renaissance Europe, at the dawn of what used to be called the Dark Ages, the Church Fathers had condemned the theatre in familiar tones of outrage:

> What tumult! What satanic clamour! What diabolic dress!
> Here are to be seen naught but fornication, adultery, courtesan women, men pretending to be women and soft-limbed boys.

This is the same voice used by the medieval clergy in their condemnation of actors:

> Some transform and transfigure their bodies with obscene dance and gesture, now indecently unclothing themselves, now putting on horrible masks.

But the Church had grown to appreciate the power of dramatic expression as a means of re-creating the meaning of the life of Christ, and imprinting biblical stories on the minds of the congregation. When in the end the Mystery plays spilled out of the churches and on to the streets, they became impregnated with common language, vulgar humour, the folk imagery and ritual preserved from pagan times, and the joy and assertiveness of a great act of communal identity. All the same, originating in the celebration of a single faith, they could not long survive its fragmentation, and could not speak for a new age.

The need now was for that vagrant secular theatre which had been living rough for nearly a thousand years. Dramatic entertainment is a perennial need: it had survived in its crudest form in the streets of Europe and anywhere else that a worthwhile crowd could be collected. *Jongleurs*, acrobats, minstrels and troubadours travelled from town to town providing what may be described as street circus. No one can say how much of the older theatrical tradition may have been preserved in folk memory, by mime artists, or even in some unrecorded tradition of performance. Certainly it is hard to believe that acting could have simply disappeared in Europe, and that the Church started it again completely from scratch.

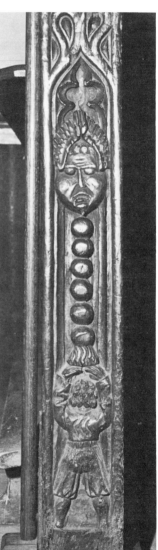

16th-century bench-ends from Abbotsham, Devon, England: acrobat and juggler

One tradition that broke out again in Renaissance Italy with uninhibited gusto, and some startling resemblances to the theatre of ancient Roman times, was the variety of professional theatre known as the *Commedia dell'Arte*, which is still played today, and which was drawn upon by Molière in the seventeenth century and by Carlo Goldoni in the eighteenth, among many other playwrights. *Commedia* actors had to be able to improvise with wit and speed along an agreed story line and within the limits of the gallery of stock characters who made the form so popular – they included the acrobatic wit called Arlecchino (Harlequin), the miserly merchant and candidate cuckold Pantalone (Pantaloon), the dashing soldier Scarramuccia (Scaramouche), and the cruel, hook-nosed hunchback Pulcinella, who lives on as Mister Punch.

A *Commedia* actor had to combine the skills of dancer, singer, acrobat, low comedian and pantomimist, and might also sing, or play a musical instrument. Many of the male characters wore masks; the women, who were played by women actors, did not. The plots were generally amorous intrigues with a vein of low farce and also of tear-jerking sentiment. In its stock characters, improvisation and comic appeal, the *Commedia dell'Arte* is strongly reminiscent of ancient Roman comedy, although no one can prove a direct line of descent, and it might be argued that the same need for a popular and lively comic theatre produced the same solutions as it had before. From the sixteenth century until the eighteenth, its vitality and gaiety infected many of the nations of Europe; its terms – *commedia, commediante, comedian* – first used in the sixteenth century, came to stand for a particular form of entertainment and, more interestingly, a new type of occupation.

Figures from the Commedia dell'Arte: *left*, Pantalone and *above* Scapino and the capitano.

In England, the changing times produced a very different response, tapping the strength of medieval drama, but also creating a generation of professional dramatists whose plays made the theatre as genuinely popular as it has ever been. With hindsight, it is possible to identify the elements that combined and interacted to begin the theatre's modern age. Before the end of the Middle Ages, travelling players were performing on English village greens, at fairs, in churchyards, guildhalls, town squares, even open fields. Records of small companies travelling together go back to the last quarter of the fifteenth century. Small bands of professional actors also performed in the halls of great houses, and may sometimes have enjoyed the patronage of the lord they entertained. The shows they gave were called 'interludes', 'games' or 'plays', and were performed between courses of banquets. Obviously they had to be short, and naturally the casts were always small, for economic rather than artistic reasons. In *Mankind*, an early Morality play dating from 1470, there are seven characters in all. The texts took second place in what was still an actor's, not a playwright's theatre.

But acting has always been a precarious profession, and it became especially precarious during the transitional period of the early and middle sixteenth century, when the age-old problem of finding employment was complicated by the theatre's growing involvement with social and political questions. Actors saw a number of attempts to control their profession, and found both life and liberty put in jeopardy. In his authoritative book, *Early English Stages*, Glynne Wickham writes that from 1530 onwards these perils were 'not the particular inventions of Henry VIII and his ministers: dramatic performances had excited sufficient opposition to provoke sporadic legislation from the start'. Professor Wickham accounts for such repeated attacks in terms of what he calls 'simply the very reasonable desire of society, as represented by its government down the centuries, to prevent breaches of the peace and the dangers to the community consequent upon hot tempers and ensuing bloodshed'. Having stressed the power of drama to give a living form to the unifying myths and beliefs of human societies, the point to be made here concerns its equal power to display the most painful sources of division, which means giving stage space to passions and ideas that endanger the established order.

Henry VIII's break with Rome inspired his ministers to adopt a form of theatrical patronage that also involved tight control over the content of plays. There is some evidence to show that the government, encouraged by leaders of the Anglican community, commissioned small theatrical companies to produce new Protestant plays in place of the traditional Mystery cycles, in another instance of the Church adapting current social patterns to its own ends. With lines like 'A dram of the turd of sweet Saint Barnaby', 'A louse of Saint Francis' and 'a maggot of Moses, with a fart of Saint Fandingo ... *In nomine Domini Pape, amen!*' there was fun of the most irreverent and lacerating kind to be had at the expense of the old order. In encouraging anti-papist feeling, however, Henry VIII was inadvertently legitimizing great national issues as subjects for plays. What he and his ministers seem not to have anticipated was the fierce reaction from conservative sections of the audience. Physical violence sometimes reached an alarming level. A play was the cause of an uprising in York in 1540, and another started a rebellion in a Norfolk village nine years later. The response of successive governments was more and more legislative control over suspect texts in the hope of preserving the peace.

Actors are often foolhardy and belligerent, as well as dedicated: political interference did not deter them. In the first ten years after Queen Elizabeth I ascended the throne in 1558, there was a rapid increase in the number of touring companies. Then in 1572 the government's aim shifted from troublesome plays to the players themselves. Parliament passed an act for 'the Punishment of Vagabonds and the Relief of the Poor and Impotent'. By its terms, actors were to be judged as 'rogues and vagabonds and sturdie beggars' unless they could prove that they were in the paid service of 'any Baron of this realm or any other personage of greater degree'. For having no master, there was a rising scale of penalties: 'For the first offence to be grievously whipped and burnt through the gristle of the right ear with a hot iron of the compass of an inch about. For the second offence to be deemed in all respects as a felon. For the third offence, death.'

Two years after the act was passed, a baron of the realm, one of the Queen's favourites, Robert Dudley, Earl of Leicester, came to the theatre's rescue. He was already patron to a company of actors who asked him for an official licence in accordance with the act. Leicester approached the Queen and obtained letters patent under the Great Seal of England which allowed his company 'to use and occupy the art of playing comedies, tragedies and interludes and such other like as they have studies providing that the same be not shown in the time of common prayer or in the time of common plague in our said City of London'.

The leader of Leicester's company was called James Burbage, a carpenter turned actor. Now that he was legally protected in his second trade, he decided to put the first to use by going to London and looking for a site on which he could build a permanent home for his company. When he got there he found that the Puritan City council had recently passed its very own legislation limiting the activities of actors: a law of 1574 regulated the performance of plays inside the City walls. Burbage jumped over the walls. He signed a lease for a patch of land outside them, in nearby Shoreditch, and in 1576 he built his playhouse and called it by the obvious name: The Theatre. The history of the London stage had been initiated by a company of five men at a cost of £666. Others soon followed their lead. A year later The Curtain was built, also in Shoreditch, beyond the wall.

Rarely in its history does a nation produce more than one intense burst of dramatic activity. The English have seen at least three such periods, and that implies specially favourable conditions for the theatre. In particular it requires a demanding and receptive audience – without that, the rest is merely academic. What makes the English theatre special is a national characteristic common to both audience and actor alike, and here I must state a theory which I offer in the spirit of the theory itself.

Intuitively, it seems, the English understand what I shall call 'the theatrical game'. This is not to retract my earlier assertion that the theatre matters to society, or that the need for drama is fed by an ancient and religious impulse. On the contrary, for the English nothing is too serious or too profound to disbar it from the status of a sport or game. In Parliament, for example, the hounding of a cabinet minister and the banter and cut and thrust of debate are practised with all the skills and attitudes of professional sportsmen. Judge and counsel, defence and prosecution, play games in the Law Courts; military manoeuvres are turned into games; games are still believed to be an essential feature of an English child's education. The invention and playing of games has delighted the English for centuries, and it denotes an attitude of mind which leaves room for a certain detachment from the authorized version of reality. For actors, this attitude illuminates their work; for playgoers, it enhances their pleasure. Impersonation and disguise as theatrical devices set no problems for a nation which domesticates them in its social conventions.

The theatre game which developed was made up of a great variety of devices which extended the choices available to dramatists and became more and more subtle in the hands of master playwrights. Members of the audience might turn out to be characters in the play; plays could be staged within plays; characters might change their names, costumes, voices, or even their sex. In the beginning all these strokes of artifice must have startled and thrilled their audience, before they passed into the familiar repertory of the plot. Many of what are now standard contrivances are found as early as the Mystery and Miracle plays, in which for example the figure of Vice is often disguised and always, in the end, unmasked. They appear and re-appear in many of the theatre's masterpieces, as part of the grammar of what they have to tell.

The ability of a Tudor audience to accept and enjoy conventions of this kind was to prove a creative influence, because it meant that dramatists could write and that actors could portray characters with an accessible internal life, confident that playgoers would appreciate the weave of reality and illusion. To this day English audiences love the theatrical game, admiring sophisticated tricks of construction, portrayal and point-of-view, and perhaps most of all enjoying the force and play of language.

So when James Burbage built The Theatre outside the jurisdiction of the City of London, the Tudor stage was set. There were experienced professional players under noble patronage, playing in permanent playhouses to a discerning and lively audience. But the century had another vital element to offer to the theatre. It happened that the English language too had emerged from its transformations in the Middle Ages, with great colloquial vigour and an enormous hybrid vocabulary. It remained for the dramatists to find a way to use it.

From the texts of the interludes of the late fifteenth and early sixteenth centuries we can see how ungainly dramatic speech was likely to be. This extract from *Mankind* dates from 1497:

> *Mankind:* Go and do your labour! God let you never thee!
> Or with my spade I shall you ding, by the Holy Trinity!
> Have ye none other man to mock, but ever me?
> Hie you forth lively, for hence I will you drife.

Fifty years later, the basic rhythm of such lines showed signs of shifting. John Heywood is sometimes described as the first writer of English comedy. The following lines are from his last play, *Johan, Johan*, whose subtitle displays its wares: it is *A Mery Play, betwene Johan Johan, the Husbande, Tyb, his wyfe, and Syr Jhan, the Priest.*

> *Tyb:* Ah, whoreson knave! Hast thou broken my pail?
> Thou shalt repent, by Cock's lily nail.
> Ye whoreson drivel. Get thee out of my door!
> *Johan:* Nay, get thou out my house, thou priestes whore!
> *Syr Jhan:* Thou liest, thou whoreson cuckold, to thy face.
> *Johan:* And thou liest, peel'd priest, with an evil grace.
> *Tyb:* At him, Syr Jhan, or else God give thee sorrow.
> *Johan:* And have at you, whore and thief, Saint George to borrow!

The language is simple and unambiguous, to say the least, yet there is a movement towards dramatic tension among the characters, instead of a debate in the manner of earlier interludes. At the same time the piece is plagued by end-stopped lines and the rhyming couplet, which make up-hill work for actors.

Literature as such has little place in this book. I believe that plays are taught in schools to their detriment, and that the most attentive reading of a dramatic text is bound to reduce it by removing it from its proper dimension. But drama and literature interact, and English literature came to the rescue of the theatre when Henry Howard, Earl of Surrey, resolved to translate books II and IV of Virgil's *Aeneid* and borrowed an Italian metre to do it. Surrey may have lacked the bite and immediacy of his great contemporary, Sir Thomas Wyat, whose verse has other strengths which would be seen in the language of drama. Yet it is Surrey who takes the credit for introducing blank verse into English, where it flourished. This is from Surrey's translation of *Dido's Hunting:*

> Like when Apollo leaveth Lycia,
> His wintering place, and Xanthus' floods likewise,
> To see Delos, his mother's mansion,
> For to repair and furnish her new choir,

Cretians and folk of Driopes
And painted Agathirth do howl and cry,
Environing the altars round about,
When that he walks upon Mount Cynthus' top,
His sparkled trees repressed with garlands soft
Of tender boughs, and tressed up in gold,
His quiver darts clattering behind his back:
So fresh and lusty did Aeneas seem;
Such loudly port in countenance doth show.

This is not yet the voice of dramatic expression, and the attempt to imitate the imagery and intonation of the classical past also brought a vein of pompousness into English literature and into some theatrical writing. But the blank verse form was crucial, and the revival of the Greek and Latin masters provided a rich source of allusion and images, as well as giving new access to the playwrights of Athens and Rome.

At the universities and the Inns of Court, learned young men wrote and performed plays on these Greek and Roman models. The text was now all-important, and I suspect that it had little life outside the institutions they were studied in. Nevertheless, by 1580 a group of undergraduates, all in their early twenties, Greene, Kyd, Thomas Lodge, Lyly and Peele among them, were learning the craft of writing plays, presumably in the hope of one day having them produced in the new permanent theatres that were springing up all over London.

Another undergraduate, sixteen years old, had just entered Corpus Christi College, Cambridge. An exact contemporary of his had not yet left his birthplace, Stratford-upon-Avon. They were Christopher Marlowe and William Shakespeare.

Marlowe, baptized in Canterbury on 26 February 1564, was the son of a shoemaker. He was educated at King's School, Canterbury, before going up to Cambridge in 1580, and his university career was cut short because of some mysterious government service abroad. There was talk that he was a spy, which seems to me an apt occupation for a playwright. After his return to London he is believed to have continued his career in espionage at the same time that he was writing his plays. Marlowe's life was short but eventful. He was imprisoned as the result of a street fight in which an innkeeper was killed, and then pardoned by the Queen. Later he was charged with the crime of atheism, but before he could be brought to trial, he himself was killed in a Deptford pub brawl in circumstances never satisfactorily explained, but possibly connected with his spying activities.

Language and drama came together in Marlowe, and flared into life, and he seems to have been fully aware of the role he was to play. He took it as his mission to free the drama from what he called 'the jigging veins of rhyming mother-wits', and that is what he did. *Tamburlaine the Great* appeared in

Donald Wolfit, crowned as *Tamburlaine the Great*, by Marlowe, directed in 1951 by Tyrone Guthrie for the Old Vic, London.

1587. It was his first work for the theatre, and because it is repetitive and sprawling it cannot be described as a great play; though it bears the hallmarks of Marlowe's inspiration by bringing to life a superb and barbaric king, the play is not sure what to do with him when it finds him. Marlowe was more poet than dramatist, more an intellectual than a man of the theatre. There is splendour in his concepts, and more particularly in his language, but his plays, when I have experienced them in the theatre, have not seemed to move; they lack the relentless drive of, say, *Oedipus*, or *The Bacchae*.

Yet Marlowe brought new qualities to the theatre. Like others, he adapted blank verse to the stage, but he made it into an English form, with a magnificence that expressed the strength of our own language rather than respect for another. In *Doctor Faustus*, which appeared in 1588, he produced a hero who was not a king and whose tragedy was of a spiritual rather than a material nature. In doing that, he made personal and individual the generalizing approach of the old Morality plays, and he allowed his characters to be changed by what they did, as Doctor Faustus is changed by the end of the play. Finally, though, it is Marlowe's words that single him out of the roster of playwrights which begins this chapter, and whose mere number is a tribute to

Frontispiece illustration from the first edition of *Doctor Faustus*

the strength of the tradition they began. His poetic vision and soaring imagery create their most brilliant effects in the great heroic set-pieces, as when Faust, having bartered his soul to the Devil, comes to face his everlasting damnation in the passage that begins:

> Ah, Faustus.
> Now hast thou but one bare hour to live
> And then thou must be damn'd perpetually!
> Stand still, you ever-moving spheres of heaven,
> That time may cease, and midnight never come;
> Fair Nature's eye, rise, rise again, and make
> Perpetual day; or let this hour be but
> A year, a month, a week, a natural day,
> That Faustus may repent and save his soul!

Even so brief an example gives a measure of the distance which dramatic language had been able to travel in the two decades since Surrey's translation of the *Aeneid*, and the revolution which had taken place since the rhyming couplets of the Interludes. Marlowe's most fitting epitaph was written in the nineteenth century by Algernon Swinburne:

> He is the greatest discoverer, the most daring and inspired pioneer, in all our poetic literature. Before him there was neither genuine blank verse nor a genuine tragedy in our language. After his arrival the way was prepared, the paths made straight, for Shakespeare.

Marlowe died in 1593. By that year, it is thought that his immediate contemporary had written at least six plays, including *Richard III* and *The Comedy of Errors*.

'All that is known with any degree of certainty concerning Shakespeare is – that he was born in Stratford-upon-Avon, married and had children there, went to London, where he commenced actor, and wrote poems and plays, returned to Stratford, made his will, died, and was buried.' That was the view of George Steevens, a great Shakespearean scholar of the eighteenth century. Modern research has produced a little more than Steevens knew, but what we have are a great many documents of a dry, official character: dates of baptism, marriage, death and burial; legal documents relating to the purchase of a house and the processes of the law. There are also some contemporary references to him as a writer, and these, taken together with the sparse details of his private life, have encouraged all sorts of attempts to flesh out the picture. The inescapable fact is that they are fantasy: history has provided us with no documented insight into Shakespeare's interior life. We have the plays, the poetry and the sonnets, and they give us an elusive, tantalizing sense of the artist, but there is no point in trying to derive a playwright's views and personality from the playwright's work.

What we can say is that Shakespeare was baptized on 26 April 1564 at Holy Trinity Church, Stratford-upon-Avon, Warwickshire. His birthday is traditionally celebrated on 23 April, but no actual record confirms it. His father, John, traded at various times in barley, timber and wool. In some documents he is styled as 'yeoman', which indicates a man of substance under the degree of gentleman. At times he was prosperous. In 1565 he was chosen as an alderman, and in 1568 as bailiff, an office equivalent to mayor. William's mother was Mary Arden, who came from an ancient family and was heiress to some land. About 1557 she married John Shakespeare; William was their first surviving child, and there were three other sons and two daughters.

Although Stratford's grammar school was a good one, no list of its pupils in the sixteenth century has ever been found. Given that John Shakespeare's position in the town would have entitled him to a free education for his children, we may take it – but here the speculation begins – that William attended the school, where he would have learned to read and write. It is thought that he would have studied Latin, and that he may have read some of the classical historians, moralists and poets, and may even have read Plautus, Terence and Seneca. He did not go on to the university, because he married when he was eighteen. We learn from the register in Stratford church that Susanna, the daughter of William Shakespeare and Anne Hathaway, was baptized in 1583. Two years later, twins were born, and baptized Hamnet and Judith. The boy, Hamnet, died at the age of eleven.

The next seven or eight years of Shakespeare's life are lost to us. Nothing is known, and so a vast bibliography of theory has sprung up to account for the missing time. Legends current long after his death have him stealing deer from a local bigwig, earning his living as a schoolmaster, going to London and gaining entry to the theatre by minding playgoers' horses, and serving as a soldier in the Low Countries. Some of the theories are simply deduced from the content of the plays – if Shakespeare knew so much about warfare, surely he must have served in the army. Ten thousand Shakespeares can be built on such a basis. None of them will do. A playwright can research his subject, talk to experts, listen to conversations, or summon the resource which theorists tend to overlook – the gift of imagination.

What happened to Shakespeare in the interval before his name begins to appear in London theatre records remains a mystery. The important thing for us is that he arrived at what seems to have been exactly the right moment. The acting profession was thriving in spite of official opposition – or maybe because of it; the drama had found its language; there was a popular and economically viable theatre. We do not know what first attracted Shakespeare to the theatre. He may have seen touring actors in Stratford, where his father,

Will Kempe as in legend he danced from London to Norwich.

as bailiff, would have had to license the first performance of visiting companies. Once he needed to express his extraordinary gifts, he could only go to London.

Again, we do not know for certain when he left Stratford or when he arrived in the capital city. All that can be said with confidence is that by 1592, at the age of twenty-eight, Shakespeare was a member of the London theatrical profession, established as an actor and playwright. He lived in Bishopsgate, a short distance from James Burbage's theatre. By 1595 he was a member of the Lord Chamberlain's Men, the most successful theatre company of the day, and already he had earned the tribute of envy. Robert Greene, one of the university playwrights, warned in a pamphlet written on his deathbed in 1592:

> There is an upstart crow, beautified with our feathers, that with his *Tygers heart wrapt in a Players hide* supposes he is as well able to bombast out a blank verse as the best of you; and, being an absolute *Johannes Factotum*, is in his own conceit the only Shake-scene in a country.

For a dying man to hold such resentment of the brilliance of a non-university writer points to one thing for certain: that his target was highly successful. Shakespeare made money, and invested it in property both in London and Stratford. For the next twenty years his daily life was writing, rehearsing and acting.

The theatre's prosperity reached a low ebb in 1597. In February, James Burbage died, but his sons Cuthbert and Richard followed in the family trade, Cuthbert as manager, Richard as actor and fellow member with Shakespeare of the Lord Chamberlain's Men. That July, another company, Pembroke's Men, gave a performance at the Swan of a play now lost, by Thomas Nashe, called *The Isle of Dogs*. The Privy Council considered that it contained 'very seditious and slanderous matter', and so ordered the closing of all theatres 'during this time of sommer'. The actors were 'comytted to prison, whereof one of them was not only an actor, but a maker of parte of the said plaie'. (This collaborator was Ben Jonson, who was obliged to spend three months in the Marshalsea prison before being released.) There was even a threat to pull down every theatre in London, but it was the Queen herself who saved the day. Elizabeth loved theatrical performances at court, and that required the continuation of a flourishing theatre.

The Burbages and Shakespeare had their own problems. The lease of The Theatre in Shoreditch expired in April, and the landlord, Giles Allen, threatened to tear it down unless he was paid a higher rent. Cuthbert, the leaseholder, would not have his arm twisted, and in December 1598 or January 1599 he anticipated Allen's threat: he, along with his brother Richard, Peter Street, the carpenter, and 'divers other persons to the number of twelve ... armed themselves ... and throwing down the sayd Theatre in very outragious, violent and riotous sort ... did then also in most forcible and ryotous manner take and carrye awaye from thence all the wood and timber thereof unto the Bancksyde ... and there erected a new playehowse with the sayd timber and woode'. Unruly the move may have been, but it was an excellent decision to cross to the South Bank, which was then packed with brothels – 'stews' – and was the venue for cock fights and bear-baiting. Every day between three and four thousand people made the journey across the Thames: they provided a ready-made audience, with few inhibitions and few rules of conduct but for a bias against boredom. The South Bank became the centre of theatrical activity. With the timbers of their old theatre, the Lord Chamberlain's Men chose a site in Southwark and there erected the most easterly of the four Bankside theatres. From 1599 onwards they presented the plays of William Shakespeare to the public at large in their new theatre, which they called The Globe.

The Globe, Shakespeare's wooden 'O', is perhaps the most famous play-house ever built, and it served London at a time when a greater proportion of its population was frequenting the theatre than at any other time in its history. It is estimated that London had about 160,000 inhabitants; of these, about twenty thousand visited the theatre every week. Since it was not the same twenty thousand every week, much more than one in eight of the population must have been regular playgoers. London must have buzzed with the theatre. With so many people longing to see plays, it is no wonder that playwrights abounded, and that they were driven to the peak of their talents.

Yet few illustrations survive of London playhouses in Tudor times. If we want to know about the physical arrangements of The Globe, and how it came to assume its shape and proportions, we have to enter yet another minefield of

Left William Shakespeare. *Right* an impression of the Globe Theatre, from a model in the Bear Garden museum, Southwark, London.

conjecture. Any idea we do have of Elizabethan playhouses we owe largely to a Dutch traveller, Johannes de Witt, who visited London around 1596 and made a drawing of The Swan to which he attached a written description. Since The Globe was not yet built, and in any case the de Witt drawing may be misleading, then reaching conclusions about The Globe from what we know about The Swan amounts to piling an inference upon an impression. Nevertheless, scholars have drawn upon other evidence too, to make informed guesses about Tudor theatres in general, including The Globe.

We can say with certainty that The Globe was octagonal in shape and open to the sky. It was built of wood and partially thatched. The precise dimensions of stage and auditorium are hypothetical, but the acting area is thought to have been immense by modern standards. There were two levels, a ground-level stage and an upper balcony. On the day of a performance a flag flew all morning and three separate blasts from a trumpeter in the roof alerted people that the hour of two o'clock was approaching, when the play would commence. Spectators entered through the only public door, which was opposite the stage. Admission cost one penny for the pit; a further penny bought a seat at the foot of the staircases to the left and right, or a climb to the top gallery; a third penny gained a spectator entrance to the first and second galleries where, according to Thomas Platter of Basle, he would have found 'the most comfortable seats which are cushioned, where he not only sees everything well, but can also be seen'. Special arrangements were made for aristocrats, who entered through the players' door behind the stage and sat in the 'gentlemen's room'. The price for the privileged was twelve pence; a view from the best seats was the poorest.

No evidence exists to tell us where what Glynne Wickham calls 'so startlingly original an idea as the Globe style Playhouse' sprang from. If it developed from inn-yards where the touring actors played, since inn-yards were rectangular, why build theatres in the round? We may be looking for logical progression where there is none. The idea of an amphitheatre could have been inspired by round medieval play-places in Cornwall, by the remains of the Roman occupation, or even by the circular bear and bull rings if an immediate precedent is required. Whatever the model, the circle is hardly an abstruse shape: it served the rituals of religion and the secular theatres of Greece and Rome. The Globe embraced man yet because it was open to the sky it did not shut out the universe. In name and concept it provides a perfect symbol of the age.

Shakespeare was a shareholder in The Globe. The Burbages – Cuthbert and Richard – held half the shares, and the other half were divided equally between John Heminge, Augustine Phillips, Thomas Pope, William Kempe (four of the twenty-six 'Principall Actors' in Shakespeare's plays as given in the First Folio list) and the playwright himself. Kempe was the leading comedian of his day. He is believed to have played Peter in *Romeo and Juliet* and Dogberry in *Much Ado About Nothing*. The year after The Globe was built, he sold his share so that, as he put it, he could 'daunst my selfe out of the world', for in 1600, perhaps to mark the new century, he took a month to dance from London to Norwich, an event he described in his *Kemps morris to Norwiche*. He seems certain to have been a broad comedian, closer to a circus clown than an actor. Consequently it is thought that the subtler parts of the Court fools in *As You Like It*, *Twelfth Night* and *King Lear* were written for his successor, Robert Armin, another of the twenty-six listed in the Folio.

By far the most remarkable actor in the company must have been Richard Burbage, because it was he who created all the major Shakespearean roles: Hamlet, Lear, Othello, Richard III and many others. The claim that he was the greatest actor of the age would have been disputed by Edward Alleyn of the Admiral's Company at The Rose playhouse. Alleyn played the heroes of Marlowe's plays; Burbage was Shakespeare's leading man. His portrait by an unknown artist depicts him as neither handsome nor striking, but with a blandness of feature common to many actors. Stories of him abound, though all apocryphal. One that demonstrates his fame is of a guide showing visitors around Bosworth Field, long after the death of the actor who had first played Richard III, and saying: 'This is where Richard Burbage fell.'

The boy players who created some of the most complex female roles ever written must also have had remarkable gifts. A boy actor had to be young, for his unbroken voice was an essential qualification, although characters like Mistress Quickly may well have been acted by men. The boys were apprenticed, probably for two or three years, to an actor who held shares in the company. Considering the parts that Shakespeare wrote for them, one is entitled to wonder whether he really expected a full account of the role, or whether the audience for a theatre without women was able to perform feats of imaginative transposition as a matter of course. In *Twelfth Night* and *As You Like It*, for example, the boys had to impersonate women who in turn were impersonating boys, and that would be literally child's play compared with the insights and resources needed for a Lady Macbeth, a Juliet, or a Cleopatra, although recent theories suggest that men played the more mature women's roles.

When it comes to the style of acting current at the time, we can only guess (having got used to conjecture), and try to console ourselves for the scale of our ignorance with the thought that at least there has been no dead weight of recorded practice to inhibit the playing of Shakespeare or the development of the theatre in later times. Still, with the reservation that playwrights are not to be automatically saddled with the views of their characters, Hamlet's famous speech of advice to the players (in Act III, Scene 2) is written with a theatrical voice that sounds more authoritative than a mere Prince of Denmark's, and to show 'the very age and body of the time his form and pressure' is very much a playwright's wish.

On the Folio list of 'principall actors' Shakespeare's is the first name, above that of Richard Burbage, which must have been a gesture of courtesy to the playwright. One of the parts he is thought to have played is the Ghost of Hamlet's father. Certainly his life was given to the theatre. With his thorough knowledge of acting, a divine gift for language, a passion for the dramatic tensions between characters, robust humour and agile wit, he wrote about two plays a year, probably with specific members of the company in mind, and he was able to rely on his audience's understanding and sophistication as much as on its rude enjoyment.

The scarcity of documented fact has enabled a long controversy about the true authorship of Shakespeare's plays to rumble down the centuries. Like some kind of literary Rorschach test, it tells more about the observers than about the subject. In part it has been motivated by a certain snobbish incredulity that anyone of his humble birth and limited education could write so well and reach so far. Not surprisingly, the pretenders to the throne have all been either scholars or noblemen or both. Francis Bacon, the 17th Earl of Oxford and even Queen Elizabeth herself have appeared as candidates. So has Christopher Marlowe, although this theory involves burying a substitute corpse in Deptford, smuggling Marlowe abroad, and paying Shakespeare to put his name to masterpieces dispatched from Italy. Perhaps the strongest reason for all this bamboozlement has been the longing to know more: one has only to imagine the emotions and excitement that would be felt around the world upon the discovery of an authentic manuscript entitled 'My Life in the Theatre' by William Shakespeare to gauge the frustration of knowing so little. Possessing the poems and plays, a skeleton of documentation, and not a shred of contemporary evidence for any of the suggested masquerades, it seems to me that there is no reason to doubt that the originality, energy and humanity of Shakespeare could have sprung from the roots we know of, and a free untutored mind.

Shakespeare holds a unique place in world literature, although I believe that his plays are best appreciated when seen in a theatre, for only then does the full magnitude of his dramatic genius appear. Ben Jonson said that Shakespeare 'was not of an age, but for all time', and I offer no further assessment of his achievements. In a strictly theatrical context, however, it is possible to describe the variety of his gifts, for he was able to write tragedy and comedy, farce and history, with a personal vision that has possessed the hearts and minds of people throughout the ages and all over the world. Above all, he applied his power of imagination and intellect not to abstract ideas but to human beings. The range of characters he created is unequalled, their emotional and psychological interplay still unexhausted. Furthermore, he expresses his insights into characters and themes with words and images that simultaneously create their speaker and the texture of the plays, so that the impression of pathos or humour or pain is unforgettable. No single play fails to echo beyond its outward confines. He continually strikes chords in his audience, drawing them into a deep identification.

As if all this were not enough, he chose to write for a medium that was not remote or bookish or scholarly. He saw to it that the most lively of forms, one that is always in danger of being seen as meretricious, could contain the most sublime, complex and enduring human experience. One of the ways he did this was to dissolve the boundary between comedy and tragedy, and let them interfuse each other. Only in the theatre could such an impact be made.

In case it is still necessary, this seems to be the place to add my own nail to the lid of a still unburied coffin. It holds the corpse of a belief, set forth in the eighteenth century by Alexander Pope and reiterated in the nineteenth century by Charles Lamb, that Shakespeare's association with the theatre does both him and his work a disservice. Pope's preface to his 1725 edition of the plays argued that Shakespeare's natural genius was hampered by his daily involvement with a working theatre, and that the theatrical form was a source of artistic defectiveness. Charles Lamb declared in 1811 'that the plays of Shakespeare are less calculated for performance on a stage, than those of any other dramatist whatever', and that reading the plays was preferable to the distraction of the theatre. Put baldly, these notions are patently insupportable, but they linger on in the deadly way that Shakespeare is often taught to the young. There is no escaping the fact that his plays were written to be performed for an audience in a theatre.

Demands are made on audiences, of course. 'O! for a muse of fire,' cries the Chorus in *King Henry the Fifth*, about to ask the playgoer to enter into the spirit of Shakespeare's theatre. He appeals to them directly:

And let us, ciphers to this great accompt,
On your imaginary forces work.

And later:

For 'tis your thoughts that now must deck our kings,
Carry them here and there, jumping o'er times,
Turning the accomplishment of many years
Into an hour-glass ...

This makes nonsense of the classical unities of time, place and action. Shakespeare's instincts were for drama wherever it was to be found. He freed the theatre from rules of style and form: what life contained, the drama might contain. In his splendid preface to the edition of the plays published in 1765, Doctor Johnson justified Shakespeare's approach as 'exhibiting the real state of sublunary nature', in which the gamut of human experience is always present.

The plays continue to be performed because the conflicts Shakespeare dramatizes are still in play. Guilt, lust for power, racialism, indecision, hypocrisy, passion and self-destruction are not archaic plagues. The sources of order and authority remain at issue. As an artist, his development and maturity were gradual. He entered the theatre comparatively late, in his mid-twenties. In eleven years, from 1589 onwards, he wrote a score of plays, mostly histories and comedies. In 1600, aged thirty-six, he produced *Hamlet* and

Paul Rogers and Jeremy Irons, as old and young Hamlet, at the Globe Theater Utah.

entered the dynamic period which contained *Twelfth Night, Measure for Measure, Othello, King Lear, Macbeth* and, in his early forties, *Antony and Cleopatra.* After that, his output lessened. *The Tempest* was his last important play. He was forty-eight years old, and tired. In the final act, Prospero says:

> But this rough magic
> I here abjure, and, when I have required
> Some heavenly music, which even now I do,
> To work mine end upon their senses that
> This airy charm is for, I'll break my staff,
> Bury it certain fathoms in the earth,
> And deeper than did ever plummet sound
> I'll drown my book.

Charles Laughton and Elsa Lanchester as Prospero and Ariel in Guthrie's production of
The Tempest at Sadlers Wells, London, 1934.

In that same year of 1612, Shakespeare retired from the theatre and returned
to Stratford. In January, four years later, he made his will. Apart from bequests
to his family and the notorious legacy of his second-best bed to his wife, he left
Richard Burbage 26s 8d for the purchase of a ring. On 23 April 1616, aged fifty-
two, he died. There is no name inscribed on his gravestone in the chancel of
the parish church of Stratford, but these words which he himself may have
written:

> Good Friend, for Jesus' sake forbear
> To dig the dust enclosed here.
> Blest be the man that spares these stones,
> And curst be he that moves my bones.

It we continue to look for the person behind the master dramatist whose
words and images have become part of the English imagination, and who is
universally acknowledged as the greatest playwright who has ever lived, we
may find him in the touching epitaph written by his friend and colleague Ben
Jonson:

> He was indeed honest, and of an open and free nature; had an excellent
> fancy, brave notions and gentle expressions.

St Paules Church

THAMESIS

The Beer Garden   The Globe

'A personal vision that has possessed the hearts and minds of people throughout the ages and all over the world.'

Above 17th-century London, with two Elizabethan theatres labelled in the foreground. *Left* The native tradition: *Mankind* in the production for *All the World's a Stage.*

Above left Charles Kean's 1859
production of *Henry V*.
Below left Henry Irving as
Benedict and Ellen Terry as
Beatrice in *Much Ado About
Nothing*.
Above Herbert Beerbohm Tree
as Falstaff, with Ellen Terry and
Mrs Kendall, in *The Merry
Wives of Windsor*, in 1904.

19th-century Shakespeare.
Left Twelfth Night, in 1853, with
Walter Lacy, Miss Heath and
Mrs Chapman.
Hamlet's advice to the players
passed largely unnoticed; (*below*)
a production from Chicago in
1873.
The Deutsches Theater in Berlin
mounted *Romeo and Juliet*
(*right*) in 1886. By 1895, however,
William Poel was advocating
a return to a more authentically
Shakespearean production:
(*below right*) *The Comedy of
Errors* at Gray's Inn, London, 1895.

Above A Midsummer Night's Dream, at Stratford upon Avon in 1981: Juliet Stevenson and Mike Gwilym as Titania and Oberon. In the same season, the Royal Shakespeare Company produced *All's Well That Ends Well* (*left*) with Peggy Ashcroft and John Franklyn-Robbins.

Above The American Shakespeare
Theatre, Connecticut, produced *Henry
IV Part I* in 1982, with Christopher
Walken as Hotspur and Ellen Tobie as
Lady Percy.
The Rustaveli Company of Georgia,
USSR, presented *Richard III* at the
Round House, London (*left*), with
Ramaz Chkhivadze, in 1980.

Overleaf The American Shakespeare
Theater's 1981 production of *Othello*
with James Earl Jones in the title role,
and Christopher Plummer as Iago.

SUCH STUFF
AS DREAMS
ARE MADE ON

What a piece of work is a man! How noble in reason! how infinite in faculty! in form and moving how express and admirable! in action how like an angel! in apprehension how like a god! the beauty of the world! the paragon of animals!

Shakespeare gives these words to Hamlet, his Renaissance Prince, and they capture the spirit of an age which proclaimed man's belief in his own divinity and the reach of his energy, both physical and intellectual. But Shakespeare was no Renaissance idealist, and his plays explored complexities of emotion and reason which took them to less elevated levels. Hamlet's speech ends: 'And yet, to me, what is this quintessence of dust?' In Italy, the mainspring of Renaissance aspirations, the expression and emphasis was to be very different. A vision of human excellence was created which lies at the heart of the Western tradition to this day, and which influenced and altered the theatre both for good and bad.

The Renaissance describes a period in European history which began in Italy in the fourteenth century and spread to the rest of Europe, taking different forms in different countries, and lasting in some of them well into the seventeenth century. The birthplace of this spirit of renewal was Florence, and by the fifteenth century it was the richest, most vigorous city in Europe. Florentines were overcome by a great surge of confidence in their republican city-state, which they were soon comparing to the Athens and Rome of the Golden Age. The ancient world became the ideal of Renaissance man, in the Renaissance version.

At that time, any Florentine who wished to be considered civilized was compelled to study the classical heritage. Whether soldier, cleric or merchant, the complete man, *l'uomo universale*, must appreciate music, painting, sculpture and architecture (but not the theatre, which was a vulgar pursuit, and apt to catch people with their pants down). Italians of the Renaissance felt it possible to be connoisseurs of everything that was thought to be beautiful. They aimed to possess a knowledge of Latin and Greek, and of history and philosophy. And the Greek philosopher who caught their imagination most strongly was Plato.

One current in Plato that attracted Renaissance interest was his abstracting, idealizing tendency: seldom a fruitful influence on the theatre, but an inspiration for the visual arts which expressed much of the Italian genius. Another and related current was Plato's theorizing about the perfect state. Very crudely, he held that desire, warmed by emotion, is governed by knowledge. In a perfect state, the forces of commerce would produce and trade in goods, but would not rule; the military would protect, but they would not rule; the forces of knowledge and science and philosophy would be guarded and encouraged, and *they* would rule. Without knowledge, the populace lack order, and so they need philosophers for guidance. The state is doomed to fall once it is ruled by traders, 'whose heart is lifted up by wealth', or by generals, when they use their armies to impose military dictatorship. The trader for economics, the warrior for strategy, but both were a scourge in public office because they submerged statesmanship in the politics of self-interest. Plato claimed that statesmanship was both a science and an art, and that its practitioner needed dedication and a thorough preparation. Only a philosopher-king was equipped to guide a nation.

This line of thinking offered a powerful ideology to the princes of Italian states, and it is hardly surprising that they grasped it:

> Until philosophers are kings, or the kings and princes of this world have the spirit and power of philosophy, and wisdom and political leadership meet in the same man ... cities will never cease from their evils – no, nor the human race, as I believe – and then only will this our State have a possibility of life and behold the light of day.

Plato's ideal of the philosopher-king was adopted by the Renaissance princes and their courts. The Prince was at the head of a higher Platonic order. Furthermore, and in accordance with Plato, he was to equate beauty with goodness.

The new prince ruled a new society centred on the city-states. The invention of printing contributed to the growth of a literate population who turned to the writings of antiquity to justify creeds of humanism and individuality not underwritten by medieval tradition. This passion for the classical world led to the rediscovery and translation of Greek and Latin texts. Sir Thomas North's translation of Plutarch's *Lives* in 1579 gave Shakespeare the material for *Antony and Cleopatra, Coriolanus, Julius Caesar* and *Timon of Athens*. Plautus supplied the sources of *The Comedy of Errors*. Authors like Petrarch and Boccaccio were inspired by the classical texts they studied. The glories of ancient Greece and Rome were to serve as models for the lords of the new age.

The Italian theatre was not in the cultural vanguard, but it could not fail to be affected by new fashions. The Florentine ruler, Lorenzo de Medici – the Magnificent – brought his own elaborate vision to the religious pageants which had been common in medieval Italy. Into the native version of Miracle plays he inserted intermezzi, pseudo-classical interludes of words and music on mythological themes. These were to become handsome entertainments in their own right. Loosely connected scenes with music and dance developed distinctly theatrical qualities. In the Uffizi Palace, in Florence, a scenic designer, Bernardo Buontalenti, renowned as an organizer of pageants and fireworks, constructed a temporary 'theatre room' where splendid fêtes were produced during the winter of 1585–6. However, Buontalenti matters, not as an architect, but as a scenic designer, or scenographer as he liked to call himself. He presented a series of intermezzi under the title *Orfeo* – six scenes linked to tell one story, though it was not the story that counted, but the visual grandeur. Until his death in 1608 he designed costumes of allegorical characters – nymphs, the planets, gods, dragons, cherubs – for the Medici extravaganzas, and constructed elaborate stage machinery which was capable of creating magical effects. His drawings and engravings for the intermezzi of 1589 were to influence the course of theatrical design.

The theatre also drew inspiration from what now appears a rather dry and dusty source, but too influential to overlook. In 1511 a book was published called *De architectura*, the same ten-volume treatise which we last met when dealing with the birth of the Christian era. Vitruvius' book was based on his own experience as well as on theoretical works by famous Greek architects such as Hermogones. It covered almost every aspect of architecture, but its outlook was essentially Hellenistic. One section was concerned with sceno-

Design for an intermezzo by Buontalenti.

graphy, and Vitruvius' Renaissance counterpart, Sebastiano Serlio, borrowed heavily from it.

Serlio was born in Bologna in 1475 and died in 1554 in Fontainebleau, where he had been employed by Francis I as a consultant on the building of the palace. His treatise *Tutte l'opere d'architettura*, much of it based on the notes and drawings made by his teacher, Baldassare Peruzzi, was published serially between 1537 and 1575. In the volume devoted to scenography, Serlio describes, among other things, his ideas for three basic permanent sets: for tragedy, palaces; for comedy, street scenes; and for satyr plays, countryside. He also explored the use of perspective in theatre design.

Linear perspective is a system of representing three-dimensional space and the objects and figures within it on a flat surface. It uses mathematical technique to render these from a single 'vanishing point', the imagined location of the viewer, and was developed in painting at the beginning of the Italian Renaissance. The technique was formulated by the Florentine architect Filippo Brunelleschi, who worked out some of the fundamental principles. In painting, the effect was to make the plane of the picture into a window on the visible world; to eyes accustomed to the very different representational methods of medieval painting, the impact was startling, almost miraculous – as if the world was being re-created. This kind of perspective also has meaning beyond the technical or visual application; it can be regarded as the symbolic expression of man's new place in taking the measure of the world. For Renaissance scene designers, this was a challenge they could not resist.

In Vicenza stands the most famous example of early experimentation with perspective in the theatre. The Teatro Olimpico was built by Andrea Palladio and completed by Vincenzo Scamozzi in 1585. It opened on 3 March of that year with an epic production of Sophocles' *Oedipus Rex*. Although constructed on the Greco-Roman model, the theatre managed to be private and elitist rather than democratic, and it was an indoor theatre – the clouds above the audience are a painted illusion. The semicircular auditorium faces a long narrow stage backed by an extravagantly designed façade with one large central opening and four other entrance doors. In these entrances are set perspective vistas of city streets. The drawback is that when performers appear on stage they destroy the effect of the perspective; Scamozzi never resolved this problem. Lighting was another difficulty, which gave rise to ingenious solutions – lamps were placed behind a row of white and red wine bottles, or vessels with coloured water, giving some compensation for the loss of natural light.

The Teatro Olimpico remains a single oddity which, despite its splendour, had little or no influence on later theatre buildings in Italy or elsewhere. Its historical importance is to have brought together many of the visual and theatrical ideas which were current at the time. Nevertheless, the spectacles and entertainments staged there must have been dazzling, and they certainly made an indelible impression on one man, the English architect and designer

Vicenza: Palladio's Teatro Olimpico.

Inigo Jones. He recorded their styles and methods and brought them back to England, where Shakespeare, Ben Jonson and their fellows were writing for a very different sort of theatre.

The age of Elizabeth I, an age of discovery and expansion, had united its literary brilliance with the vigour of its popular theatre. In 1603 Elizabeth died, and the throne fell to James I of England and VI of Scotland. A golden monarch of the Renaissance was succeeded by a graceless king, riddled with insecurity because of his doubtful claim to the English throne. One of the ways James chose to reinforce his sovereignty was by showing off on a monstrous scale. Since royal processions had been a glory of the monarchy from the thirteenth century onwards, he chose to turn his entry into London with his Queen into a gaudy and fantastic progress.

James I was a staunch believer in the Divine Right of Kings, and in addition to the age-old symbols of power – processions, crowns, sceptres, orbs, which are still the paraphernalia of monarchy – James hit on yet another way of blazoning the notion of his absolute authority. He encouraged his wife, Queen Anne, in her passion for mounting elaborate court entertainments, called Masques, at the Palace of Whitehall.

These masques were hugely expensive, lavishly executed propaganda exercises: they glorified the King, thinly disguised as an allegorical figurehead, and it was classical allegory that carried the message. What created the impact was visual delight, and this was the province of the designer. Anne's choice fell on the young painter and architect who had studied in Italy and served at the Court of her brother, King Christian IV of Denmark. Entire control of the masques was placed in the hands of Inigo Jones.

In their study of Inigo Jones, Stephen Orgel and Roy Strong call him 'the most important single figure in the arts in seventeenth-century England'. He was baptized in London on 19 July 1573, the son of a clothworker. Little is known of his early life, but it is thought that he was apprenticed to a joiner. He had completed his tour of Italy by 1603, and in 1605, after his return from Denmark, Queen Anne employed him to design the scenes and costumes for a masque. From then until the outbreak of the Civil War in 1642, he was continuously under royal patronage, principally as a surveyor of works to James I and Charles I. The genius of Inigo Jones found many expressions; in this story he appears as a theatrical innovator, the man who altered forever the emphasis of dramatic presentation.

> Our revels now are ended. These our actors,
> As I foretold you, were all spirits and
> Are melted into air, into thin air,
> And, like the baseless fabric of this vision,
> The cloud-capp'd towers, the gorgeous palaces,
> The solemn temples, the great globe itself,
> Yea, all which it inherit, shall dissolve
> And, like this insubstantial pageant faded,
> Leave not a rack behind. We are such stuff
> As dreams are made on, and our little life
> Is rounded with a sleep.

In this speech from *The Tempest*, which can be dated about 1610–11, Allardyce Nicoll suggests that Shakespeare's Prospero likens the passage of life to the masque which has just been performed in honour of his daughter Miranda's marriage. He, the rightful Duke of Milan, had followed the practice of Florentine princes and English kings by commanding an entertainment to celebrate a special occasion. The goddesses Iris, Ceres and Juno had appeared, and a band of nymphs had danced with country reapers to mark the royal occasion. Prospero's images of ephemeral splendour may convey Shakespeare's response to the masques he would certainly have seen. The melting into air, the towers, palaces, temples – this is the style and content of the royal masques.

The Tempest was Shakespeare's last major play, and he retired soon after it was written, perhaps because of an inner conviction that he had no more to write. But that conviction may have been reinforced by the more conscious understanding that the theatre in which he had worked all his adult life was in eclipse. It is difficult to escape the impression that Shakespeare knew that there was no part for his 'rough magic' in the performances whose engineer and impresario was Inigo Jones.

No theatrical form could have been more alien to Shakespeare. To begin with, the masque was exclusive to the Court – no groundlings here. Instead of allowing language and imagination to paint the scene between them, the masque took décor as its central feature. The vast stage and seating arrangements were temporary. A masque would be given for a couple of grand performances, and then the entire structure was removed. The King sat on his throne at the central point of the perspective. No other member of the audience could enjoy the effects so completely as he. Seated to either side of him were his guests and those members of his Court who were not performing, for these affairs were amateur dramatics on the grandest scale, although assistance was sometimes enlisted from professional actors. The area between throne and stage, the space where allegory and reality were joined, was the scene of the dancing which ended the masque and which often went on till dawn, compared with the less than an hour's duration of the masque itself.

Inigo Jones was encouraged to allow his brilliant imagination to run riot. Each masque was endowed with fantastic settings and magical effects which were intended to bewitch the spectator as one scene gave way effortlessly to another. In Christ Church Hall, Oxford, in August 1605 he used revolving screens, copied from the Italians, for the first time. He used backcloths, shutters and, painted to give the illusion of perspective, flats which could be slotted into grooves and fitted onto a turn-table called *machina versatilis*, revolving to show the audience different facets of an apparently permanent and solid setting. Most important of all, he swept away the old concept that one side of the stage could represent, say, Africa, and the other Asia, and that the audience must remember which was which (a concept which was to dog the theatre in France). Jones made a unity of place within an ornamental arch which echoed the triumphal arches of Roman emperors and Renaissance princes; it was called the proscenium arch (Latinized from the Greek *proskenion*, in front of the stage), and was to become the enduring frame of the theatre.

Yet the spirit of the masque was its transitory beauty. Jones and his colleagues laboured hard to produce a bubble of illusion which was never intended to be permanent – a fact which may account for the impression of sadness that permeates so many contemporary descriptions of the performances. When the masque was over the magic evaporated. This same quality was the burden of a famous dispute which blew up between Inigo Jones and his chief collaborator, the playwright Ben Jonson. The conflict ran deep, and still does: it was the perennial battle of spectacle against content.

Samuel Daniel, himself a writer of masques, accepted rather lamely that the

Proscenium border and standing pastoral scene, for *Florimene*, 1635, by Inigo Jones.

'pompe and splendor of the sight takes up all the intention without regard [to] what is spoken'. Later he was to admit that 'the only life consists in shew; the arte and invention of the Architect gives the greatest grace and is of most importance'. Thomas Dekker, best known for his comedy *The Shoemaker's Holiday* (1600), and who used elements of the masque in his plays, complained of being at 'the hard-handed mercy of Mychanitiens'. But Ben Jonson suffered nothing gladly and said few things lamely: his complaints were broadsides, and he frequently displayed the temperamental weakness of the man who cracks nuts with steamrollers. Aggressive and burly, he could be argumentative well beyond the point of spite, and was given to venting his spleen on colleagues, who for their part tended to forgive him, possibly reminding themselves that his first trade had been laying bricks.

Jonson's comedy *Volpone* (1606) contains many soaring passages of poetry counterpointing his exultant exposure of almost all of the seven deadly sins, and most of all greed. His major comedies express distaste for the world he lived in, and a youthful delight in prodding the sores of its follies and vices. Even so, he was able to write eight masques for performance at Court, and found words to glorify the King as an ideal monarch and the society he ruled as immaculate. Conflicting thoughts and passions warred in Jonson, and he was cross-grained enough to enjoy the contest. He was a delicate lyric poet, yet two

'Until philosophers are kings, or the kings
and princes of this world have the spirit and
power of philosophy – then only will this our
State have a possibility of life and behold the
light of day.'

Above the Teatro Olimpico at Vicenza, with
its illusionistic perspective, designed by
Palladio and completed by Scamozzi in 1585.

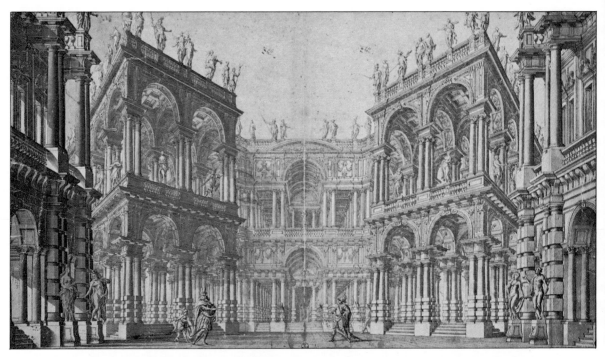

Left the perspective designs of the Bibienas at the turn of the eighteenth century marked the fruition of the epoch that was initiated by Serlio (1475–1573) and (*below left*) his teacher, Peruzzi. From the Gabinetto dei Disegni e delle Stampe, Florence.

The designs for the Medicean intermezzi at Florence, by the brilliant scenographer, Bernardo Buontalenti, would have been known to the young Inigo Jones.
Below L'Inferno, from *La Pellegrina*, 1589.

Intermezzo designs, from *La Pellegrina*,
1589, by Buontalenti.
Above Dei e segni planetari.
Right La montagna delle Amadriadi
(Biblioteca Nazionale, Florence).

Three designs for masque costumes by Inigo Jones.
Far left a lady masquer, *c.*1610.
Left a star, from *The Lord's Masque* by Thomas Campion, 1613.
Right A torchbearer as an 'oceania' from *The Masque of Blackness* by Ben Jonson, 1605.

Below the establishment of Italian scene design: a set by Borgonio, 1651.
Overleaf Parigi and Callot's vast setting of the entombment of Typhon on Ischia, an intermezzo performed for a Medici wedding in the Uffizi Palace in 1616.

of his most successful plays, *Epicoene* (1609) and *Bartholomew Fair* (1614), are written entirely in prose; he castigated Shakespeare for verbal extravagance, yet penned verses which acclaimed him equal to the dramatists of classical antiquity. But the duality of his nature was most conspicuously exposed in his attitudes towards Inigo Jones and the masque.

Jonson gained royal attention at the beginning of the new reign. When Queen Anne was travelling south from Scotland in 1603 she saw his *Entertainment at Althorpe*; two years later, Jonson's *The Masque of Blackness* was presented at Court, and this brought him into a working relationship with Inigo Jones which progressed from a harmonious beginning to a sour conclusion. Jonson's duality showed itself as early as 1606, when his masque *Hymenaei* was performed to celebrate the marriage of the Earl of Essex to Lady Frances Howard. Jonson introduced four 'humours' who disrupt the ceremony but are expelled by 'reason' so that the gods favourable to marriage may enter for the celebration. In the context of the work as a whole, this is a minor moment, and the anti-masquers have no lines, but Jonson was soon to remedy that, and in the course of time he wrote a number of anti-masques.

The battle between Ben Jonson and Inigo Jones raged on for several years, and is best told in the combatants' own words:

Ben Jonson: Court masques have either been or ought to be the mirrors of man's life.
Inigo Jones: Masques are nothing else but pictures with light and motion.
Jonson: If Ben Jonson is prepared to write masques, let no Englishman dismiss them as a trifle.
Jones: Shall we who are the poor engineers for shadows, and who frame images of no result, seek to avoid them by flying to an Army of Authors, as idle as ourselves?
Jonson: It is a noble and just advantage that the things subjected to understanding have of those which are subjected to sense; that the one sort are but momentary, and merely taking; the other impressing and lasting, else the glories of all these solemnies had perished like a blaze, and gone out, in the beholders' eyes. So short lived are the bodies of all things, in comparison of their souls. And though bodies of times have the ill-luck to be sensually preferred, they find afterwards the good fortune (when souls live) to be utterly forgotten. This it is hath made the most royal princes, and greatest persons (who are commonly the personaters of these actions) not only studious of riches, and magnificence in the outward celebration or shew, which rightly becomes them; but curious after the most high and hearty inventions, to furnish the inward parts, and those grounded upon antiquity and solid learnings: which though their voice be taught to sound to present occasions, their sense or doth or should always lay hold on more removed mysteries.

But no matter how eloquent Ben Jonson's words, King and Court were seduced by the dynamic visual imagination of Inigo Jones, which must have been overwhelming when translated into reality. He was encouraged, if encouragement was needed, to become more and more extravagant. Jonson responded by making fun of his opponent. It has been suggested that the puppet master, Lantern Leatherhead, in *Bartholomew Fair* is based on Jones. In case the dig escaped him, Jonson addressed him more directly:

Oh, to make Boardes to speake! There is a taske!
Painting and Carpentry are the Soule of Masque!
Pack with your pedling Poetry to the Stage!
This is the money-gett, Mechanick Age!

It was Jones who won the contest. He responded with ever more lavish masques, and continued to enjoy royal patronage. In 1619 he was commissioned to build a new Masquing Hall, the Banqueting House in Whitehall. There the great temporary stage and seating arrangements were erected, and there courtly extravagance ran riot.

On 27 March 1625, James I died at his favourite country residence, Theobalds, in Hertfordshire. His successor, Charles I, married Henrietta Maria, the sister of the French king, Louis XIII, and in the first masque of his reign the Queen not only appeared as a masquer but also played a speaking part. The growing Puritan reaction against extravagance and display, for which the masque stood as a perfect symbol, was voiced by the barrister William Prynne. His description of women actors as notorious whores was construed as an attack on the Queen, and Prynne was prosecuted for High Treason, fined, and had his ears cut off. His cause was not so easy to curtail.

Although King Charles was heading for bankruptcy, he continued both to finance the masques and to sanction them with his presence. In 1613, a masque in his honour cost £20,000 – the equivalent of about £700,000 today – for a single performance. Admittedly the sum was raised by lawyers of the Inns of Court, but the masque was felt as a deliberate snub to public discontent. Yet in 1640, for the last masque ever presented – *Salmacida Spolia* by Sir William Davenant, Jones's new collaborator – the production and especially the machinery was costlier and more complicated than ever. Staging the masque was not the only parade of waste. It turned out that *Salmacida Spolia* could not be performed in the new Banqueting House because the great Rubens ceiling, Charles's memorial to his father and the Stuart dynasty, was being damaged by the torches used to light the performances. The King's solution was to have another masquing hall built nearby.

The finale of *Salmacida Spolia* (from the edition of 1640, the only printing) gives the flavour of 'that rich and nobly foolish line of courtly entertainments':

From the highest part of the heavens came forth a cloud far in the scene, in which were eight persons richly attired representing the spheres. This, joining with two other clouds which appeared at that instant full of music, covered all the upper part of the scene; and at that instant, beyond all these, a heaven opened full of deities; which celestial prospect, with the chorus below, filled all the whole scene with apparitions and harmony.

Song VI
To the King and Queen, by a Chorus of All
So musical as to all ears
Doth seem the music of the spheres,
Are you unto each other still,
Turning your thoughts to either's will.

All that are harsh, all that are rude,
Are by your harmony subdued;
Yet so into obedience wrought,
As if not forc'd to it, but taught.

Live still, the pleasure of our sight,
Both our examples and delight;

So long, until you find the good success
Of all your virtues in one happiness;

Till we so kind, so wise, and careful be,
In the behalf of our prosperity,

That we may wish your sceptres ruling here,
Lov'd even by those who should your justice fear,
When we are gone, when to our last remove
We are dispatch'd, to sing your praise above.

After this song the spheres passed through the air, and all the Deities ascended, and so concluded this Masque, which was generally approved of by all strangers that were present, to be the noblest and most ingenious that hath been done here in that kind.

The invention, ornament, scenes, and apparitions, with their descriptions, were made by Inigo Jones, Surveyor General of his Majesty's Works.

What was spoken or sung, by William Davenant, her Majesty's servant.

The subject was set down by them both.

The music was composed by Lewis Richard, Master of her Majesty's Music.

FINIS.

Davenant, who will be seen successfully spanning the chasm that severed English social and theatrical history, acknowledged the changing world. One of his characters, Philogones, speaks these words of comfort for a king who had to suffer repeated and savage attacks:

> O who but he could thus endure
> To live and govern in a sullen age
> When it is harder far to cure
> The people's folly than resist their rage?

The Puritans were in the ascendancy. The masque as a form was dead and gone. All that is left are some of the designs by Inigo Jones, preserved in the library of the Duke of Devonshire at Chatsworth. Yet in addition to symbolizing an incurable political division, the masque had powerfully dramatized the conflict between spectacle and content, between the scenic designer and the author. What was a triumph in the creation of theatrical illusion was disastrous for the inner life of the drama. To put it as bluntly as possible, Inigo Jones represents all that was and is superficial and spurious in the theatre. That is not to deny his genius, but rather to argue that it was never used to enhance a play of any worth, and furthermore that a theatre of 'production values' cannot leave room for any other kind. With the popularity at Court of the masque, the value of language was debased, and that cost the theatre very dear. In a sense the masque is important to this story by default. It is tempting to speculate whether Shakespeare at the height of his powers might have welded these two worlds of show and meaning into a single poetic vision, but when he declined the challenge he probably answered the question.

But the palace of the Stuart kings was not the only centre of theatrical life, and London provided an alternative theatre where the satires of Ben Jonson and others appeared side by side with tragedies whose authors would have found Aristotle's pity and fear a disappointing response. What they aimed to provoke was horror, and the content of Jacobean tragedy, stained with blood and quaking with thunder, tells a lot about what was waiting behind the brittle façade of London high life. The masques were expensive diversions in which the monarchy attempted to boost its own morale and to project a show of splendid security. When the show was over, the strains and fissures remained, and it was these that the Jacobean playwrights identified. Their plays were seldom given at Court, of course, but the paradox is that many of the courtiers who had so delighted in the masques should also have been drawn to the public playhouses. The English middle class which had supported Shakespeare's theatre had grown more and more Puritan by 1640, and took no delight in the biting comedies of Ben Jonson, John Marston or Thomas Middleton. The darker plays provoked violent reaction.

Possibly to accommodate the courtiers, or more likely because the King's Men were exasperated by the freaks of the English weather, theatres began to acquire protection from the elements. The Blackfriars Theatre was more or less a roofed-over version of Shakespeare's wooden O. In Drury Lane, an old cockpit – literally a place for cockfights – had been adapted for theatrical performances. A fire in 1619 destroyed the original, but it was rebuilt as the Phoenix, the first theatre in the West End of London.

Some of the plays performed in these new venues were written in a vein of murderous cynicism and morbid passion which makes deliberate nonsense of the Renaissance idealism equating good with beauty. Here, beauty of language, and sexual beauty, far from being emblems of good, are likely to be the outward forms of evil. Like the plays themselves, they are intimations of violence to come. Although some critics have dismissed the plots as melodramatic, they work in deadly earnest when they are played.

The Duchess of Malfi, by John Webster, dates from 1613–14 and tells the story of an aristocrat who falls in love and marries her steward. So incensed are her brothers, a cardinal and a duke, that they enlist the help of a villainous agent, Bosola. The duchess is subjected to torment, and made to witness vile pageants which culminate in a cruel dance of madmen. Finally they strangle her and her children. The duke's response to the sight of his sister's corpse is a line of ornate hypocrisy: 'Cover her face, mine eyes dazzle: she died young.'

Incest is the theme of John Ford's play *'Tis Pity She's A Whore*. A brother, Giovanni, woos his sister, Annabella, gains her love, marries her off, then forestalls the husband's revenge by killing Annabella and in a famous scene enters brandishing her heart, impaled on his dagger. In *The Changeling*, by Thomas Middleton and William Rowley, Beatrice Joanna hires an impoverished gentleman, De Flores, to murder the man her father wants her to marry because she is in love with another. She fails to perceive that De Flores

Helen Mirren as the Duchess of Malfi, at the Royal Exchange Theatre, Manchester, 1980.

himself has designs on her and therefore accepts the commission more than willingly. He murders her betrothed, but instead of accepting the money she offers discloses his passion for her. Her shock arises from her pride and hauteur. She who has commissioned De Flores to kill another man speaks of him as the would-be murderer of her honour, and scolds him for the viciousness of the language he has used to make his longings known. 'I cannot see which way I can forgive it,' she cries, 'With any modesty.' De Flores retaliates: 'Pish! You forget yourself! A woman dipped in blood, and talk of modesty!' Like Macbeth, she becomes the victim of her own wickedness. De Flores calls her 'the deed's creature', and in the end he murders her.

The Jacobean catalogue of savagery is long, with horror piled on horror. The plays are clotted with images of blood and death. It has been suggested that these playwrights were piling on the agony in order to satisfy the jaded palates of their audiences, but this judgment begs the question of why taste should have changed in that direction. It would not be so very strange if the plays and their audiences were to have anticipated the internecine rage of the Civil War to come. There is a parallel in the twentieth century for similar subconscious prophecies. The psychologist Carl Jung noted that many of his patients' dreams in the 1920s and 1930s were full of a horror which he diagnosed as anticipation of the terrible future of Hitler's Germany. Sometimes a nation will choose the theatre to do its collective dreaming.

The fabric of English society tore apart in 1642 with the outbreak of the Civil War. Parliament banned all plays, and recommended instead 'the profitable and seasonable considerations of Repentance, Reconciliation and peace with God'. Illicit performances were raided, and audiences fined on the spot. At the start of 1649, Puritan soldiers raided a theatre, and in the riot that followed, a property crown was paraded by the soldiers and mocked. A week later, on Tuesday, 30 January, outside his Banqueting House, Charles I was executed.

The English theatrical tradition could not be immune. Ben Jonson, rehabilitated by the Stuarts, did not live to see his country at war with itself. He died in 1637 and is buried in Westminster Abbey. His great antagonist, Inigo Jones, having been compelled to relinquish his office as Surveyor of Works, was arrested, temporarily stripped of his estates, and heavily fined. Later he was pardoned, and he was working for the Earl of Pembroke at Wilton House in the year of King Charles's execution. He died in 1652, and was buried with his parents at St Benet, Paul's Wharf. There the monument he had provided for in his will was destroyed by the Great Fire of 1666.

For almost two decades the theatre in England lay dormant. When it recovered, it was under the approving eye of another king, with a taste for theatre acquired across the Channel. The theatre of the English Restoration, though, would never attempt to revive the royalist grandeur which French drama was ready to embody in its own golden age.

THE VICES
OF MANKIND

The effects associated with Heaven and Hell were truly prodigious and might well have seemed ... the result of magic. Truth, the Angels and diverse characters were to be seen descending from a great height ... From Hell, Lucifer arose, how one could not tell, on a dragon's back. The dry and withered staff of Moses suddenly burst forth with flowers and fruit ... Water was seen to change into wine ... The eclipse, the earthquake, the shattering of rocks and other miracles that accompanied the death of Our Lord were represented with still further miracles.

This description comes from a contemporary account of a Passion play staged at Valenciennes, in France, in 1547. It lasted twenty-five days, and had its stations strung out over a considerable distance, perhaps as much as 100 yards. Paradise was on the left, Hell on the right, with Jerusalem and other stops of interest in between.

The production at Valenciennes was one of a rash of extravaganzas which broke out in the more ambitious cities of fifteenth-century France, and seem to have thrown up an assortment of Cecil B. de Milles. In 1536, in Bourges, a magnificent production based on the Acts of the Apostles was mounted in the ruins of a Roman amphitheatre, inside the city's medieval walls. The auditorium was renovated and given tiers of galleries, costumes were lavish, a great cast was assembled from the community, and members of the clergy received special dispensations to play the main sacred roles.

The festivities began with a solemn Mass, followed by a great procession to the theatre. In the arena, two wagons were used, in the English manner, one to hold Hell, the other Heaven. They framed the action, which went on with the help of all sorts of ingenious devices and machines: Lucifer spat fire, a dragon flapped its wings, a miniature boat sailed on real water and capsized on cue. The spectators could see earthquakes, gruesome tortures, and executions in which hands and heads were severed from bodies and bowels were ripped out. A certain theatrical madness was in the air, as it often can be when money is no object to staging. The backers represented the city's most reputable commercial and social interests: they expected the production to repay their investment both in cash and prestige.

It happened that this particular show was a flop. Too few people came, money was lost, costumes and masks were sold off, and Bourges never repeated the experience. But with so much theatrical vitality at large in the provinces, Paris could not be outdone. Undeterred by the poor reception of the Bourges play, the capital decided to revive it in 1540. A group called the Confrérie de la Passion held a monopoly of all religious drama in Paris, by letters patent granted them in 1402 by Charles VI. It was an association of merchants, tradesmen and representatives of the professions, and was governed in 1540 by a committee of four: an upholsterer, a butcher, a florist and a barrister. The productions of the Confrérie (Brotherhood) differed from those mounted by its provincial cousins in at least one important respect – their location. They were played indoors, mostly in the Hospital of the Trinity, near the Porte St Denis, which was their permanent home until 1539. Forced to leave by the Hospital's ramshackle condition, the company moved into the Hôtel de Flandre but petitioned King Francis I, in verse, for a proper theatre to be built in the Roman style.

The petition was written in a fanciful, flowery tone, and suggested that the new theatre should be dedicated to the greater glory of His Majesty. Francis I turned it down flat, but the reverence of the French theatre for the classical past, and longing for an established position in the nation's life, were portents of its future direction. And although no one now knows where the *Acts of the Apostles* was performed, we do know that the production was enormously successful. It was played for a total of thirty-five days, not consecutively but spaced over a period of six months, using Sundays, saints' days and holidays. Apparently the effects were rather like those of a modern television serial or soap opera, except that whereas nowadays it is theatres, restaurants and the like which suffer because people stay at home for fear of missing an episode, in 1540 it was the Church which found itself having to cancel whole services for want of a congregation.

It was a brief success. Two years later, when the Confrérie announced its intention of playing the *Mystery of the Old Testament* the *procureur général* of the Paris Parliament responded with a stinging condemnation. He declared that these part-time producers and actors were 'uneducated people ... who have never learned their ABC'. According to him they were 'so uncouth in speech, lacking in vocabulary and faulty in pronunciation that they will often split one word in three, pause or break the sentence in the middle of a clause, make an exclamation out of what should be a question, or use some emphasis, gesture or accent which runs counter to the sense'. The effect was to cause such public ridicule and uproar that the play, 'far from edifying the audience, turns into a public scandal'. It would have been unthinkable in England for a high legal official to take so moralistic a line in defence of severe formal criteria of language and decorum. One implication for the French language was a devaluation of the verbal exuberance and colloquial strength represented by writers such as Villon and Rabelais; this had a direct influence on the theatre, not in terms of language alone, but of popular expression. Common speech was for louts and bumpkins; it was going to be very difficult for playwrights to put the lower orders on their stages other than as figures of fun.

The Italian comedians at the Théâtre de l'Hôtel de Bourgogne in 1689.

At the same time, the *procureur général*'s remarks were more than the voice of snobbery. Semi-amateur productions of sacred drama expired in France, not from the religious dilemmas that bedevilled Protestant England, but from natural causes. The public wanted something more polished and contemporary. Yet although the Confrérie de la Passion was forbidden to perform religious plays, it did not altogether disappear. By way of compensation for the loss of religious drama, it was granted a monopoly for presenting 'secular mysteries', as long as these were 'honourable and legitimate'. In 1548, the year of the ban, it moved into new quarters on the site of the old Hôtel de Bourgogne, formerly the town residence of the dukes of Burgundy. Although it began by putting on its own performances, after 1578 the Confrérie leased its premises to companies of professional actors, but it still kept its legal stranglehold on Parisian theatrical life, and was the focus of all kinds of litigation, royal petitions and political intrigue before it was finally dissolved in 1676.

In the first decades of the seventeenth century the company of the Hôtel de Bourgogne was under the direction of Valleran le Conte, and was not in permanent residence but also made provincial tours. This company called itself the *Comédiens du Roi* – the King's Players – and its principal rivals were the *Comédiens du Prince d'Orange*, who actually occupied the Hôtel de Bourgogne on several occasions in the 1620s, while le Conte's company was on tour. In those days the Paris audience was not enthusiastic enough to support even one company in permanent residence. Perhaps its taste was blunted by the memory of the last tottering years of the Confrérie's Mystery plays. Peter Arnott also claims, in his *Introduction to the French Theatre*, that 'while amateur acting, in all countries and at all periods, has been considered totally respectable, the shift to professionalism brings a stigma and a sharp decline in social status ... to attempt to earn money by performing roles in public is automatically to incur ... suspicion and outright hostility'.

Still, the actors were persistent, and Paris was not the only town big enough to be worth playing, in a country as large and populous as seventeenth-century France. The *Comédiens du Prince d'Orange* were at Rouen in 1629. Their principal actor, Montdory, who had served his apprenticeship under le Conte, received a comedy from a young local lawyer called Pierre Corneille. Both Montdory and the company's director, Lenoir, were eager to move to Paris permanently. The problem was where to present their work.

The next turn in the story provokes the intriguing question of what comes first, the play or the playhouse? Even today, theatre people are always on the lookout for empty buildings suitable for conversion and not too dear to run. But convenience is not the only factor, or even the chief one. Theatrical historians tend to look for purely theatrical answers. The argument runs that a drama company adapts some more or less suitable space, then eventually enshrines the resulting improvisations in a permanent building. I would argue that the audience also dictates the kind of space which is chosen and the way it is used, as it did in ancient Greece and in Elizabethan London. Convenience and availability may have suggested the initial shape – the ancient Greek circular threshing floor, the Tudor inn – but the eventual structure expressed a deeper relationship between the drama and the society that used it. French society in the seventeenth century was fiercely aware and protective of its own values and divisions: its theatres would reflect that fact.

The theatre which the Confrérie had built on the site of the old Hôtel de Bourgogne was long and narrow, and used over half the floor space for the pit or *parterre*, which had no fixed seats. Behind the *parterre* rose a bank of tiered seats, cramped and uncomfortable, which was called the *amphithéâtre*. There were overhanging boxes or *loges*, and there may have been still another tier, which the French called *le paradis* as the English call it 'the gods'. All this left little room for the stage itself, which was about 25 feet square. But Montdory's troupe could not possibly afford to build from scratch – it had to go prospecting. What it found, after a few years of occupying temporary premises in the Hôtel d'Argent, was a tennis court.

In Shakespeare's *Henry V*, the French Dauphin makes a gift of tennis balls to the English king. It is an insulting gift, and produces an angry response:

When we have match'd our rackets to these balls,
We will, in France, by God's grace, play a set
Shall strike his father's crown into the hazard.

This game is not our modern lawn tennis, which dates from the 1870s, but the outlandish game of Royal Tennis, which has a fiendishly complicated scoring system and the unusual quality of permitting a player to miss the ball but still win the point. One variety of this game, which the French call *jeu de paume*, was played in an indoor court, whose design supposedly owed much to medieval monastic life and architecture. At one time there were said to be as many as 250 courts in Paris, but the game was played less and less in the sixteenth century, for reasons that do not seem hard to understand. The *jeu de paume* where Montdory's company set up shop was in the Marais district.

Montdory was not alone. In 1643 a theatrical group made up mostly of amateurs aged between sixteen and twenty-seven leased a court in the Rue Mazarine. Within two years the company was bankrupt, and its founder, Jean-Baptiste Poquelin, the son of the King's upholsterer, was sent to prison. Fortunately his father discharged his debts, and in 1645 he left Paris to tour in the provinces. By then he had already changed his name to Molière.

The *jeu de paume* lent itself readily to theatrical invention. Like the Confrérie's purpose-built structure it was long and narrow – approximately 110 by 38 feet – and only required the erection of a stage at one end to make a simple playhouse. Seats were arranged on the floor of the court and in the spectators' gallery. Changing rooms built for the tennis players could be taken over by the players. But there the advantages end, because from the actor's point of view the *jeu de paume* exerted a coercive influence on the style and manner of performance. The acoustics were hopeless, the sightlines unyielding. The ideal place to be seen and heard was downstage centre, but then the actor would have to belt out his lines while practically rooted to the spot. The temptation would be to exaggerate and over-emphasize, simply to try to keep a hold on the audience. (It is said that Montdory, while playing Herod, so exerted himself that he suffered a stroke which left him partially paralysed and voiceless.) The audience too became restless. In time, wealthier patrons bought seats on the stage itself, and so cramped the action even further. And if all that were not handicap enough on a small stage, the problem of scenery intervened to hinder communication.

The multiple staging of the French Mystery plays was so deeply ingrained in the consciousness of the French theatre that it clung on long after the disappearance of the circumstances that made it necessary. Much the same system was used indoors, and for secular plays, in the early seventeenth century. The open stage became imprisoned by the *compartements*, each of which represented a different location in the play. The convention was that the place from which the actor entered governed the stage – the practice was called *décor simultané*. If he or she entered from a *compartement* representing the Roman Forum, then the audience understood that the whole stage was now the Forum. But let another actor enter from a different *compartement*, and the play's location shifted. With the actors constantly marooned at downstage centre, and the audience needing instant recall in order to work out where the action was now supposed to be, the result was mutual frustration. It was Pierre Corneille, Montdory's young lawyer-cum-playwright, who began the process of eliminating the clumsy relic:

> The common sense which is my constant guide led me to devise a unity of action by involving four lovers in a single plot, and gave me such repugnance for the barbaric practice of displaying Paris, Rome and Constantinople on the same stage that I compressed the location of my play into one city.

This is Corneille writing in a mood of self-congratulation after his first success, *Mélite*, a comedy of thwarted love, presented by Montdory in 1629. Corneille had been born in 1606, the son of middle-class parents in Rouen. He was educated by Jesuits, and went on to read law. Since his father was *maître des eaux et des forêts*, the younger Corneille was able to buy posts in the Rivers and Forests and in the local Court of Admiralty, which oversaw the navigation of the Seine. While writing his plays he conscientiously discharged these duties for more than twenty years, and he remained a devoted family man, a father of seven, with roots sunk firmly in the soil of provincial values, a compound of respectability, shrewdness and materialism. With success, Corneille became touchy about criticism and resentful of competition, even though he was long regarded as a supreme master of the drama. His contemporaries thought of him as socially inept, and even those who acknowledged his genius in the theatre considered him boring to the point of incoherence in conversation.

The sixteenth century had seen a number of comedies derived from ancient Greek or Roman models, and incorporating features of the native French 'farce', which comes from a verb meaning to stuff, because they were originally comic passages in common speech, 'stuffed' into the liturgy as part of revels celebrated at the turn of the year until about the mid-fifteenth century. Corneille's early plays mark a transition into a more native form of comedy. Filled with misunderstandings, deceptions, threatened duels (never portrayed on stage), disguises and a proliferation of complications, they were set in smart, fashionable Paris, and were a hit with the smart, fashionable audiences that went to see them. Corneille's critics – and they were many – accused him of pandering to the town by the cheap trick of using Paris place names to give his plays a dash of local colour. That kind of touch would not have been out of character: Corneille was to become known for prefacing his works with obsequious dedications that almost grovelled in their hope to secure pensions and favours. Certainly the titles of his early plays – *La Galerie du Palais, La Place Royale* – suggest who he wanted to impress, and how crudely he was prepared to go about it. The playwright defended himself against detractors by claiming to describe 'how elegant folk actually converse. The first play to cause laughter without the aid of stock buffoons'.

For the next eight years Montdory continued to present the plays of Corneille to packed houses, with the usual theatrical side-effects: success bred further success, and that bred the envy of the less successful. Montdory gained financial backing, and the great distinction of being summoned to play at Court. On the other hand the Hôtel de Bourgogne was appalled by the smaller company's triumph, and started what turned out to be a lengthy running battle. The *Comédiens du Roi* intrigued and plotted against their rival, and even managed to lure away some of its actors and writers. But in spite of all the treachery and double-dealing, time and again Montdory productions won a better response from the public. Slowly the theatre came to occupy the attention of fashionable Paris, but it was more than just a source of gossip – people were actually going to see plays. The climax of the feud was reached in January 1637, when Montdory presented his greatest triumph, Corneille's tragic masterpiece, *Le Cid*. Its immediate impact was a result not only of the play's unique and splendid strengths, but also of a particular quirk of French culture.

Since the Middle Ages, the French have – but for one notorious lapse – cultivated order, embraced rules and laws, and professed a special attachment for logic. This national characteristic has been displayed in almost every aspect of life, and therefore not least in art. In the seventeenth century this formal propensity was asserted in the way the French laid out their gardens, designed their buildings, and did their thinking. René Bray wrote: 'The generation of Descartes and of Corneille, de Chapelain and [Guez] de Balzac ...

organized Parnassus as Richelieu organized the kingdom. It was the generation of order.' What is remarkable about this statement is that in addition to one philosopher and one dramatist, the two other names mentioned belong not to creative writers but to critics. Most people working in the modern theatre have had grounds for complaint about contemporary critics, but their power is insignificant compared with the dominion of their counterparts in seventeenth-century France, because it was the critic, not as reviewer but as theorist and cultural legislator, who would play the cardinal role in the evolution of French classical drama.

This vague term 'classical' is more apt than usual when applied to the age which laid down the standards of French drama, because those standards were consciously based on the classical past. Whereas English drama was able to incorporate some of the themes and much of the popular vigour of the Mystery and Morality plays, in France there was no organic transition. The emphasis on grandiose spectacle offered nothing to playwrights, and the banning of religious plays in 1548 left a sudden void just at the time when the Renaissance was resurrecting the models of antiquity. Plautus, Terence and Seneca were readily imitated, and the attempt to follow the same principles of dramatic construction led to the close study of classical theorists such as Aristotle and Horace. Aristotle's account of Greek tragedy was taken as a prescription, and rules were derived from it which all drama became obliged to follow, or be counted immature or primitive.

First among these rules come the 'three unities' – action in a single location, in a single time span of not more than a day, and developing as a single sequence, uncluttered with subplots. A further requirement was *vraisemblance* – true-seemingness, probability. This may have been the most important of all the criteria: the action must be true to life and internally consistent. Here there was a generalizing principle involved – it was not enough for an event or observation to be 'true', it should also be representative rather than exceptional. Strict rules of decorum and taste – *les bienséances* – should also be observed: characters must behave and speak as their rank and social position required, and must remain 'in character', as the play portrayed them. In accordance with good taste, curtains were lowered before death scenes to avoid indecorous unpleasantries. Some said that all this amounted to a discipline essential to the creative process; others felt the bony clutch of pedantry. The dispute was fiercely argued throughout the seventeenth century, and it broke over Corneille's head in 1637, with the first performance of his tragedy *Le Cid*.

In England we judge an actor by his Hamlet; in France the test is Rodrigue in *Le Cid*, one of the great male roles in the French repertoire. The play is set in Spain, and tells a complicated story of star-crossed lovers, both possessed of high moral principles and heroism. Their private fate is played out against the backdrop of Rodrigue's epic fight against the Moors, which wins him the Moorish title of 'Cid' (Lord). In Seville, Rodrigue and Chimène are in

Pierre Corneille (1606–1684), and his masterpiece *Le Cid*, performed by Jean Vilar and Gérard Philipe of the Théâtre Nationale Populaire.

love and plan to marry. Their fathers quarrel, Rodrigue has to fight on behalf of his ageing father in the resulting duel, and he kills his lover's father. The tragedy at the centre of the drama is that Chimène is in duty bound to seek revenge, although still in love with Rodrigue, who loves her still, and even admires her sense of duty. Rodrigue survives her efforts, and the play ends with the possibility that they may be united after all.

At this remove, the controversy has evaporated, but 350 years ago Corneille was accused of plagiarism, immorality, disregard for truth and artistic impropriety. Finally the issue was settled from above, and certainly from outside, by the intervention of Cardinal Richelieu himself, the chief minister of Louis XIII, and the most powerful figure in all France, if not in Europe. In 1634 he had created the *Académie française*, an institution whose object was to establish the literary language by compiling an authoritative dictionary, and to maintain standards of literary taste. Richelieu persuaded Corneille to submit his play for judgment by the Academy, and the verdict was that *Le Cid* was guilty of definite irregularities.

The Academy found that although Corneille had observed the formal rules, the setting was Spain, not Rome or Athens; much of the incident was improbable; and the end of the play was happy, not tragic. A tone of moral outrage found its way into this affair, and there is no doubt that personal jealousies and rivalries raised the temperature, but underlying the whole debate was an institutional longing for order, restraint and social harmony. Corneille defended himself, but did not reject the idea that it was right to legislate for the kind of art the age required. He took the Academy's adverse verdict to heart, and his later plays are simpler and have classical settings. The forces of order triumphed. Yet *Le Cid* was a tremendous public success, in spite of official attitudes, since live plays are not written, and live audiences do not respond, according to command.

Another of the features which give a more formal quality to French tragedy, in addition to the 'classical' rules and the social and political factors that have allowed various French governments to think of Culture practically as an instrument of policy, is the form it was written in. English drama found blank verse, French drama the alexandrine, a line of twelve syllables, used in rhyming couplets. The greater length calls for greater literary dexterity than the ten syllables of blank verse, and the rhymes emphasize the artificial quality of the verse and bring out the nature of the metre, while the best blank verse is often an unobtrusive presence binding together the tones and rhythms of colloquial speech. The combination of rhyming couplet and alexandrine gave to French drama a sophisticated literary language, and to French acting a declamatory quality still to be heard in the intonations of the Comédie-Française and perhaps echoed in the solemn resonances of French political rhetoric. Since all the plays of Corneille and Racine, and many of Molière's, are written in alexandrines, they are peculiarly difficult to translate, and this has had the effect of making them less playable in other languages.

In France, the rules and their enforcers had been too powerful for Corneille to ignore. Even so, they could still be attacked and ridiculed, and that was the pleasure of the playwright whose début in the *jeu de paume* on the Rue Mazarine ended in bankruptcy for his company of ten, the *Illustre Théâtre*. After that setback, Molière toured the provinces in the south for thirteen years, playing in great towns such as Avignon, Montpellier and Toulouse, and learning his craft as an actor as well as a dramatist. For some years he was based at Lyons, where he saw and was powerfully influenced by Italian companies performing the *Commedia dell'Arte*. The plots of this genuinely popular entertainment are delightfully familiar, not to say predictable: meddling father opposes love match and wants daughter to marry pedantic, rich, old fool; young lovers are aided by clever devious servant – Brighella, Scapino, the ancestors of Figaro. Molière's early plays are mostly farces, adaptations of Italian models. He wrote brilliant parts for himself, and one contemporary observed: 'One doesn't know whether to admire the author more for the way he has written the play, or for the way he acts it.'

France had a new young king who liked to be entertained. Academicians and critics may have looked down their noses at comedy and the *Commedia dell'Arte*, but Louis XIV enjoyed them, and that was Molière's passport back to Paris. In 1658 he secured the patronage of Louis' eighteen-year-old brother, formally known as 'Monsieur', the Duke of Orleans. He brought Molière and his company to Court, and on the evening of 24 October they presented two plays before the twenty-year-old King Louis XIV. The first was a tragedy by Corneille called *Nicomède*, in which they hoped to flatter the King – its hero is a young, handsome, generous prince. *Nicomède* sank like a lead weight. It was the afterpiece, *Le Docteur amoureux*, a farce by Molière from the company's provincial repertoire, which caught the royal fancy and turned out to be the hit of the evening. The King granted permission to the *Troupe de Monsieur* to occupy the theatre of the Petit-Bourbon, and in 1661 it moved into a hall in the Palais-Royal, just around the corner from the Louvre.

A year after settling in the Palais Royal, Molière wrote *L'Ecole des femmes*, which tells the story of a man whose solution to the problem of unfaithful wives is to find a girl too ignorant and artless to look away from her husband. Arnolphe finds the right sort of girl, but before he can marry her she falls in love with a younger man, who confides in Arnolphe without knowing of his intentions. Arnolphe is going to bury Agnès in a convent when her father comes to the rescue and the young lovers marry. The play brought accusations of bad taste, immorality, impiety and slander (and a pension of 1000 *livres* from the King). Molière's crushing replies were delivered in two short pieces, *La Critique de l'Ecole des femmes* and *L'Impromptu de Versailles* (sending up his theatrical rivals of the Hôtel de Bourgogne), both played in 1663. These remarks are spoken by characters in the *Critique*:

> You people are funny with your rules, with which you embarrass the ignorant and deafen the rest of us every day.

> I've noticed one thing ... that those who talk the most about the rules, and know them better than anyone else, write comedies that nobody considers good.

> ... if the plays that are according to the rules are not liked, and if those that are liked are not according to the rules, then the rules must necessarily have been badly made. So ... let's consult nothing about a play but the effect it had on us. Let's allow ourselves to go wholeheartedly to the things that grip us by the entrails, and let's not seek out arguments to keep ourselves from having pleasure.

Molière's advice still gives the clinching argument against importing extrinsic criteria into the theatre; whether academic, literary, social or political, they are likely to deter those for whom plays are simply a source of refreshment and recreation. That is not to say that Molière gave his audience an easy ride. Comedy could address the present day, where tragedy was safely distanced to far countries or to ancient times. In his great plays of the next ten years, Molière put the French society of his own day under the scrutiny of eyes which saw deep into human character and its typical vices and excesses: that was comedy's business, he said. *Tartuffe* was first performed in 1664, and was a ferocious satire on religious hypocrisy that came too close to the mark not to raise desperate opposition from religious circles. Alceste in *Le Misanthrope* (1666) is a man who cannot pretend, and dislikes pretence in others; his predicament is that society does not work without pretence, and by dealing with such a theme, Molière draws comedy onto the ground of tragedy. In *L'Avare* (1668), *Le Bourgeois gentilhomme* (1670) and *Le Malade imaginaire* (1673), he exposed and satirized avarice, snobbery, and the medical profession, and brought to these themes the penetrating humour and fond ear for absurdity which were the weapons of a melancholy temperament.

Yet it was tragedy, the hallmark of a confident society, which the theorists of French classicism proclaimed to be the highest form of dramatic achievement. And while Corneille may be viewed as the forerunner, by the 1660s, when the last of his tragedies appeared, he was already considered passé, his characters too stark and overpowering. Times were changing. High society, the Court lords and ladies whose tastes had to be taken into account, wanted plays of a subtler mould, works which would reflect the image they had of themselves – polite, gallant, sensitive. The muscular idealism of Corneille

Molière (1622–1673), and a 19th-century drawing of him as Orgon unmasking Tartuffe.

gave way to the psychological realism of one of the world's great tragic writers, Jean Racine.

Racine was born in 1639 in the desolate little town of La Ferté-Milon, sixty miles east of Paris. Orphaned at the age of four, he was brought up by his grandmother and educated on charity at the convent school of Port-Royal des Champs, outside Paris. These bleak facts are the keys to his emotional and intellectual development. He was drawn early to the theatre, which must have offered a thrilling contrast to the drabness of his daily life. But it was the charitable institution which had charge of his education that was to shape his character and talent, and to bring out and sharpen the inner conflicts which are voiced in much of his work.

Port-Royal was the centre of Jansenism, a movement in the Roman Catholic Church which in its moral strictness and belief in predestination offers some parallels with Calvinism. Its schools provided an education renowned for thoroughness and severity. (For example, Racine received a broad grounding in Greek, which was unusual at the time.) But it was the general thrust of Jansenist thought that dominated the boy's schooling. Named after its Dutch founder, Cornelis Jansen, Bishop of Ypres, the movement came into direct

Le Malade imaginaire, by Molière, in performance at Versailles.

conflict with the teaching of Rome. Regular churchgoing, faith and charity were not the paths to salvation – that goal could only be reached through the direct gift of God's grace. The pleasures of this world were condemned, and the theatre was believed to be the invention of the devil. Man, they taught, was fundamentally corrupt. The severity of Jansenist belief and practice was to haunt Racine all his life.

At the start of his career, however, Racine took easily to high society, and also turned out to be adept at the theatre game. His first play, *La Thébaïde*, was produced in 1664 by Molière's company, but after what he considered was a botched performance of his second play, *Alexandre le Grand*, in 1665 he gave it to the Hôtel de Bourgogne, without bothering to let Molière know. Few people were fond of him, and he could be competitive, ungenerous to rivals, witty, cruel, and often insensitive, but his gift as a dramatist was unique. Inside the formal limits of the classical mode, his tight plots and intense psychological realism combine to create a theatrical atmosphere of the most passionate concentration. The King was his admirer and supporter; honours came in showers. Between 1664 and 1677 he wrote ten plays which conquered both Court and public. Then he abandoned the theatre, for reasons which have never been satisfactorily explained.

Above and right Jean Racine (1639–1699), with the frontispiece to the 1672 first edition of his works. *Opposite* the great French actress Elisa Rachel (1820–1858) in *Phèdre*.

One clue to Racine's departure lies, I believe, in his last great work, *Phèdre*, which is suffused with guilt, sensuality and illicit pleasure. The Jansenist doctrines which he had absorbed under pressure at Port-Royal were surfacing again. *Phèdre* is the first great part for a woman which was actually played by a woman, Marie Champmeslé, who was Racine's mistress for some time, and played many of his heroines. For *Phèdre*, he coached her line by line. The theme itself is sexual passion. Plagued with guilt at her unnatural love for her stepson, Hippolyte, and believing that her husband, Thésée, is dead, Phèdre is persuaded by her old nurse and confidante, Oenone, to declare her passion to the young man. He is in love with another and rejects her advances. Disaster ensues when Phèdre succumbs to jealousy and Thésée returns. The conflict between her moral conscience and the fatality of her passion drives her in the end to take poison as the only honourable escape, but not before the death of Hippolyte, whom Oenone has accused of having tried to seduce her mistress.

The play is written with such overt passion that it is hard not to sense Racine's personal involvement in every line. It is his undoubted masterpiece, and this could be the second reason for his sudden retirement: he may have recognized that he could not surpass it. For *Phèdre* represents French dramatic verse at its most sublime, more spare and economic than Corneille's,

exploring the irrational world at the heart of so much great drama with a tense lucidity generated by the stresses between passion and controlled form. When this quality in the writing echoes the theme of the play itself, which is the conflict between duty and desire, the individual and the social, French classical tragedy finds its purest definition.

Phèdre is to French drama what *Hamlet* is to English, a sort of proving ground which succeeding generations rediscover and confront. But there the comparison ends, and not only because *Hamlet* is not the most monumental of Shakespeare's tragedies. Racine is the master of a different tradition, ruthlessly austere and disciplined in his story-telling and language. There are no rambling subplots, no comic diversions, apparently not one inessential syllable. A few statistics help to point the differences: Racine's dramatic vocabulary is 2,000 words, Shakespeare's 24,000; *Phèdre* is 1,600 lines long, *Hamlet* nearly 3,800. In Racine the tyrannous unities of time and place work to create a sense of claustrophobia, of characters locked into the isolation zone of their own relationships. The effect is both vital and arresting: to experience it in the theatre brings out the power still stored in those classical conventions which the English theatre has never really managed to re-create.

Both Corneille and Racine wrote comedies. Molière wrote no tragedies. The age saw tragedy as the more noble form, and a certain snobbery resulted, producing a condescension towards comic writers which was deeply resented by Molière. He vented his feeling in the *Critique de l'Ecole des femmes:*

> ...if you were to put a plus for difficulty on the side of comedy, perhaps you would be making no mistake. For, after all, I think it would be much easier to strike a lofty pose upon grand sentiments, to brave fortune in rhyme, accuse destiny, and hurl insults at the gods, than to enter into the ridiculous side of men and represent everybody's defects agreeably on stage. When you paint heroes, you do what you like... But when you paint men, you must paint from nature... In a word, in serious plays, to avoid blame it is enough to say things that are sensible and well written; but in the other kind this is not enough, you have to be funny; and it's quite an undertaking to make people of breeding laugh.

The irony is that of all the playwrights of the French Golden Age, it is Molière who has emerged as the most universal. Perhaps his work has presented fewer problems in translation, since in comedy the ultimate criterion is laughter, while the fact that a play like *Phèdre*, as well as being made for the stage, is also a dramatic poem, faces would-be translators with an extra dilemma. At any rate the comic spirit that lives in Molière's plays was to influence other writers in other lands, while the impact of Corneille and Racine has been felt more exclusively in their native land. Molière also remained closer to his audience because, like Shakespeare, he was a man of the theatre – actor, director and manager, as well as writer.

Combining the role of courtier and artist, and mindful of where his support and backing lay, Molière considered himself a servant of the King. In time, he provided elaborate comic ballets for Court spectacles, so that like his father, the royal upholsterer, before him, he could be called a purveyor of extravagant furnishings to the Court. But he never disowned his sources. He brought farce in from the streets and refined it to suit his new, sophisticated audience. Some of his plays show him more subdued and critical, reflecting the world he moved in. He himself wrote that: 'The function of comedy is to correct the vices of mankind.' At the same time he never succumbed to the self-importance which has been known to afflict comic talents impressed with their new prestige. His wit and insight did not inhibit his love of buffoonery and 'low' humour, and he was ready to use any weapon that would enhance his attacks on pretence and dishonesty of all kinds. His plays are part of the standard repertoire in France, and are played throughout the world, as if to reaffirm the proposition that plays survive only if the issues they embody remain unresolved, and that there are some issues which seem likely to stay that way this side of Armageddon.

It was while playing *Le Malade imaginaire* on the night of 17 February 1673 that Molière collapsed and was carried home to die. A priest was called, but none came, and he died unable to repent of his life as an actor. This was a serious matter, because all through the seventeenth century the French Church automatically excommunicated actors, and as late as 1730 it refused burial to the prominent tragic actress Adrienne Lecouvreur. The Sun King himself had to intervene to obtain a stealthy funeral, conducted in the night. In fifteen years Molière had staged ninety-five plays of which he had written thirty-one and acted in almost all of them.

In 1680, Louis XIV ordered the actors of the Hôtel de Bourgogne to join with the company formed after Molière's death by merging his company with Montdory's former company of the Marais. They were housed in the Rue Guénégaud, and took the title of *Le Théâtre Français*. In honour of the great actor-dramatist the company was also called *La Maison de Molière*. Today it is best known as the Comédie-Française.

Reflecting its historical origins, the organization of the Comédie-Française closely resembles that of the Confrérie de la Passion. (The constitution was originally laid down by the King, but it is a measure of the theatre's importance that amendments were made by Napoleon on his way to Moscow.) Merit governs a player's admission to the company. For his first appearances, the actor may choose his own part in comedy or tragedy. If successful, he is made *pensionnaire*, and given a fixed salary; later he may become a full member or *sociétaire*, replacing someone who has retired or died and receiving a share or part share of the company. In most cases, twenty years' service is demanded before retirement and the receipt of a pension, but there have been numerous instances of actors – Sarah Bernhardt for one – who have stormed out in fury, believing that they had been deprived of the parts which their talents deserved. The longest-serving member of the company is called the *doyen*.

The foundations of the Comédie-Française were laid during France's golden age of drama. Both Corneille and Racine lived to see the theatre institutionalized and given national importance. Corneille died in 1684, Racine in 1699. Together with Molière, they had created a dramatic literature worthy of the great nation that dominated Europe's cultural and political life throughout the seventeenth century. It was a literature that prized rational elegance and formal intelligence, and a drama whose respect for the classics of ancient Greece and Rome reflected its conscious desire for grandeur and magnificence. Yet Racine, who saw passion as the agent of disorder and discipline as the armature of feeling, said that the golden rule was to delight and touch, and neither of his professional rivals would have disagreed. They made a theatre that was varied and powerful, and popular well beyond the reaches of the Court. They showed, and their country recognized, that to a civilized nation the theatre counts as a social staple, a plain necessity.

The stage of the Comédie-Française in 1726.

Molière. Jouëlet. Poisson. Turlupin. Le Capitan-Matamore. Arlequin. Guillot Gorju. Gros Guillaume. Le Dottor Grazian Balourd. Gaultier Garguille. polichinelle. Pantalon. Scaramouche. Philippin. Briguelle. Trivelin.

'The cool paradox of passion treated dispassionately'

Above French farce meets *Commedia* in this 1670 painting at the Comédie Française. The scene was improbable, but the situation not impossible. The figure third from the right is thought to be Molière.
Left a scene from Molière's *Tartuffe*, in the *All the World's a Stage* production.

Left Versailles, by Pierre Martin: French
formalism in a *Vue Perspective du Grand
Trianon*, 1722. The Restoration dressing-
room is recalled less formally (*above*) by
Thomas Rowlandson (1756–1827).

Overleaf (*left*) Beryl Reid as Lady Wishfort in
Congreve's *The Way of the World* (Royal
Shakespeare Company, 1978) and (*right*)
Colley Cibber (1671–1757), a famous Lord
Foppington in Vanbrugh's *The Relapse*.

Wilde's *The Importance of Being Earnest* at London's Haymarket Theatre, in 1967. *Left* Robert Eddison muses to Pauline Collins and Flora Robson; while John Standing and Pauline Collins, and Helen Weir and Daniel Massey pair off (*below*).

Right Noel Coward and Gertrude Lawrence, forever captured as Elyot and Amanda, in a publicity still for Coward's *Private Lives*.

THE PLAY

CTORIAL

With which are incorporated
THE PLAY   THE PLAY SOUVENIR   "THE STAGE SOUVENIR"

"PRIVATE LIVES"

VOL. LVII

NOEL COWARD   GERTRUDE LAWRENCE

MONTH

The black comedy of manners. Joe Orton held the mirror of art up to his own excessively way-ward nature in (*left*) *Entertaining Mr Sloane,* and (*below*) *Loot.*

SILK STOCKINGS AND WHITE BOSOMS

At three o'clock in the afternoon of 25 May 1660, King Charles II left his ship, the *Royal Charles*, and was rowed ashore at Dover, where he knelt to thank God for his safe return. Four days later, he entered London, while the bells pealed, the cannon roared, and his subjects rejoiced. So ended nine years of royal exile and eleven years of Puritan government, during which time the Puritan ethic had been translated haphazardly into law. All governments of zealots are tempted to control the means of public expression, and tend to view them more or less in terms of their propaganda function. The fact that the theatre is a favourite target confirms the medium's power to influence and change people's lives. The Puritans' approach was less directly political, more nearly superstitious, in the way it seemed to say that plays are art, art is beautiful, the beautiful is pleasant, the pleasant damnable. Their distrust of the theatre's powers of seduction was scandalized enough to suggest their own deep response, just as some modern supporters of censorship seem, with the thoroughness of their researches into the shocking, to advertise a greater than usual wealth of erotic imagination.

In 1642 the Puritans closed the theatres and outlawed performances (maypoles and morris dancing were also banned, with proper consistency). Their efforts were not entirely successful, and plays were still put on, almost as a challenge, in public houses, inns and private homes, although there was always a danger of raids by the military. Plays were also given at Christmas and at Bartholomew Fair, which was held at West Smithfield in late August. But with the collapse of the Commonwealth and Puritan control in 1660, the English theatre was free to enter into its second great age, the period now known as the Restoration, though it extends for some time after the reign of Charles II.

The euphoria which greeted the King's return set the mood of his reign, exciting and exuberant. With King and Court restored to a confidence they had not felt since the previous century, and an expansive upper-middle class, new currents of moral licence and intellectual inquiry began to flow. In philosophy John Locke founded the school of empiricism – the theory that experience is the only source of knowledge. In science, the new direction is typified by the name of the organization founded in the year of the Restoration and incorporated two years later under the title of the Royal Society of London for Improving Natural Knowledge. Superstition, fanciful beliefs, anything that could not be proved and demonstrated was rejected. England was entering a period when cleverness outranked feeling, and wit was admired above sincerity. The cynics and debunkers came into their own. At the centre of this new freedom stood the King. Described as having a 'noble laziness of mind', he, like the gentlemen writers who were his friends, was a connoisseur of amusement. The theatre was to reflect and encourage the ebullient pursuit of pleasure, with wit, outrageous romps and satires.

All the same, although the general climate was permissive, the established order was not so lax, or so secure, that it would permit subversion. The dangers of satire were pointed out to the King only a few months after his return, among others by a cunning theatrical manager called Thomas Killigrew, who also had a remedy in mind. He suggested that Charles should issue Patents – licences – to two theatres only, and that those theatres should be held answerable to the Crown. Killigrew had followed Prince Charles into exile in 1647, and was Groom of the Bedchamber to the new King. Few were surprised when he became the holder of one of the two Patents which Charles agreed to establish.

Shakespeare's Globe had been turned into tenements during the Commonwealth, and many of London's other theatres had been demolished. Those that survived soon came to be regarded as obsolete, and for reasons which concerned the audience rather than the actors. The old theatres could accommodate every section of society except one – the Court itself. There was no Royal Box in the wooden O, or in its roofed-over equivalents such as the Blackfriars. If Elizabeth I wanted to see a play, the actors had come to her, and performed as best they could in the great hall of one of her palaces. On the Continent, princes and noblemen did visit the playhouses, and during his exile Charles had come to know the theatre as an elegant social event, with its own special amusement and excitement. It was a pleasure that he and his courtiers did not want to lose.

If the King and his Court were going to visit theatres, then somehow they would have to be made comfortable. At the very least the King should not have to brave the wind and rain. But building from scratch was expensive, and the search for a covered space led to another Royal Tennis court, this one in Lincoln's Inn Fields. It looks as if the English were following the French example, though in London the credit for the idea went to Inigo Jones's former collaborator, Sir William Davenant.

Davenant was born in 1606. Claims – probably his own – that he was the illegitimate son of Shakespeare and the hostess of the Crown Inn at Oxford are discounted, but it is thought just possible that Shakespeare was Davenant's godfather. His authorship of various Court Masques before the Civil War had led to him being made Poet Laureate, in succession to Ben Jonson, in 1638, and Charles I knighted him in 1643 for his services to the royalist cause. In the last years of the Commonwealth he managed to circumvent the ban on plays by describing his work as 'music and instruction', and received permission in 1656 to present the first part of *The Siege of Rhodes*, which some consider the first English opera. With the Restoration he gained the patronage of the Duke of York, the future James II, and he became the second Patent holder. The tennis court in Lincoln's Inn he named the Duke's House, and his company of actors, under Thomas Betterton, the Duke's Players. Killigrew's company were the King's Players. It took the new Patent holders two or three years to transform English theatrical architecture.

Very little is known in detail about the disposition of actors and audience in the tennis court theatres. The most immediate English influence would have been Shakespeare's open-air stage, which jutted out into the audience, used no scenery, but had doors and a balcony at the back. In adapting the tennis courts, French and Italian ideas are thought likely to have been enlisted: a proscenium arch framed by entrance doors and balconies, with the scenery set behind it; in front of the arch a deep platform where the actors played in the blaze of two great chandeliers, but still close to their audience.

Here for the first time duchesses rubbed shoulders with civil servants to witness the spectacular displays that were presented, especially by Davenant. Painted scenery decorated the most important scenes in a play, and was changed in full view, much to the delight of the audience. Everything came new and was regarded as original. The two licensed companies must have worked in an atmosphere of constant excitement, on a great wave of theatrical energy. And the spectators – noisy, cheerful, affected, mischievous – responded with high spirits. Samuel Pepys recorded on 2 July 1661:

> To the Duke's Theatre to see Sir William Davenant's opera, *The Siege of Rhodes*, this being the fourth day that it hath begun, and the first that I have seen it. Today was acted the second part, which Sir William wrote for the opening of his theatre. We stayed a very great while for the King and Queen of Bohemia; and by the breaking of a board above our heads, a great deal of dust fell into the ladies' necks and the men's hair, which made good sport. The King being come, the scene opened; which indeed is very fine and magnificent and well acted, all but the Eunuch, who was so much out that he was hissed off the stage.

Following the converted tennis courts came new, purpose-built theatres. Killigrew moved to the Theatre Royal, Bridges Street, in May 1663. When fire destroyed it nine years later, he at once set about commissioning a replacement, and in March 1674 the Theatre Royal, Drury Lane, designed by Sir Christopher Wren, was opened to the public. Davenant's most famous theatre was in Dorset Gardens, and was eventually to give rise to a Theatre Royal, Covent Garden, in 1732. These buildings occupied the middle ground between the City of London and Whitehall Palace, the area known today as the West End.

The auditoria of Restoration theatres accurately reflect the society for which they were designed, one in which a booming middle class could afford the high price of theatre tickets. The anonymous author of *The Country Gentleman's Vade Mecum*, published in 1699, described the layout in some detail. There was an upper gallery crammed with servants, and then came the boxes, 'one peculiar to the King and Royal Family, and the rest for the Persons of Quality ... unless some Fools ... crowd in among 'em'. Then came the middle gallery 'where the Citizens Wives and Daughters, together with the *Abigails*, Serving-men, Journey-men, and Apprentices commonly take their Places; and now and then some disponding Mistresses and superannuated Poets'. Down in the Pit seethed the various '*Judges, Wits* and *Censurers* ... in common with these sit the *Squires, Sharpers, Beaus, Bullies* and *Whores*, and here and there an extravagant *Male* and *Female Cit*'.

Occupying their prescribed social strata, the audience were lively, talkative and critical. They went as much to be seen as to see, for the theatre was a place to meet and talk. Above all, it was the ideal setting in which to make assignations with the opposite sex, and that gave the King a further incentive to become a regular and enthusiastic playgoer. In the theatre he could pursue his sexual fancies as venturously as he pleased, because the Restoration brought a vital innovation to the English stage: Charles II's Royal Warrant licensing the new theatres in London specified that only women should play women's parts.

> I come, unknown to any of the rest
> To tell you news, I saw the lady drest,
> The Woman playes today, mistake me not,
> No Man in Gown, or Page in Petty-Coat...

With these words a male actor introduced Margaret Hughes, the first woman to appear on the London stage, in the role of Desdemona. Next he led her forward and asked the audience:

> And how d'ye like her, come what is't ye drive at,
> She's the same thing in public as in private;
> As far from being what you call a Whore,
> As *Desdemona* innur'd by the Moor?

Having learned to pardon the elephantine archness of other such introductions, actresses breathed new life into the Restoration theatre. Not only did they bring original insights and accurate observation to the female characters of plays from the past, but they also inspired new plays in which women were treated as intellectually equal to men, and in some cases as intellectually superior. On the other hand, Restoration drama produced no women characters with the fierce will of a Lady Macbeth, the moral determination of a Portia, or the ferocious independence of a Katherina. Some of their most brilliant new parts were as witty freelances in the battle of the sexes.

Since the new reign welcomed innovation, the way was also clear for women to write for the theatre. Women playwrights quickly rose to their opportunities. Katherine Philips, who wrote under the pseudonym of 'The Matchless Orinda', and died in 1664 at the age of only thirty-three, was the first woman to have a play, *Pompey*, professionally produced on the London stage. Aphra Behn, who followed in the footsteps of Christopher Marlowe by spying for her country in the Dutch Wars, was the most famous woman dramatist, and often more daring than her male counterparts. Her play *The Amorous Prince*, first performed in 1671, has a risqué first scene in which a half-dressed couple rise from their bed. *The Dutch Lover* contains the lines: 'I never made love so well as when I was drunk. It improves my parts and makes me witty; that is, it makes me say anything that comes next, which passes nowadays for wit.' Her most celebrated play was *The Rover*, produced in 1677, which dealt sympathetically with arranged marriages and has the often-quoted line: 'Come away; poverty's catching.'

Aphra Behn (1640–1689)

The guarded emancipation of women in society, and more particularly of actresses in the theatre, brought to the fore an entirely new genre of plays which has come to be known as the comedy of manners. We have seen Ben Jonson and Molière writing comedies of contemporary life, but theirs were comedies of morals. They wanted to teach society a lesson, and were concerned with how people *ought* to behave. The comedy of manners is about the way people *do* behave: the censure, if any, is implied not proclaimed. At the heart of the English comedy of manners lies the cool paradox of passion treated dispassionately in the acutely observed social context of the time.

In a dreadful play by the Duchess of Newcastle called *Sociable Companions*, a character says: 'Wit was killed in the war.' 'You are mistaken,' comes the complacent reply, 'it was only banished with the cavaliers; but now it is returned home.' Eight years were to pass before the wit and word-play which are definitive attributes of the English comedy of manners could be heard on the stage. Sir George Etherege was the first playwright to lay down the strict ground rules of the genre in *She Would If She Could*, written in 1668 when he was thirty-four, and *The Man of Mode; or, Sir Fopling Flutter*, written eight years later. The central action of the plays concerns the quest by both sexes for amorous adventures. Etherege, himself a fashionable gentleman, depicted the fops and ladies of quality whom he knew and the audience easily recognized. The characters live for the pleasures of the moment, the men indolent, the women hopeful of dangerous escapades. Although the style is intended to reflect everyday reality, the language is constantly heightened and polished to the point of making wit seem the medium of daily social exchange. There is no hint of criticism of the way of life portrayed: its manner and mores are taken for granted.

The attitude of William Wycherley is more at odds. Many writers tried to imitate Etherege, and few succeeded, but Wycherley made himself a master of the genre, and adapted it to his own more trenchant view of the world. Coarse, savage, obscene, he often equivocates between manners and morals, and was deeply influenced by Molière, especially in his two outstanding works, *The Country Wife* and *The Plain Dealer*, both produced in the mid-1670s. In these plays he is preoccupied with sexual desire at its most coarse and direct, yet cannot conceal his objections to the new permissiveness and to the current standards of behaviour, both male and female. 'Lord,' says his Lady Fidget in *The Country Wife*, 'why should you not think that we women make use of our reputation, as you men of yours, only to deceive the world with less suspicion? Our virtue is like the statesman's religion, the quaker's word, the gamester's oath, and the great man's honour, but to cheat those who trust us.' Wycherley never quite moves wholeheartedly into the comedy of manners: he cannot make himself airy and buoyant enough, and stands a little outside, refusing to keep a sense of disappointment and disapproval from darkening his plays.

It was not until the final decade of the seventeenth century that the comedy of manners found its most brilliant expression in the works of William

Congreve. He was born near Leeds in 1670, the son of an army officer who served in Ireland, where Congreve was educated first at Kilkenny and then at Trinity College, Dublin. He won fame early, at the age of twenty-three, when his play *The Old Bachelor* took the town by storm. Dryden said that he had never read so brilliant a first play. In 1694 *The Double Dealer*, a finer play, was not so well received, but Congreve was acclaimed again in 1695 for *Love for Love*. By now he was one of the leading literary figures of the day, and was rewarded by a government sinecure, his appointment as a commissioner for licensing hackney coaches, at a hundred pounds a year. Perversely, Congreve's most popular play was a tragedy called *The Mourning Bride*, produced in 1697. Three years later came his masterpiece, *The Way of the World*, which flopped.

Ann Pitt as Lady Wishfort, in *The Way of the World* by Congreve.

So disenchanted was Congreve that he never attempted another play, though he did not abandon the theatre altogether, and wrote two libretti as well as collaborating on a translation of Molière's *Monsieur de Pourceaugnac*. In 1705 he was associated with Sir John Vanbrugh (himself the author of at least one Restoration classic, *The Provoked Wife*, of 1697) in the opening of the Queen's Theatre, or Italian Opera House, in the Haymarket, and wrote an epilogue to its first production. The rest of his life he spent in broad tranquillity. He enjoyed a serene temperament, avoided quarrels, and was called by John Gay, the author of *The Beggar's Opera*, the 'unreproachful man'. The love of his life was Mrs Anne Bracegirdle, the actress who played most of his heroines. In later years he transferred his affections to the Duchess of Marlborough, and it is almost certain that he fathered her daughter, Lady Mary Godolphin, who later became Duchess of Leeds. Congreve died in London after a carriage accident five days before his fifty-ninth birthday, on 19 January 1729.

Congreve towers above his contemporaries. He was gifted both with wit and feeling, qualities which do not always appear in equal measure in the comedy of manners. According to William Hazlitt: 'Every sentence is replete with sense and satire, conveyed in the most polished and pointed terms.' In *The Way of the World*, Congreve's genius reached its peak. The plot is confused and confusing, but it hardly matters, for the brilliance of the play lies in the language and in the subtle relationship between Mirabell, in love despite himself, and Millamant, wanting to be loved but not enslaved. 'Here she comes i'faith full sail, with her fan spread and streamers out, and a shoal of fools for tenders,' Mirabell exclaims, providing one of the best first entrances for an actress ever written. Millamant is late but cannot remember the reason. 'Why was I so long?' she asks her maid, Mincing.

Mincing: Oh mem, your la'ship stayed to peruse a pecquet of letters.
Millamant: Oh ay, letters – I had letters – I am persecuted with letters – I hate letters – nobody knows how to write letters; and yet one has 'em, one does not know why. They serve one to pin up one's hair.
Witwoud: Is that the way? Pray madam, do you pin up your hair with all your letters? I find I must keep copies.
Millamant: Only with those in verse, Mr Witwoud, I never pin up my hair with prose. I fancy one's hair would not curl if it were pinned up with prose.

The wit sparkles and flows. Mirabell and Millamant circle each other, fence, thrust, parry and riposte. In the end love conquers all, and in a famous scene the two lay down provisos for their future:

Millamant: ... Positively, Mirabell, I'll lie a-bed in a morning as long as I please.
Mirabell: Then I'll get up in a morning as early as I please.

Millamant: ... I won't be called names after I'm married; positively I won't be called names.

Mirabell: Names!

Millamant: Ay, as wife, spouse, my dear, joy, jewel, love, sweetheart, and the rest of the nauseous cant in which men and their wives are so fulsomely familiar. I shall never bear that. Good Mirabell, don't let us be familiar or fond, nor kiss before folks ... nor go to Hyde Park together the first Sunday in a new chariot, to provoke eyes and whispers, and then never be seen together again; as if we were proud of one another the first week, and ashamed of one another for ever after that. Let us never visit together, nor go to a play together, but let us be very strange and well-bred; let us be as strange as if we had been married a great while, and as well-bred as if we were not married at all.

Mirabell: Have you any more conditions to offer? Hitherto, your demands are pretty reasonable.

Congreve and his contemporaries were the first to explore and shape the form which has become an accepted part of English theatrical tradition. In the second half of the eighteenth century it was to be refined and perfected by Richard Brinsley Sheridan, whose best play, *The School for Scandal*, stands in the front rank. Sheridan, having inherited the Restoration comedy, discarded the licentiousness but retained the wit. Like the playwrights of the Restoration, he was working in a very different vein. Let the playwright grow too critical, too distanced from the society he idealizes even while he may be satirizing it, and the audience will not be flattered enough to come again. The subjects of the comedy must be made to feel what Dryden was reading in their minds when he wrote (but surely did not believe):

Our ladies and our men now speake more wit,
In conversation, than those poets writ.

Let the playwright merely hold the mirror up to nature, foregoing all verbal brilliance and contrived eventfulness, and the audience will be bored by its own ordinariness. Yet there should not be too absurd a discrepancy between the audience and its image on the stage, so comedy of manners does require a lively audience and a lively society. Restoration comedy encouraged good conversation, the inventive use of language, and people's desire to be as witty in themselves as their theatrical reflections: comedy of manners needs the audience to be persuaded that it recognizes itself.

Yet for a society to observe itself so closely, for an audience's standards to become so involved with its image of itself, implies a degree of self-consciousness which is the opposite of the original function of theatre. Manners had become a matter of display and fashion, and fashion must have arbiters and setters. The sideways glance had arrived: if drama was going to make appearances important, it would be embarrassing to be caught liking

Laurence Olivier and Vivien Leigh in their first London appearance together as Sir Peter and Lady Teazle in *The School for Scandal* by Sheridan.

what others did not like. Superficial questions are the hardest to judge. An audience is likely to recognize when its deepest interests are engaged; to differentiate between one engrossing mode and another, it needs critics.

This need was realized at the time of the Restoration when the First Night Ritual was inaugurated. It was fashionable to be seen at the play, and fashionable to see successful plays early. Plays were discussed, analysed, praised or dispraised, and the whisper went round. Guidance must be provided. No wonder then that the Restoration gave birth to a breed which theatre people have always regarded with suspicion, caution and, on rare occasions, awe.

The art of criticism – and it is only rarely practised as an art – was born with the comedy of manners. Restoration comedy was to be written, and looked at, in detachment, and this is well illustrated by the sort of playhouse which the times produced. The proscenium arch is the key: it distances the action from the audience by setting it inside a frame, so that the spectator is better able to say: 'I'm not part of what is going on. I can recognize others, but what has this to do with me?' Critics, as a breed, have to be the most detached spectators of all. From the outset they were mistrusted and resented, and quickly became the targets for actors and dramatists. Wycherley fired his burst in *The Plain Dealer*, and Sheridan in *The Critic*.

In recent years the critic has become a maker of literary rather than theatrical judgments. Too many practitioners write as if they were still trying to satisfy their university tutors. Modern critics have broken with two great traditions in theatrical criticism. By abolishing wit from their columns they have renounced a faculty which in any case is no true loss to the would-be cultural legislator. By giving up the job of verbally re-creating the performance witnessed, they have jettisoned one of the most valuable contributions made by earlier critics in the English language, which was to give permanence to the passing traffic of the stage. Film and video are not capable of capturing theatrical atmosphere, or recording the particular gesture or inflection which unlocked the imagination of an audience. I hope that criticism may simply be going through a temporary crisis of confidence parallel to the one that figurative art now seems to be recovering from, following the impact of photography. Hazlitt, Scott, Shaw, Beerbohm, Montague, Agate and Tynan sometimes illuminated plays, and sometimes got them hopelessly wrong: what they also did was to treasure up great performances and great productions whose inner qualities have otherwise evaporated into time.

The Restoration theatre made one other lasting contribution to the theatre. It engendered a passionate, sometimes unhealthy, interest in the private lives of the performers, a fascination with backstage life that has persisted and extended to colonize the lives of film and TV stars too. The interest was certainly quickened by the advent of actresses, who attracted admirers, gossip and intrigue. If a member of the public wanted to be thought of as fashionable (and they usually did), then knowledge of the backstage rivalries, the squabbles and the bedroom adventures of the female stars was essential. Actresses were a titillating novelty. Doctor Johnson confessed to his friend, the actor David Garrick: 'I'll come no more behind your scenes, David; for the silk stockings and white bosoms of your actresses excite my amorous propensities.' Their private lives were often quite as torrid as any character they portrayed on stage.

Nell Gwynn is probably the most famous actress of the Restoration, but her talent was, and is, the subject of debate. It has been said that to describe her as an actress is to do the profession an injustice; others claim that she was a gifted and witty comedienne. Certainly the twentieth century is in no position to criticize the seventeenth for judging actresses in terms of their sexual glamour, though the seventeenth was likely to be more straightforward in expressing its interests: 'Nelly was eased of her virginity by Mr Hart at the same time as Lord Buckhurst sighed for it,' one gossip wrote. 'But His Majesty carrying off the prize, we must leave her under Royal protection.'

Samuel Pepys was a keen theatregoer, not a knowledgable critic. In serious or tragic roles he considered Nell a dreadful performer, but there is something persuasive about his view of her acting in lighter vein:

2nd March, 1667. After dinner with my wife to the King's house to see *The Maiden Queen*, a new play of Dryden's ... and the truth is there is a comical part done by Nell which is Florimel, that I never can hope ever to see the like done again, by man or woman ... But so great a performance of a comical part was never, I believe in the world before as Nell do this, both as a mad girl, then most and best of all when she comes in like a young gallant; and hath the motions and carriage of a spark the most that ever I saw any man have. It makes me, I confess, admire her.

Nell Gwynn (1650–1687) from Sir Peter Lely's portrait.

Mrs Barry and Mrs Boutell had an infamous backstage row. They played together in a scene where Mrs Barry had the lines 'Die, sorceress, die: and all my wrongs die with thee' and then actually stabbed her unfortunate colleague, though not fatally. Other actresses resisted the rumour mill:

> Mrs Bracegirdle's unblemished reputation contributed not a little to make her the Cara, the darling of the theatre. And though she might be said to have been the universal passion, and under the highest temptation, her constancy in resisting them served but to increase the number of her admirers. Her youth and lively aspect threw out such a glow of health and cheerfulness on the stage that few spectators that were not past it could behold her without desire.

When she died of cancer in 1730, she lay in state in the Jerusalem Chamber of Westminster Abbey, the only actress ever to do so.

Two actresses whose private lives would certainly not have qualified them for such an honour were Kitty Clive and Peg Woffington. Their enmity was legendary. Peg Woffington was renowned for her impersonation of men on stage, in what were called 'breeches parts'. On one occasion she sailed into the Green Room after a loudly applauded performance as Sir Harry Wildair. 'By God,' she said, 'half the audience thinks me to be a man.' To which Kitty Clive replied: 'By God, madam, the other half *knows* you to be a woman.' On her return to Covent Garden after an unexplained absence, Peg Woffington was asked by the actor James Quin where she had been. To Bath, the famous health spa, she told him. 'What took you there?' he asked. 'Oh, pure wantonness,' she replied. 'And were you cured?' Quin enquired.

These spicy tales are not repeated for the sake of wantonness. They make an important point about the theatre of the time. The audience's obsession with the actresses and with their irregular lives – which sometimes spilled on to the stage, when they played parts which were semi-autobiographical – led to a decline in the standard of plays. Wit hardly mattered. The recurring theme of Puritan reaction emerged again when the future Bishop Jeremy Collier published a broadside called *A Short View of the Immorality and Profaneness of the English Stage* in 1698. Sir Richard Steele, then a captain in the army, and later to become a dramatist as well as the critic and essayist of *Tatler* and *Spectator* fame, took Collier's line. He condemned licentiousness and favoured a kind of sentimental moralizing which seemed to satisfy middle-class taste.

When performers take precedence over plays, the theatre becomes decadent and tawdry. So it did in England in the eighteenth century. Actors dominated. In 1756 Theo Cibber reported:

> I have heard of an actor who humorously told his brother comedians that, whenever he had a part where the redundancy of the author ran into too great a length in the scenes, he had recourse to a whimsical expedient for

the shortening of them. He had the whole part wrote out, and then gave it to his cat to play with. What Puss clawed off, the actor left out; yet he generally found enough remained to satisfy his audience.

The theatrical profession's desire to please its audience and to accommodate the soft-centred public morality of the time was paramount. The plays of Shakespeare came in for particularly obnoxious treatment. An appalling poet, Nahum Tate, was a chief offender (and was rewarded with the poet laureateship in 1692). In 1681 this numskull took *King Lear*, omitted the Fool, preserved Cordelia to survive and marry Edgar, and consigned the old King to a peaceful and honourable dotage. 'And Cordelia shall be queen!' her rapturous subjects chorused. For a hundred and fifty years the Nahum Tate version remained the standard acting edition of the play: Shakespeare's did not resurface until 1838, when William Charles Macready played the original text.

Colley Cibber's adaptation of *Richard III* added a now famous line which modern actors find difficult to resist. 'So much for Buckingham!' says Richard, after learning of the duke's execution. Often the changes seem capricious, if not unintelligible. In *Macbeth* the lines:

The devil damn thee black, thou cream fac'd loon,
Where got'st thou that goose look?

were sanitized as:

Now friend, what means thy change of countenance?

Much of the blame for the decline belongs to the monopoly of the two great Patent houses, Drury Lane and Covent Garden, which were not so much interested in producing plays that mattered as in seeing to it that the seats were filled. Their rivalry was interminable, and to some theatre historians a source of fascination, but it was peripheral to the main events, which were happening elsewhere while the old pros slugged it out. In 1728, John Rich's theatre in Lincoln's Inn Fields produced a ballad opera by John Gay which Drury Lane had rejected. It was called *The Beggar's Opera* and was a phenomenal success: the wags said that the piece 'made Gay rich and Rich gay'. With music selected by John Pepusch from well-known airs, it is a lighthearted political satire, coloured by characters from the underworld. However it was not lighthearted enough to appease Sir Robert Walpole, whose government it ridiculed, and the following year he had Gay's sequel, *Polly*, suppressed.

In 1729, with the success of Gay and Rich as a spur, Thomas Odell, a man without much knowledge of the stage, opened a similar playhouse, Goodman's Fields, in London's East End, but he soon retired. Then in 1737 the infamous Licensing Act was passed to ensure that all new dramas were submitted for approval to the Lord Chamberlain, and only the two Patent houses were allowed to operate as places of entertainment. Nervous owners of

Frontispiece to *The Beggar's Opera* by Gay, première in 1728.

the smaller theatres immediately closed their doors. But even the most ruthless governments discover sooner or later that no legislation can entirely prevent people from doing what they most want. Henry Giffard, who had taken over Goodman's Fields, and was particularly artful, described his house as 'the late Theatre', and announced that he would present a 'Concert of Vocal and Instrumental Music, divided in two parts. Tickets at three, two and one shilling.' It looked innocent enough, but those who paid their money were able to see plays 'performed gratis by persons for their diversion'. Giffard could not be accused of illegally taking money for what happened between the two halves of the 'concert'.

On Monday, 19 October 1741, Giffard presented Shakespeare's *Richard III*, announcing (not quite accurately) that the part of King Richard was to be played 'by a Gentleman Who never appeared on any Stage'. The following day a critic wrote that the anonymous actor's reception was 'the most extraordinary and great that was ever known upon such an Occasion'. The actor was David Garrick. With one performance he introduced a style of acting that

David Garrick as Romeo in *Romeo and Juliet* and *overleaf* as Abel Drugger in *The Alchemist* by Ben Jonson.

punctured the heavyweight histrionic approach which had dominated the English stage. James Quin, a champion exponent of the old apoplectic school, observed sourly: 'If this young man be right, then we have all been wrong.'

Of French and Irish descent, David Garrick was born on 19 February 1717 at Hereford, where his father, Peter, a captain in the English army, was on recruiting duty. The Irish blood came from his mother, Arabella Clough, the daughter of a clergyman at Lichfield Cathedral. When Garrick was nineteen, his parents sent him to the academy opened in 1736 by Samuel Johnson, near Lichfield. The schooling did not last long: after a few months, on 2 March 1737, teacher and pupil set off for London. Johnson later reported that he had twopence-halfpenny in his pocket, and Garrick three halfpence.

In the capital Garrick entered his name as a law student at Lincoln's Inn, but a legacy enabled him and his brother to set up Garrick & Co., wine merchants. His new trade took him to places of entertainment where he met the actor Charles 'Wicked Charlie' Macklin and Charles Fleetwood, the manager of Drury Lane, who produced Garrick's comedy *Lethe, or Esop in the Shades* in 1740. Macklin's performance as Shylock in *The Merchant of Venice* is said to have powerfully influenced Garrick's conception of acting. In the same year of 1741, at the theatre in Goodman's Fields, he made his first appearance as an actor, appropriately wearing a mask, substituting for a sick Harlequin. After that he was given several parts, played in Ipswich for the summer, but did not dare tell his family that he had entered so low a profession until his astonishing début in *Richard III* enabled him to break the news to his elder brother.

Garrick's legend was born in that one night. The originality of his style, which the age thought naturalistic, savaged the pompous vocalizing which had dominated the previous generation. Gone were the stately attitudes and the throbbing recitations echoed from the French. Garrick was electrifying because he conveyed reality. Alexander Pope enthused: 'That young man never had his equal as an actor, and he will never have a rival.' In the weeks and months after his début (he played 150 performances as Richard, at a salary of £2 a night), Goodman's Fields was filled with fashionable celebrities who came, saw and were conquered. It was said that a dozen dukes a night attended the performances. To a less sturdy temperament, the adulation might have proved fatal. Fortunately Garrick, although sensitive and highly strung, was blessed with the common sense that a pupil of Doctor Johnson's could be expected to possess. And like his teacher, he was also a great survivor.

Garrick was the first superstar of the English theatre. His audience flocked to see him no matter what he played. Although rather small for a conventional leading man – he was known affectionately as 'Little Davy' – he must have had the one quality which posterity cannot recapture: presence. When Garrick came on to a stage, his personality worked magically on his audience, who were also dazzled by his versatility. He took on roles as diverse as the simple-minded Abel Drugger in Ben Jonson's *The Alchemist*, the voluble Francis Archer in George Farquhar's *The Beaux' Stratagem*, and the great Shake-spearean parts – Hamlet, Macbeth, Richard III and Lear (in the Nahum Tate version). On top of this he wrote plays, of which *The Clandestine Marriage*, written with George Colman the Elder, is the most frequently revived, and songs – the lyric for *Heart of Oak* is the most famous. Soon he was lured to Drury Lane. In 1746 a young man called Richard Cumberland, then in the sixth form at Westminster School, but later to become a prominent dramatist, wrote this account of Garrick as the young Lothario in Nicholas Rowe's *The Fair Penitent:*

> Little Garrick enters young and light and alive in every muscle and feature; heavens what a transition! It seemed as if a whole century had been stepped over in the transition of a single scene; old things were done away, and a new order at once brought forward, bright and luminous, and clearly destined to dispel the barbarisms and bigotry of a tasteless age, too long attached to the prejudices of custom, and superstitiously devoted to the illusions of imposing declamation.

By 1747, when he was thirty, Garrick's friends in the City helped him to raise £8,000 for his share in buying the lease and furnishings of Drury Lane Theatre and renewing the Patent. That September he opened the theatre with Macklin as Shylock, but the first words to be heard in the refurbished house were by Samuel Johnson, his old friend, who wrote a prologue setting forth Garrick's theatrical principles, his devotion to Shakespeare and his intention to reform plays and players, and ending with a famous appeal:

> The drama's laws the drama's patrons give,
> For we, who live to please, must please to live.
>
> . . . .
>
> 'Tis yours this night to bid the reign commence
> Of rescued nature and reviving sense.

In Garrick's company, his reforms were immediately self-evident. He did not surround himself with indifferent performers so that he would be shown off to greater advantage. Instead, he recruited leading players to share the limelight, and they included Macklin, Kitty Clive and Peg Woffington. (He was deeply in love with Peg Woffington, and they had an intense affair, but her extravagances and infidelities persuaded him not to marry her.) He warned his new troupe that they had joined a regime in which the discipline would be harsh. Garrick was, in effect, the first real director that England had known. He imposed a degree of stylistic unity on the hitherto self-indulgent performances of his actors and actresses, and one of them said that 'he hammered his conceptions into our minds'.

He was also determined to reform audiences. Infuriated by the gossiping fops and wits who sat on stage just a few feet away from the actors, Garrick banished them to the auditorium, which he enlarged. The apron, a forestage in front of the curtain, on to which the old brigade had marched to strike an attitude before launching into long soliloquies, served no purpose for the new naturalistic style, and Garrick did away with it. He introduced new lighting by having footlights and sidelights, which were oil lamps with reflectors. He forbade members of the audience to come backstage during the play, and discontinued the practice of reduced entry fees for those who come late or left early. He travelled abroad to find the best scene designers, and through his lifelong friendship with Doctor Johnson he brought the theatre into the world of letters and scholarship.

Garrick's career coincided with, and to some extent inspired, the first wave of provincial theatre building throughout England. Within twenty years of his début, Bristol, Bath, Norwich and many other centres were putting up theatres which incorporated Garrick's innovations. Devoted to Shakespeare, he inaugurated an annual Jubilee at Stratford-upon-Avon. He made the theatre attractive and available to people who might otherwise have felt excluded. More important, he insisted that the theatre could speak to the human imagination at its greatest stretch.

Like many great actors, Garrick's private personality was full of contradictions. He was accused of being vain, avaricious, mean and arrogant. Yet he and his wife, the Viennese opera singer Eva Maria Veigel, whom he married in 1749, were famous for their hospitality, and it turned out after his death that he had made many anonymous gifts to charity. When he realized that he was

putting on weight he gave up youthful parts and concentrated good-humouredly on maturer roles, so it may be said that his vanity was not quite so entrenched as his critics liked to suggest. It is true that he was fond of making money, but that trait is not rare among those who work in insecure professions.

After a series of farewell performances, Garrick retired in 1775. All his life he had suffered from kidney ailments, and early in 1779 he was taken ill while staying with his old friends Lord and Lady Spencer at Althorp Park, Northamptonshire. He died in London on 20 January, a month short of his sixty-second birthday, and is buried in Poets' Corner, Westminster Abbey. But it is as an actor, the ephemeral profession, that he is chiefly remembered, and nowhere better or more lovingly than in the discussion of Garrick's Hamlet in Henry Fielding's novel *Tom Jones*:

> 'Indeed, Mr Partridge,' says Mrs Miller, 'you are not of the same opinion with the town; for they are all agreed, that Hamlet is acted by the best player who ever was on the stage.' – 'He the best player!' cries Partridge with a contemptuous sneer: 'Why, I could act as well as he myself. I am sure if I had seen a ghost, I should have looked in the very same manner, and done just as he did. And then, to be sure, in that scene, as you called it, between him and his mother, where you told me he acted so fine, why, Lord help me! any man, that is, any good man, that had such a mother, would have done exactly the same. I know you are only joking with me; but, indeed, madam, though I was never at a play in London, yet I have seen acting before in the country; and the King for my money: he speaks all his words distinctly, half as loud again as the other. – Anybody may see he is an actor.'

A monument to David Garrick in Lichfield Cathedral bears Doctor Johnson's epitaph: 'I am disappointed by that stroke of death which has eclipsed the gaiety of nations and impoverished the public stock of harmless pleasure.' The ascendancy of the actor and the exclusion of uncomfortable contemporary themes had indeed taken the harm out of theatrical pleasure, though Johnson did not mean to belittle his friend, and the philosopher Edmund Burke observed that Garrick had raised the character of his profession to the level of a liberal art. That kind of praise from Burke was an Establishment seal of safety. There was nothing disturbing in the theatre he knew. For the next hundred years in which the actor was to command the drama, some of the most desperate battles fought out were those between playwright and performer.

A WORLD
TURNED
UPSIDE-DOWN

When the Lord Chamberlain licensed the King Street Theatre in Bristol in the 1760s, the letters patent called on behalf of King George III for 'the Strictest Regard to such Representations as any way Concern Civil polity or the Constitution of our Government that those may Contribute to the Support of our Sacred Authority and the preservation of Order'. Travelling companies could still get round the Licensing Act of 1737 by the use of blatant subterfuges, and they went on doing so long into the nineteenth century, but that made them dependent on the good will and blind eye of local magistrates. The plays of Goldsmith and Sheridan were splendid entertainments in the amiable vein of the comedy of manners. The reign of the actor in the Patent theatres required an atmosphere of warm approval. These conditions created a theatre of enjoyment and recreation, and brought all sorts of technical improvements, but they did not encourage any radical innovation in English drama.

The next great burst of theatrical energy had no single geographical or national identity, and is linked with the age of political and social change which Europe was about to enter. Yet one of the most interesting centres of activity had the unlikely setting of a political backwater with a quiet populace. At a time when commercialism and the poetic drama were in continual conflict – and the drama more often the loser – the theatre of playwrights and ideas found its place in the peaceful, orderly Duchy of Saxe-Weimar, in eastern Germany.

In the eighteenth century Germany consisted of a flock of independent states of which Saxe-Weimar was one of the smallest and poorest, exerting little influence on social or religious affairs. On the other hand the Duchy was good farming country, and its Court was renowned for its active cultural life and love of music – Johann Sebastian Bach had been Court Organist for eight years from 1708. In Weimar, it was said, there were ten thousand poets and only a few inhabitants. The Court was small, but in combination with a thriving middle class it supported its own theatre, which displayed a taste for what can only be described as a bizarre style of classical drama inspired by ancient sources. The giant of Weimar's theatre was an invited guest, the phenomenal figure of Johann Wolfgang von Goethe – poet, novelist, scientist, statesman, and one of the most versatile and gifted men in all the history of European culture. In his youth he was a rebellious, passionate poet, but the more successful he became, the closer he drew to the traditionalists at the Court of Weimar, who reverenced the classical past.

Goethe, who was born in the free city of Frankfurt am Main in 1749, was drawn into Weimar's affairs by the young heir to the dukedom, Karl August. The two first met in 1774, when Goethe was already famous as the author of *Götz von Berlichingen*, a historical play originally written to be read, but performed in Berlin in 1774, and of the wildly successful novel, *Die Leiden des jungen Werthers*. Both works captured the imagination of the exuberant Karl August. The play reflected the brute vitality of the sixteenth century, and came as a powerful antidote to the refined affectations of its author's own time. It was regarded as the first work of authentic genius produced by a cultural movement of which Goethe was a leading light, and which came to be known as *Sturm und Drang*, literally Storm and Stress. The *Sturm und Drang* grew in reaction against French classical taste; it exalted nature and the human individual, and was opposed to established authority. In the theatre, it produced what its name suggests it should, a bombastic, expressionistic style of acting. The grandeur of Shakespearean characters was the ideal.

Goethe's novel, *Werther*, gave expression to what Thomas Carlyle called 'the nameless unrest and longing discontent which was then agitating in every bosom'. It has been described as a sentimental book, a tear-jerker, dealing with a blighted idyll, a young man's love that ends in suicide. But its true theme was what the eighteenth century called enthusiasm, the disastrous effects of striving for absolutes in all things. Karl August found himself in harmony with these passions, and he invited Goethe to Weimar in 1775, the year of his eighteenth birthday, when he became the reigning Duke.

The new ruler quickly provided the kind of preferment that comes seldom to authors and hardly ever to young ones. In 1776 he appointed Goethe to his Cabinet and in 1782 he made him his minister of finance and granted him the noble rank which entitled him to style himself *von* Goethe. At the same time Goethe had the post of director of both the Court Amateur Theatre and the professional Court Theatre, but his role more closely resembled that of a minister of culture. Yet although he carried out his responsibilities with great diligence and seriousness, he also kept writing both poetry and plays, and it was in the early 1770s that he began to write his masterpiece, *Faust*, a play in verse which he worked on for most of his life.

With Goethe at the centre, Weimar soon came to be regarded as the cultural capital of Germany, and attracted the attention of men of letters from all over Europe. One of these was the playwright Friedrich Schiller, who was thirty-five years old when he and Goethe embarked on a close friendship and collaboration, in 1794. Together they created a unique theatre in Weimar, although it was a hot-house creation, and in many ways a theatre gone wrong. Both Goethe and Schiller were idealists: their expressed aim was to lay down a body of work for the generations to come, no matter what a contemporary audience might make of these monuments for posterity. The results were highly stylized. They used masks and even a Greek chorus. This was subsidized theatre at its purest: the poets and playwrights were absolutely free from commercial pressures, able to do just what they pleased. Yet Goethe's genius was never fully at home in the collective and practical world of the theatre. In spite of his passionate interest in the drama and in the

Johann Wolfgang von Goethe (1749–1832).

production of plays, he seemed to lack a true theatrical instinct: ideas dominate feeling, momentum stops for intellectual discussion. Even *Faust*, which in literary terms is an undoubted classic, does not rate anywhere near so highly in the theatre, where its vast scope and undramatic nature restrict production to occasional experimental ventures. It was Goethe's collaborator who displayed the true talents of the dramatist.

Schiller was born in Marbach in 1759, the son of an army officer. After a solid grammar school education to the age of thirteen, he spent eight years at the Military Academy, where he studied medicine, and was then appointed medical officer to a Stuttgart regiment. He was twenty-two years old when he published his first play, a stirring protest against stifling convention and corruption in high places, *Die Räuber* (*The Robbers*). It is furious stuff, and the style conveys the flavour, with lines like: 'Command? You, reptile, command? Command me?' or: 'I defy the tyrant destiny!' or again:

Hermann: ... Your uncle –
Amalia: (*rushing at him*) You are lying –
Hermann: Your uncle –
Amalia: Karl is alive!
Hermann: And your uncle –
Amalia: Karl is alive?
Hermann: Your uncle, too – Do not betray me. (*Rushes off.*)
Amalia: (*Standing as if petrified, then starting up wildly and rushing after him*) Karl is alive!

This kind of high-tension dialogue can only be exchanged in melodrama. Some of the stage directions intensify the colour: '*Franz writhes on his chair in fearful convulsions*' and, in his writhing, '*shoots himself*'.

The Robbers is specially important for its influence on the nineteenth-century theatre, because it was the first of its kind. A virtuous maiden importuned by an evil count, a stolen birthright, a father left naked in a dungeon by a villainous son, the usurped brother leading a band of robbers to obtain justice – the quintessence of melodrama. Although much of *The Robbers* may now seem ludicrous, in its day it was irresistible for its energy and passion. It was also a casualty in the battle between poet and commercial manager.

The manager was Baron Wolfgang Heribert von Dalberg, honorary director of the National Theatre at Mannheim, who decided to produce the play but then grew nervous of the content, and so reduced it to conventional eighteenth-century morality. The playbills read like a Hollywood poster of the movie-mogul period: 'the portrait of a lost and mighty soul'; 'a man to weep for and hate, to detest and love'. But in spite of Dalberg's excisions, the play retained so much of Schiller's power that when it was first performed, on 13 January 1782, the theatre was turned into a madhouse. Women fainted, men raised their fists. Schiller, who went absent without leave to attend the

Johann Christoph Friedrich von Schiller (1759–1805) and – out of doors – the first reading of *The Robbers*

sensational first night, was subsequently confined to barracks and ordered to write no more seditious literature. When the play was produced in France, it prompted audiences to cry 'The world is turned upside-down!' – one of Schiller's own lines. The English banned it. Yet again the theatre was provoking society into thinking differently about itself, a fact which the leaders of the new French Republic recognized when they made Schiller an honorary citizen in 1792.

Sturm und Drang was a German prelude to the Romantic movement whose history became so entangled with the egalitarian and libertarian currents of the French Revolution and the history of nationalism that it has formed a kind of Black Hole of definitions, sucking in the most wildly contradictory elements. One of its sources was the philosophy of Jean-Jacques Rousseau, who emphasized the value of the natural world and the essential goodness of human beings, ideas which now seem quietist and nostalgic in view of the violent change and urban dominance that the 'age of revolution' brought with it. Certainly the analogy between social and artistic revolution seems to be based on a liaison which both artists and revolutionaries have been ready to break as their needs required.

As it happens, it is quite difficult to think of the European theatre of the time as being revolutionary in the political sense at all. Perhaps that is because the best theatre calls for a sense of communal unity which the age could not provide. Theatrical revolutions do not spill real blood, even though a deep enough change in the drama can provoke its own violent reactions, and orthodoxy is bound to defend itself, especially when the change is inventive, sudden and daring enough. Fittingly, it was in France that the next theatrical revolution took place. It happened on the stage of the Comédie-Française on 25 February 1830 with a play called *Hernani*, by Victor Hugo. The curtain rose on a bedroom set where an old woman dressed in black heard a knock at the door and said: '*Serait-ce déjà lui?*' – 'Can that be him already?'

The moment that line was said, pandemonium broke out. To foreign ears, the question hardly sounds offensive enough to have sent the conservative occupants of the stalls and boxes booing into battle against the wildly counter-applauding regiments of the cheaper seats, but that is what happened. The point was – and it is a particularly French point – that the offence lay not in what the line said but in what it *was* – or rather what it was not. It was not an alexandrine. Victor Hugo had smashed the subtle rhyming couplet in which all French drama had been written since the seventeenth century. The Bastille of French classicism had fallen, and Romanticism had triumphed.

English theatre stood firm, and admitted no revolution at all, either artistic or political – for wasn't the one likely to be tainted with the other? Instead it imported melodrama, though the word came from the French. Literally it means drama with music – interludes in which music was used to express the actions while the actors mimed them – a technique later to be adopted by silent films, and then naturalized in films and television, which have developed the use of music to enhance and counterpoint images into a minor art. The term 'melodrama' also seems to have been used in the early nineteenth century in order to legitimize plays staged outside the licensed theatres.

Melodrama flourished first of all in London, then described as 'the richest town in the world, the biggest port, the greatest manufacturing town, the Imperial city, the centre of circulation, the heart of the world, a whirlpool, a maelstrom'. In this heady concentration of humanity, it became one of the most popular theatrical forms ever known. The most frequently offered explanations suggest that melodrama thrived because it was escapist enter-tainment centred on implausible, undemanding and unsubtle plots in which the villains and heroes were singular and easily identified, and thrills and emotion were laid on with a trowel. Such reasoning may be too facile to account for its enormous popularity in England and Europe, where more people were now going to the theatre than at any time in history. Queen Victoria herself made eight hundred visits – presumably eight hundred times that she was amused. For a form to be so attractive to all levels of society there had to be sound and important reasons.

The twentieth century has good reason to see itself as confused and chaotic; consequently it tends to take the compensating view that in times past society was more stable, more easily defined, and its ills more readily diagnosed. But for much of the nineteenth century too the world was in turmoil and must have felt just as threatening and insecure. Fragmented rural populations were draining into the cities, and the cities' own populations expanding, faster than any community could cope with. Melodrama, with its obligatory happy ending, with virtue always triumphant over evil, provided moral certainties. Of course it was also unabashed and energetic entertainment, given in theatres whose splendid opulence (by gaslight, anyway) created a world of well-upholstered security. To that world, anything so remotely immaterial as a decline in theatrical literary standards was simply an irrelevance.

Much of the nineteenth century represents one of the most arid periods in all dramatic literature. Authors of any worth regarded the theatre as meretricious and second-rate. Those who wanted the freedom to explore the truth of their society and follow their characters where their imagination led them were writing novels. Another, less noble, reason for the scarcity of important plays was the simple matter of finance. Contrary to a belief not yet extinct among theatrical impresarios, playwrights have to earn a livelihood. In the nineteenth century, despite the numbers that filled the theatres, the first great English melodrama, *Black-Ey'd Susan*, made its author, Douglas Jerrold, exactly £60 in 1829.

Today, of the price paid for every theatre ticket, the playwright will receive a percentage ranging from five to ten per cent, and occasionally more. That level of reward is a fairly recent development. In the nineteenth century, play-wrights received no royalties at all. They sold their work outright at the going rate, which was around £50. As a result there was bitter hostility between the playwright and the impresario. One writer described the theatrical manager as one who 'in most instances, received his education in a bar room, possibly on the far side of the counter'.

That derision came from Dion Boucicault, who had been baptized with the most fitting of Christian names for a future man of the theatre, Dionysius. He was the first playwright to demand and get a share of the profits. He wrote between 100 and 150 plays, the more famous including the melodramas *London Assurance* (1841) and *The Corsican Brothers* (1852). Boucicault had tremendous facility in both farce and melodrama, and a flair for knowing what the public wanted. His play *The Streets of London* changed title according to the city where it was being performed, and might modulate into *The Sidewalks of New York*.

As if melodrama and inadequate returns were not handicaps enough, the artistic famine mattered very little to the really dominant figures in the nineteenth-century theatre: this was the golden age of that august and imposing theatrical personage, the actor-manager. Although the two occupa-tions have rarely been combined since the late 1930s, the actor-manager was for almost 250 years the paramount force in the theatre, and especially in Britain. Of course, to achieve such status the man would first have to prove himself as an actor, and restraint was unlikely to be his forte in either role.

This brings us up against the inherent difficulty of doing justice to the power and presence of dead actors.

The passing moment is the actor's natural element. The experience of playgoers belongs to the performance they witness, and it is bound to vary, because on any given night the actor may perform very well, or very badly, or merely indifferently. The audience will base its opinion on that performance: if the actor is off form, reputation counts for nothing. That is one of the reasons why opinions of actors disagree. Posterity has no direct means to judge. It cannot reproduce a performance by an actor of a bygone age, and cannot recreate voice and movement. Even if it could do the latter, as it can today, I have already argued that there is no instrument that will register an actor's personality and presence as an audience perceives it in the heat of a live performance. That magic belongs to a living actor before a living audience. That is why to be in a darkened auditorium, responding to actors who in turn respond to the audience, is one of the most sublime and rewarding ways to explore our common imagination, and why at the end of the performance people sometimes feel what Prospero summed up:

> These our actors,
> As I foretold you, were all spirits, and
> Are melted into air, into thin air...

At the same time, it is not difficult to answer the question whether Burbage or Garrick or Molière would have been regarded as great actors today, or Champmeslé, Mrs Siddons or Eleonora Duse as great actresses. Given that their talent and personality caught the imagination of their contemporaries, there is no reason to doubt that if they had been born in a different age they would have scaled their talent, and adapted their style, to the time. That ability is essential to an actor's success. One of the contributions actors make is to reveal the manner, the taste, the favourite modes of expression, of the times they live in.

Yet the supremacy of the actor, I have suggested, is not always best for the theatre as an art. If actors are allowed to dominate, the theatre may easily become an arena for jostling egos, for exhibitionism. The actor-manager was frequently guilty of this kind of indecent display; paradoxically, he was also the means by which classical plays – especially the plays of Shakespeare, since they offered the greatest parts – were kept alive.

The archetypal actor-manager usually decided to venture on his own in his mid to late thirties. By then he could feel confident of his abilities, which would have been underlined by good notices and praised by friends and admirers. Now he would form his own company, which is to say that he financed and organized a theatrical troupe in which he, the actor-manager, retained the best parts. More often than not he was married, and his wife would play the female leads. Towards his company he was both tyrannical and paternal. His word was law. Productions were ruthlessly tailored to ensure that the actor-manager was shown off to best advantage – usually centre-stage in bright light. The supporting players, including the aforementioned wife, were nearly always less talented than he: it did not do for a satellite to shine too brightly.

The actor-manager was a benevolent despot driven by a need to serve himself, but with himself the community at large. Only a few ever reached London. For most, the provinces were their principalities. They played as many as eight different major roles, Monday to Saturday. They toured the length and breadth of Britain, week after week, living in rented rooms – the legendary 'theatrical digs' – making up in shabby, cold dressing-rooms, and changing trains at Crewe on Sundays. They inspired the first wave of provincial theatre-building throughout the country. In their fur-collared overcoats and Homburgs, they combined an air of theatrical flamboyance with the grave respectability of an alderman.

Thomas Betterton was among the first to combine the work of actor and manager, and was the leading player of the Restoration stage. He was a member of Davenant's company, and three years after Davenant's death in 1668 the company moved to a new theatre in Dorset Gardens, which combined with the Theatre Royal, Drury Lane, in 1682. Thirteen years after that, Betterton led a strike of his fellow artists which resulted in him setting up his own troupe by reopening the theatre in Lincoln's Inn Fields. He launched his career as actor-manager with the first performance of Congreve's *Love for Love*. In 1705 he moved to a new theatre in the Haymarket designed by Sir John Vanbrugh, and there he successfully presented himself in comedy and tragedy until 1710, the year of his death. His wife, Mary Sanderson, was one of the first English actresses.

Betterton was large and rotund, an unlikely shape for an actor famous for his Hamlet. His fellow actor Anthony Aston wrote of him:

> Mr Betterton, although a superlative good actor, laboured under an ill figure, being clumsily made, having a great head, short, thick neck, stooped in the shoulders, and had fat short arms which he rarely lifted higher than his stomach ... He had little eyes and a broad face, a little pock-bitten, a corpulent body, with thick legs and large feet. He was better to meet than to follow, for his aspect was serious, venerable and majestic – in his latter time a little paralytic. His voice was low and grumbling; yet he could time it by an artful climax which enforced universal attention even from the fops and orange-girls.

Those 'little eyes' and 'corpulent body' were counteracted when the actor took the stage. Pepys recorded on 28 May 1663: 'And so to the Duke's house; and there saw Hamlet done, giving us fresh reason never to think enough of Mr. Betterton.'

Garrick was thirty when he took over the Theatre Royal, Drury Lane, where he presented himself and an unusually fine company for the rest of his career.

He spent most of his professional life as an actor-manager. So too did John Philip Kemble, who was born in 1757, the year Garrick turned forty. Kemble was one of twelve children of a Midland actor-manager, Roger Kemble, and his actress wife, Sarah Wood, who founded an extraordinary theatrical family. The eldest child was Sarah Siddons, the greatest tragic actress of her day; two other brothers, Stephen and Charles, were also actors. Of Stephen it was said that he could play Falstaff without padding. Charles fathered another famous actress, Fanny Kemble, whose talent saved him from bankruptcy.

But it was John Philip who took the acting profession into the nineteenth century. He was successively manager of Drury Lane and Covent Garden. As an actor, he was the noblest Roman of them all, bringing a stately, stentorian approach to classical parts. He was dignified, certainly impressive, and probably dull. His style suited the time but was rendered obsolescent on the night of 26 January 1814, when Edmund Kean made his début as Shylock at Drury Lane. Kean was a comet in the theatrical cosmos – passionate, original, tempestuous – whose private life and drinking habits were his downfall. He was not strictly speaking an actor-manager, for most of his career was spent in the employ of others, but he did, from time to time, 'don the purple', the grandiose phrase used by the profession to describe venturing into management.

Left John Philip Kemble, in a caricature of 1789. *Right* Edmund Kean (1787–1833) as Shylock at Drury Lane.

Kean's great rival was William Charles Macready, who, like Kemble, was at various times manager of both the Patent houses. Between the two there was great competition, which was encouraged by press and public. Macready hated being an actor and would have preferred to lead the life of a gentleman, because he resented the lowly social status accorded to members of his profession. He was a snob with an ungovernable temper and a host of enemies. Yet he is an important figure in this story because he instituted a number of reforms which show that he was a deeply serious artist. He insisted on rehearsals for all members of the company at a time when it was customary for the leading players to meet the rest of the cast for the first time during the course of a performance. He even insisted that the extras should rehearse the crowd scenes. His unpopularity among the members of his company must have been acute. Perhaps Macready's most important contribution was to rescue some of Shakespeare's texts from the mangling inflicted by Restoration actors and writers. He presented plays by distinguished authors, but all were in the melodramatic or poeticizing mould and proved to have little or no staying power – Robert Browning's immobile *Strafford*, Bulwer-Lytton's fustian *The Lady of Lyons* and *Richelieu*, and Byron's deadly *The Two Foscari*.

Perhaps the most typical of all actor-managers of the period was Samuel Phelps, born in 1804 and thirty-nine years old when he took over Sadler's Wells and made it the home of Shakespeare in London. After a long apprenticeship touring the provinces, he did a lot to raise the quality of Shakespearean production. He hardly ever appeared in a contemporary play, preferring to vary the Shakespeare diet with adaptations of novels by Sir Walter Scott.

All of these actors subjected the theatre to their own needs and fancies, and put good parts before good plays. They were ruthless towards their colleagues and their authors. Yet it was they who made the theatre a popular institution, and kept the classical repertoire alive from generation to generation.

Society admired the actor-manager's gifts but did not respect his position. Kean, for example, was thought of, with some justice, as a 'rogue and vagabond'. But it was Macready's yearning for respectability that eventually gained the upper hand, in the person of an actor-manager of genius, whose achievements transformed the status of actors, and entitled them to be welcomed into the Establishment as respected and valued members. This man was Henry Irving, born John Henry Brodribb in Somerset in 1838. He changed his name when he became an actor at the age of eighteen, and during the next three years he portrayed 428 characters on stage – an apprenticeship it would now be quite impossible to receive. His training ground was the English provinces, and it was not till he was thirty-three years old that he conquered London, on the night of 25 November 1871, in a play called *The Bells*, by Leopold Lewis.

The Bells started life as *Le Juif Polonais* (*The Polish Jew*), by the French writers Emile Erckmann and Alexandre Chatrian, and had been presented at the Théâtre Cluny, in Paris. Irving's association with the piece came about when he made the acquaintance of Leopold Lewis, a solicitor, who had adapted it into English. Irving was instantly drawn to the leading character, Mathias, and saw him as a vehicle for his own gifts. He bought the rights from Lewis and worked on the adaptation, sensing his opportunity to play the part in London. The actor had recently been seen by the lessee of the Lyceum Theatre, one Hezekiah Linthicum Bateman, who admired him enough to sign him on a three-year contract, though he saw Irving as a character comedian. Irving had other ideas, and he made it a condition of the agreement that he should play *The Bells* at the first suitable opportunity. In 1871 the opportunity came.

Sir Henry Irving (1838–1905) as Mathias in *The Bells*: the role that made him famous.

The Bells is a melodrama, but compared to other plays in the genre it has a fairly original plot and greater psychological insight. The plot concerns a murderer who escapes the gallows but is destroyed by his own conscience. Mathias, the prosperous innkeeper and respected burgomaster of an Alsatian village in the year 1833, is about to give his daughter in marriage to the local police chief. Only Mathias knows that his present prosperity is the result of a murder committed fifteen years before, when during a stormy winter night he killed a Jew for gold. The Jew had been driving a sledge, and although Mathias escaped undetected, as he gets older and more successful he becomes haunted by the sound of the sleigh bells. Somehow he manages to keep the dreadful hallucination under control and believes that when the police chief becomes his son-in-law he will be finally safe from the law.

Then one day he goes to a fair and sees a mesmerist who is capable of putting people into a trance and making them reveal their innermost secrets. The scene plays upon Mathias's mind. The night before the wedding he dreams he is before a court of law. He resists the searching questions of the prosecutor, but the judge summons a mesmerist who hypnotizes the unwilling Mathias into re-enacting his crime. He is found guilty and sentenced to be hanged. In the morning Mathias's family come to wake him for the wedding. He starts from sleep and, clawing at the imaginary rope around his neck, staggers from his bed before dying in terror.

Irving rehearsed the play for a month. In France, the burgomaster had been conceived as a remorseless villain, but Irving introduced a more sympathetic note, trying to portray a man whose life was shattered by one moment of weakness. On the first night, the Lyceum was half-empty, and to begin with the audience was mystified by the play, but by the end it had succumbed to Irving's power. There was also something in the content of the play which captured these Victorians' imagination: in the century of Doctor Jekyll and Dorian Gray, a character who led a successful public life but nursed a criminal secret was a resident in the popular imagination. David Mayer, who edited Irving's personal script for publication, observed:

> *The Bells* offered to theatre audiences the opportunity to share vicariously the experience of criminal action, guilt, fear of discovery, and eventual retribution... In sharing emotions which touched on their own unconscious fears, first activating and then assuaging them, the audience gained a temporary but pleasurable respite from these fears.

On the first night, when the final curtain fell, the audience sat in shocked silence, disturbed only by the flurry of attendants helping a lady who had fainted in the stalls. Irving's biographer, his grandson Laurence, wrote: 'A tumult of cheers and round upon round of applause brought up the curtain once more. There was Irving, bowing in modest acceptance of their acclaim; there was Lewis wringing the actor's hand.' When the applause had died away and the audience shuffled out into Wellington Street, the editor of the *Daily*

Telegraph, a Mr Levy, who had seen the performance, said to his drama critic, Clement Scott: 'Tonight I have seen a great actor at the Lyceum – a great actor. There was a poor house. Write about him so that everyone shall know he is great.'

In his dressing-room, Irving received the praise and congratulations of his friends. Probably exhausted, but surely exhilarated, he joined his wife, Florence, and together they set off home across London in a brougham. She was an ill-natured woman, and she waited until they were crossing Hyde Park Corner before she turned to him and asked: 'Are you going to make a fool of yourself like this all your life?' Irving ordered the driver to stop. He got out without a word, left his wife to continue the journey alone, and never spoke to her again. He had his own journey to make, and no one would be allowed to stand in his way. His performance that night had brought him command of the English theatre, and he intended to keep it.

Irving was not endowed only with a genius for acting, but also with a sense of service. In raising acting from a disreputable profession to a vocation he surrounded himself with a mystical aura, a priestly aestheticism. His long romance with his leading lady, Ellen Terry, was discreet and private. He made a virtue of good taste to attract an intellectual and middle-class public – a formula that has been followed in the English theatre ever since. Despite his tampering with Shakespeare's texts, and doctoring plays so that all was subjugated to his own talent and position, he and his fellow managers took the drama to every corner of Britain. The theatre was never more available to people at all levels of society, all over the country – there were upwards of a dozen theatres in Manchester, for example, and as many again in and around Newcastle. Regularly he toured the British Isles, where his name was synonymous with great acting. He played in America, and was admired by the French. So widespread was the Irving mystique that country children would wait at railway sidings to see his famous profile in the carriage window as the train sped by.

In May 1895, Irving received a letter from Lord Rosebery, the Prime Minister, telling him that Queen Victoria intended to confer the honour of knighthood in recognition of his services to art. On the night it was announced, he was playing Don Quixote and had the line: 'Knighthood sits like a halo round my head,' to which Sancho Panza's reply, 'But, master, you have never been knighted', naturally brought a storm of laughter and cheers. In July he went to Windsor Castle to receive the accolade. The Queen said: 'I am very, very pleased,' and as I have put it elsewhere, when she tapped Sir Henry's shoulders with the sword, she inadvertently decapitated the rogue and vagabond. The status of the actor in society would never be the same again. Throughout the Western world, the English actor or actress recognized by the State would have a special place of honour, one which would be shared by members of their profession no matter what their nationality.

Irving never retired. In 1905 he returned to his Bradford hotel after performing in Alfred Lord Tennyson's tedious play, *Becket*, and there collapsed and died. He is buried in Westminster Abbey, and is the emblem of the orthodox stage. Yet his career had not been free from savage critical attack, especially from the critic of the *Saturday Review*, a young Irishman called George Bernard Shaw, and there was truth in Shaw's complaints. Sir Henry never produced a new play of any importance. He played only Shakespeare and melodrama. The Lyceum Theatre was the temple of the star system of which Irving made himself the high priest.

Yet a man with Irving's theatrical instincts must have sensed that there were changes in the air. In 1881 he saw and apparently recognized one symptom of the new theatrical forces at work in Europe, when the Meiningen Players visited London and played at Drury Lane. The company belonged to George II, Duke of Saxe-Meiningen. It boasted no stars, and was dedicated to ensemble playing, each part given its due weight and importance, the antithesis of all the Lyceum stood for. Their crowd scenes were carefully and splendidly staged, and when Irving saw them he immediately improved his own, but he took little else from the Meiningen Players. He believed too strongly in his own genius to move an inch from centre-stage.

Another kind of change was the arrival of a real English, or rather Irish, playwright on the London stage. Oscar Wilde's best play, *The Importance of Being Earnest*, was staged in the year that Irving received his knighthood; it was no one-man vehicle, and its underlying satire of Victorian high society would almost certainly have been distasteful to Sir Henry. The play was a late and timely reappearance of the comedy of manners, with the special edge of Wilde's own detachment from contemporary society, his keen wit, and his equally keen observation. *The Importance of Being Earnest* captures for ever a number of social types who obviously existed, but whom Wilde enabled his contemporaries to recognize and laugh at: the languid Englishman was one, the Victorian society dragon, in the shape of Lady Bracknell, was another.

Perhaps the comedy of manners has been taken over by the 'domestic' and 'situation' comedy of television. One of its last appearances on the London stage came with a flourish in the generation after Wilde, and from a master of the form, Noel Coward, whose plays *Hay Fever* (1925) and *Private Lives* (1930) stand beside the best of Congreve, Sheridan and Wilde. Coward also drew attention to prevailing types and attitudes, and he caught (or perhaps invented) a tone and rhythm of speech that lent itself to the barbed and economic humour for which he was renowned, and which was to be imitated to the point of plagiarism by the very people he satirized.

Wilde and Coward may represent the last hurrah of the comedy of manners, seeing that the genre seems to require a leisured upper class, either unaware of any great pressure from below, or able to ignore it. Not that very much of the English or European drama of the nineteenth century had room for the people 'below', and their absence except as caricatures is one of its glaring weaknesses – a sign of its refusal to come to terms with what was happening in the cities it served. The irony is that Europe had already produced a playwright who was able to deal with this kind of theme, though neither of his two important plays was performed until the following century.

Georg Büchner was a German playwright, poet and revolutionary who died in 1837, in his twenty-third year, without ever hearing a word of his spoken on stage. He is best known for his drama of the French Revolution, *Dantons Tod* (*Danton's Death*), written in 1835, but he also left an uncompleted work, *Woyzeck*, which lay dormant until the manuscript was discovered in Munich in 1879. *Dantons Tod* was first performed in Berlin in 1902. Not until 8 November 1913 did *Woyzeck* receive a production, a hundred years after its author's birth. Its influence was only strengthened by the lapse in time. *Woyzeck* can be described as the first modern play, the first working-class tragedy, centred upon a man at once victim and criminal.

Büchner was born into a medical family who lived in Goddelau, in the Grand Duchy of Hesse-Darmstadt. As a boy, he preferred science to the classics, although he loved folksong, poetry, especially Shakespeare, Homer,

Georg Büchner (1813–1837).

Goethe and the German Romantics. On summer afternoons he and his friends would go into the beech forest and read Shakespeare's plays. He soon became an atheist and a convinced revolutionary. At eighteen, in the autumn of 1831, he set off for Strasburg to study medicine, and in 1833 he moved to Giessen to continue his studies. There he learned to despise the petty restrictions of a German principality and organized a Society of Human Rights in March 1834. But he was dogged by ill-health, and was struck down by meningitis, recovering to study medicine by day and philosophy at night.

In five weeks early in 1835 he wrote *Danton's Death*. The work was done in his father's laboratory, and Büchner had to hide the manuscript under his medical books when his father came in. He wrote:

> I feel as though I had been annihilated by the dreadful fatalism of history. I find a terrible uniformity in human nature, an inexorable force... The individual: mere foam on the wave, greatness pure chance, the mastery of genius a puppet play, a ridiculous struggle against an iron law to acknowledge which is the highest good, to defeat impossible. I'm no longer in the mood to bow my head to the dress uniforms and street-corner orators of history. I am accustoming my eyes to blood.

The voice of modern man, at once frustrated and militant, is unmistakable. *Danton's Death* proclaims the contemporary themes of death, amorality,

Danton's Death by Büchner, performed at the National Theatre of Great Britain, 1982.

meaninglessness. Danton's sexuality is interpreted by Büchner as inseparable from a death wish. Contradictions of character, reminiscent of Hamlet, and easily acceptable in the light of what modern drama and Freudian psychology would reveal, are astounding in the knowledge that the play was written in 1835.

But it is the fragment, *Woyzeck*, which has the greater charge. The play was based on the case of Johann Christian Woyzeck, who was publicly executed for the murder of his mistress in Leipzig in 1824. In it, Woyzeck, a soldier, is besieged by life which he yearns to understand. He teeters on the edge of insanity, hears voices, hallucinates. In the end, his world falls apart, and his voices order him to murder Marie, the mother of his child. It is impossible to categorize *Woyzeck* – its power breaks loose of definitions. The dialogue is taut, the story told in a series of sharply defined encounters, the atmosphere bleak and poignant. Here the drama of the twentieth century has its secret genesis. Some extracts illustrate the point:

Woyzeck: When you're poor like us sir... It's the money, the money! If you haven't got the money ... I mean you can't bring the likes of us into this world on decency. We're flesh and blood, too. Our kind doesn't get a chance in this world or the next. If we go to heaven they'll put us to work on the thunder....

Woyzeck: Oh, self-control. I'm not very strong on that, sir. You see, the likes of us just don't have any self-control. I mean, we obey nature's call. But if I were a gentleman and had a hat and a watch and topcoat and could talk proper, then I'd have self-control all right. Must be a fine thing, self-control. But I'm a poor man....

Woyzeck: On and on, on and on. Scrape and squeak – that's the fiddles and flutes. On and on. – Sh. Music. Who's speaking down there? (*Stretches himself full-length on the ground.*) What's that you say? Louder, louder. Stab the she-wolf dead. Stab. The. She-Wolf. Dead. Must I? Do I hear it up there too? Is that the wind saying it? I keep on hearing it, on and on. Stab her dead. Dead.

If this voice sounds just a little familiar now, it is because of the echoes it has created in our own time. It belongs to the protagonist who is neither noble nor superhuman, to the captive in the lower depths.

THE MASTER BUILDERS

Anyone who wishes to understand me fully must know Norway. The spectacular but severe landscape which people have around them in the north, and the lonely shut-off life – the houses often lie miles from each other – force them not to bother about other people, but only their own concerns, so that they become reflective and serious, they brood and doubt and often despair. In Norway, every second man is a philosopher. And those dark winters, with the thick mists outside – ah, they long for the sun!

These are the unmistakable tones of Henrik Ibsen, the playwright whose images of claustrophobic prison-households, flawed respectability and life struggling to escape from under the sediment of convention have come to form an inseparable part of our picture of the nineteenth-century 'Victorian' world. Generations of playwrights have laboured in his shadow. It was Ibsen's work that restored vitality to the theatre and brought it back into the mainstream of the time, after its long drift on the surface. His profound and revolutionary themes have triumphantly survived their early rejection and are appreciated throughout the world. Yet the plays he created are rooted in the small provincial towns, the fjords, the snow and ice, of his native land. Much of the framework of twentieth-century drama was built between 1860 and 1900, and that drama – as if to provide a lucid symbol for what it would express – was born in the frozen north, in Norway, Sweden and Russia. The creation of a new sort of theatre was made all the more possible because these countries had no strong theatrical tradition of their own. The drama was free to change.

Henrik Johan Ibsen was born on 20 March 1828 in the small timber port of Skien, about 100 miles southwest of the Norwegian capital, Christiania, which is now called Oslo. He was the second child of Knud Ibsen, a merchant, and his wife Marichen. In a unique fragment of autobiography, he recorded:

I was born in a house in the main square. This house stood directly opposite the front of the church with its steep steps and lofty tower. To the right of the church stood the town pillory, and to the left the town hall, with its cell for delinquents and 'lunatic-box'. The fourth side of the square was occupied by the Grammar School and Lower School. The church stands isolated in the centre.

Skien in the years of his childhood Ibsen called an 'unusually gay and sociable town', although he also remembered that from his window he saw only buildings, 'nothing green'. The first seven years of his life seem to have been happy, but that contentment was shattered when, in the mid-1830s, his father went bankrupt.

Financial ruin – which will crop up again in this story – resulted in a move from Skien to Venstop. After it happened, Ibsen's father became aggressive, coarse and domineering; his mother, Marichen, who had loved the theatre, turned inward and sad, terrified of her husband and shamed by his failure. Her unhappiness and the family disgrace were to be compounded when gossip claimed that Henrik was not his father's son but the child of a former admirer of Marichen. The truth of the rumour appears unlikely, but both bankruptcy and the idea of illegitimacy had deep effects on Henrik and are recurring themes in his work.

In 1844, aged sixteen, Henrik was apprenticed to an apothecary in Grimstad. Some months after his eighteenth birthday, one of the maids in the house where he lived, Else Sofie Jensdatter, ten years his senior, bore him a son whom she named Hans Jacob Henriksen and who was to lead a sad erratic life, plagued by drink. Although Ibsen supported him for his first fourteen years, he kept the incident as one of the darker secrets of a lifetime spent bringing secrecy to light.

Ibsen showed early signs of an intense intellectual curiosity, and a temperament that allowed him to accept nothing without question. He rejected the views of religion and general morality which he was offered, his attitude to the relations between men and women was already unconventional, and he held republican opinions in a Norway reigned over by Swedish kings for all but the last year of his life. The young radical was profoundly excited by the European revolutions of 1848 which began in January with the rebellion against Bourbon rule in Sicily. It seemed autocratic rule was under siege all over the continent. The upheaval that must have given Ibsen and like-minded Norwegians most encouragement was the revolt against being incorporated into Denmark which broke out only a few hundred miles away, in the twin duchies of Schleswig and Holstein.

The turmoil in Europe inspired Ibsen to write his first play, a verse tragedy called *Catalina*; as he himself explained later, it dealt with a theme to which he would return, 'the clash of ability and inspiration, of will and possibility, at once the tragedy and comedy of mankind and of the individual'. Politics and nationalism were more overt in *The Burial Mound*, his first play to be performed, in 1850. It did not succeed, and he eked out a living as a journalist until the following year, when he accepted an invitation to join the recently established Norske Theater in Bergen, primarily as 'dramatic author'.

Bergen has preserved streets and houses which date from the mid-nineteenth century. There is an inescapable feeling of small-town captivity, prying neighbours, ingrown respectability – narrow streets and narrow-mindedness. Here Ibsen pursued a life in the theatre which he was later to describe as 'a daily abortion'. Yet this background and early experience were to teach him a lot about the theatre, as well as enriching the work of his maturity. At the Bergen theatre he was involved in upwards of a hundred productions, and between 1851 and 1857 he saw five of his own plays staged, though only one of them, *Feast at Solhaug*, was well received.

Ibsen left Bergen in 1857 to become artistic director of the Norwegian Theatre in Christiania. The following year he married Suzannah Thoresen, and in 1859 their only child, Sigurd, was born. In 1862 the theatre went bankrupt, and Ibsen found poorly paid temporary work as literary adviser to another playhouse, the Christiania Theatre. These were unhappy years – a time of mounting debts, attacks of depression, public indifference and even hostility. He continued to write plays – *The Vikings at Helgeland*, *Love's Comedy* and *The Pretenders* – and all of them improved on his earlier work, but the second of the three, *Love's Comedy*, was rejected and labelled 'an offence against society'. Fortunately *The Pretenders* was a critical success whose favourable reception helped to win Ibsen a state pension and a grant for foreign travel. For the next twenty-seven years he lived abroad. Only twice in that time did he return to Norway, and then only for brief visits.

When the ice broke in the spring of 1864, Ibsen set out for Berlin, travelled by train to Vienna, and then went south towards the sun:

> I ... crossed the Alps on 9 May. Over the high mountains the clouds hung like great dark curtains, and beneath these we drove through the tunnel and suddenly found ourselves at Mira Mara, where that marvellously bright light which is the beauty of the south suddenly revealed itself to me, gleaming like white marble. It was to affect all my later work, even if the content was not always beautiful.

Recalling that journey to Italy, he later remembered 'a feeling of being released from the darkness into light, of emerging from mists through a tunnel into sunshine'.

Ibsen lived in and around Rome. He explored the ancient ruins and admired the art he found in the south. He wrote to his colleague Bjørnstjerne Bjørnson, the foremost Norwegian writer and dramatist of the day: 'If I were to name the most important result of my coming here, I should say it was that I have rid myself of that aesthetic attitude, that forcing of oneself into isolation and self-sufficiency, that formerly held sway over me.' It is a queer notion to think of Ibsen relaxed and warm in the sun, while his thoughts were of ice cathedrals and avalanches. It turned out that he was one of those authors who have found it easier to write about their homeland from the perspective of exile. In the summer of 1864, his first in Italy, he reported: 'For some time I have been working on a big poem'. A year later, at Ariccia, he decided to turn the poem into a poetic drama, and *Brand* was completed in three months. After his experiences in the Norwegian theatre he was so disenchanted with the restrictions the stage imposed that he wanted his new verse play to be read, not acted. It was published in Norway in 1866, and caused a sensation. By the end of the year the publishers were already preparing a fourth edition.

It was *Brand* that first saw Ibsen venturing into the symbolism which distilled his dramatic imagination and has since proved to be part of the dramatic vocabulary which later playwrights inherited and explored. On the most practical level, the play has been described as a polemical work attacking the parochial complacency of Norwegian life. Beyond that, the significance of the hawk, the Ice Church, the final voice crying through the thunder, is less direct, and has given rise to a chorus of interpretations. In literary terms, these may support the criticism that the play is overloaded and lacks control. In the theatre – where it was first performed in Stockholm in 1885 – what happens is that the symbols and images go to work, as dreams do, on the broader, less ordinarily rational understanding that an audience contributes to a performance. Whether the kernel of the work is seen as a statement of the necessity to follow one's private conscience, or as the denial of convention, or as a painful reminder that 'He is the God of Love', seems to matter less to the playgoer than to the reader. The effect of *Brand* on stage is to make the audience listen to the author's original and powerful voice, and possibly feel a sense of relief, even more than a century later, at hearing things that still need saying. Above all, some will be left with the conviction of the play's deep spiritual majesty.

After writing *Brand*, Ibsen's imagination was released. In his next play, *Peer Gynt*, also a poetic drama written to be read rather than acted, he created a world out of Nordic myth and legend, whose settings include a desert, the sea, and the Hall of the Troll King. Fantasy and reality interfuse, and the last act is in the nature of a dream. Again, its readers took the play to be a satirical exposé of Norwegian provincialism. There was an uneasy feeling that the playwright was a revolutionary, and so he was, although his revolution took place in a setting more down to earth than frozen mountain tops and sunless fjords.

In 1877, *The Pillars of Society* appeared. The play marks the end of his poetic period and is the first of the 'social satires' for which he became famous. It was his next play, *A Doll's House*, published at the end of 1879, that created a major scandal and brought Ibsen his first international success. Played against a background which evoked what Henry James called 'the pervasive air of small interests and standards, the sign of limited local life', it contains this careful description of the scene of the action:

> *A comfortably and tastefully, but not expensively furnished room ... a piano ... a round table with armchairs and a small sofa ... a stove lined with porcelain tiles ... a couple of armchairs, a rocking-chair ... a small table. Engravings on the wall. A what-not with china and other bric-à-brac; a small bookcase with leather-bound books. A carpet on the floor; a fire in the stove. A winter day.*

The theme of the drama to be played out in this conventional room is described by Ibsen himself, in the notes he made while the play was taking shape in his mind:

There are two kinds of spiritual laws, two kinds of conscience, one for men and one, quite different, for women. They don't understand each other; but in practical life, woman is judged by masculine law, as though she weren't a woman but a man.

The wife in the play ends by having no idea what is right and what is wrong; natural feelings on the one hand and belief in authority on the other lead her to utter distraction. A woman cannot be herself in modern society, with laws made by men and with prosecutors and judges who assess female conduct from a male standpoint.

She has committed forgery, which is her pride; for she has done it out of love for her husband, to save his life. But this husband of hers takes his standpoint, conventionally honourable, on the side of the law, and sees the situation with male eyes.

Spiritual conflict. Weighed down and confused by her trust in authority, she loses faith in her own morality, and in her fitness to bring up her children. Bitterness. A mother in modern society, like certain insects, goes away and dies once she has done her duty by propagating the race. Love of life, of home, of husband and children and family. Now and then, as women do, she shrugs off her thoughts. Suddenly anguish and fear return. Everything must be borne alone. The catastrophe approaches, mercilessly, inevitably. Despair, conflict and defeat.

In *The Pillars of Society*, Ibsen retained the traditional happy ending; not so in *A Doll's House*. According to his biographer, Halvdan Koht, the play 'knew no mercy; ending not in reconciliation, but in inexorable calamity, it pronounced a death sentence on accepted social ethics'. In the last moments of the play, Nora Helmer leaves her husband. The final stage direction reads:

The street door is slammed shut downstairs.

That departure has been described as 'the loudest slamming door in drama'. Halvdan Koht recalled that: '*A Doll's House* exploded like a bomb into contemporary life ... Ibsen was hailed, not only as a revolutionary champion of intellectual liberty, but as the especial champion of women, and those who were against revolution, against social and moral upheaval, against female emancipation, came to see in Ibsen their greatest and most dangerous enemy.'

Instead of verse, Ibsen had now turned to what he called 'the much more difficult art of writing the genuine, plain language spoken in life'. He was a brave artist, always ready to experiment and reach out. He never repeated, or tried to repeat, a previous success. Each play is different from its predecessor not so much because of any conscious programme, but rather because he wrote what he was compelled to write. His next play, *Ghosts*, took all his courage. He predicted that it would 'probably cause alarm in some circles; but that can't be helped. If it didn't there would have been no necessity for me to have written it.'

Top A Doll's House with Johanne Dybwad as Nora in the 1926 production at the Christiania Theatre. *Above left* Duse as *Hedda Gabler* in 1906. *Above right* the playwright: Henrik Ibsen (1828–1906).

In *Ghosts*, the theme of hereditary venereal disease becomes a metaphor for the harms done in the past which can make life intolerable for the living. After leaving her husband, Mrs Alving is persuaded by Pastor Manders, whom she loves, to return home. She does so and gives birth to a son, Oswald, who has inherited his father's syphilis. (This was long before the discovery of penicillin, when the disease was likely to cause irreparable physical damage, and finally insanity.) The play was published in an edition of 10,000 copies in December 1881. 'My new play has come out,' Ibsen wrote in a letter, 'and has created a violent commotion in the Scandinavian press. Every day I receive letters and newspaper articles, some for, some against.' Public readings were given in out-of-the-way places, and people flocked to them. The critics were less enthusiastic:

'*Ghosts* is a repulsive pathological phenomenon which, by undermining the morality of our social order, threatens its foundations.'

'Complete silence would, in our opinion, be the most fitting reception for such a work. *Ghosts* is the most unpleasant book we have read for a long while.'

'The book has no place on the Christmas table of any Christian home.'

'The play is one of the filthiest things ever written in Scandinavia.'

Ibsen defended himself – 'My book contains the future!' Michael Meyer, his English biographer, observes:

Ibsen's contemporaries saw *Ghosts* primarily as a play about physical illness, just as they had seen *A Doll's House* primarily as a play about women's rights. With few exceptions, they failed to realise that the true subject of *Ghosts* is the devitalising effect of a dumb acceptance of convention ... *Ghosts* is a play about ethical, not physical debility. The importance of waging war against the past, the need for each individual to find his or her own freedom, the danger of renouncing love in the name of duty – these are the real themes of *Ghosts*, as they are the themes of every play which Ibsen wrote from *A Doll's House* onwards.

Nothing deterred Ibsen from exploring the places where eyes were supposed to be kept averted. *An Enemy of the People*, *The Wild Duck* and *Rosmersholm* all reveal the development of his genius.

The last twelve years of his writing life, before a stroke in 1900 left him helpless, produced yet another change in direction. With *The Lady from the Sea*, *Hedda Gabler*, *The Master Builder*, *Little Eyolf* and *John Gabriel Borkman*, there is a movement away from his portrayals of the social structure and towards a more psychological style. In his last play, *When We Dead Awaken*, a merciless piece of self-analysis, though seen by many of his admirers as flawed and unfulfilled, his vision of humanity is aimed at the mountain top, at the final freedom of the spirit. One of his great achievements was to establish that tragedies could be written not only about gods, kings or great leaders, but about the lives of self-enclosed middle-class families, the kind of people who were to be shocked by his plays, and to some extent still are. His vision found sublime drama, and all the resources of the human spirit, where few playwrights had looked before him.

The influence of Ibsen pervades modern drama. In his own lifetime, his work was argued, discussed and analysed all over Europe, and this is a measure of a different kind of contribution to the drama. When he started writing plays, the contemporary theatre as a medium for serious thought was in the dumps. No self-respecting author had time for it. Ibsen changed all that, and nowhere was the change felt more strongly than in England.

A young Scot, William Archer, became Ibsen's first translator into English, and his version of *The Pillars of Society* was the first of Ibsen's plays to be produced in London, in 1880. In 1899, when his translation of *Ghosts* had its première, the critics did not need to think twice: it was 'an open drain', 'a loathesome sore unbandaged', 'a dirty act done publicly'. By then the fatal germ had already been passed, and as the result of a chance encounter. In the early 1880s, Archer used to visit the Reading Room of the British Museum every day, and would often sit next to a man who drew his attention partly because of his unusual colouring – pallid skin, bright red hair and beard – and partly because of the man's odd combination of interests – Karl Marx, for example, but also the score of Wagner's *Tristan and Isolde*. The man was George Bernard Shaw, and he and Archer soon became friends. Archer introduced him to the work of Ibsen, and so began the process that turned the young Irish novelist and critic to the theatre as an outlet for his prodigious creative and intellectual energies.

Shaw was born on 26 July 1856 in Dublin, the third and youngest child of George Carr Shaw and Lucinda Elizabeth Gurly. He was tutored by an uncle in his early years, before briefly attending a Protestant and then a Catholic day school. He started work in a land agent's office before he reached sixteen, and the genteel poverty of much of his early manhood was a source of continuous frustration.

Music, not the theatre, was at the centre of the Shaw household. His mother's music teacher, George John Vandeleur Lee, a magnetic figure in Irish musical circles, was an important influence in Shaw's life. After his departure for London in 1875, Mrs Shaw left her husband and followed Lee, earning a living as a singing teacher. In London, Shaw began to write novels, but his fiction failed utterly. After the meeting with Archer, and now under the influence of Ibsen, he turned to plays. Not far from the British Museum, at 55 Great Russell Street, he was one of the actors in a rendering of *A Doll's House* with an unusual cast. Years later he described the events of 15 January 1886:

The private reading took place on a first floor in a Bloomsbury lodging house. Karl Marx's youngest daughter played Nora Helmer; I impersonated Krogstad at her request, with a very vague notion of what it was all about.

That vagueness was soon to be transformed into brilliant advocacy. Shaw, like many commentators, viewed Ibsen as an 'issue-playwright'. When he talked of 'the gospel of Ibsen' he was turning his latest hero into a crusade. Shaw had long believed that art was the 'most effective instrument of moral propaganda in the world'; he took Ibsen as proof of that contention. My own view is that his enthusiasm was based on a misreading of Ibsen, and that when he published *The Quintessence of Ibsenism* in 1891, he might more accurately have called his defence *The Quintessence of Shavianism*, for Shaw, in accordance with his own temperament, divorced the playwright from the emotional complexity of his characters and focused instead on his intellectual power. Ibsen believed that plays could change the nature of man, and therefore the moral and social order. Shaw's aims may have been similar, but his doctrine was exactly opposite. He believed that plays could change the moral, but more especially the social order, and thereby change the nature of man.

Shaw's career as a crusading dramatist began when he tried to write a play with William Archer (Archer to supply the plot, Shaw the dialogue) – a surprising venture, given the nature of the Shavian ego, whose vast dimensions he does not conceal in this account of the collaboration:

> Laying hands on his [Archer's] thoroughly planned scheme for a sympathetically 'well-made play' of the Parisian type then in vogue, I perversely distorted it into a grotesquely realistic exposure of slum-landlordism, municipal jobbery, and the pecuniary and matrimonial ties between them and the pleasant people with 'independent' incomes who imagine that such sordid matters do not touch their own lives.

The play was shelved for eight years before being produced in 1892. Shaw, now the sole author of this social propaganda, called it *Widowers' Houses* ('I must, however, warn my readers that my attacks are directed against themselves'). It was given two performances and brought the author his first taste of notoriety.

The next play revealed Shaw's gift for self-mockery. In *The Philanderer* he satirized himself, invented an 'Ibsen Club', and even ridiculed the socially emancipated 'New Woman', so poking fun at two of his favourite causes. No producer could be found for the play until 1905. In the meantime he wrote *Mrs Warren's Profession* (1893, but not produced until 1902), which provoked such a furore that the author was able to observe that he 'once more shared with Ibsen the triumphant amusement of startling all but the strongest headed of the London theatre critics clear out of the practice of their profession'. Ostensibly, the subject of *Mrs Warren's Profession* is prostitution:

> *Mrs Warren:* ... all we had was our appearance and our turn for pleasing men. Do you think we were such fools as to let other people trade in our good looks by employing us as shopgirls, or barmaids, or waitresses, when

we could trade in them ourselves and get all the profits instead of starvation wages? Not likely.

The humour, the irony, the social paradox – in fact the essence of Shaw – were all apparent. The Lord Chamberlain, still the censor of plays, refused a licence. But the play, like its author, was intensely moral. 'I should be quite content,' he insisted, 'to have my play judged by, say, a joint committee of the Central Vigilance Society and the Salvation Army. And the sterner the moralists the members of the committee were, the better.'

In the 1890s, besides writing plays, he was music critic for the *Star* (as 'Corno di Bassetto') and for the *World* (as 'G.B.S.') and was superbly wide-ranging in his digressions. More important, except perhaps for Wagnerites, from 1895 to 1898 he was theatre critic for the *Saturday Review*, and a superb one. He campaigned hard against the artificialities of the Victorian stage, and took for his special target Sir Henry Irving, who stood as the great barrier to the 'New Drama' he championed. Shaw contended that the true critic is 'the man who becomes your personal enemy on the sole provocation of a bad performance, and will only be appeased by good performances'. In Irving's case he ignored the good performances. He became Irving's personal enemy not only for what he considered the highest motives, but also because he allowed his objectivity to be clouded by personal resentment, for it must be said that Shaw would have liked nothing better than to have Irving produce one of his plays.

Plays Pleasant and Unpleasant was Shaw's first volume of plays, and was published in 1898. In addition to the ('unpleasant') plays already named, it included *Arms and the Man*, which satirized romantic war and love (and which was itself romanticized, without Shaw's permission, in the Oscar Straus operetta, *The Chocolate Soldier*), the one-act *Man of Destiny*, about Napoleon I, and described by Shaw as a 'bravura piece to display the virtuosity of two performers', and *Candida*, in which a wife chooses her Christian Socialist husband in preference to a green young poet.

His output was enormous. As well as the plays, he wrote prefaces and essays, and lectured and campaigned for his socialist beliefs. All his work combines the same penetrating intelligence with an original, if sometimes deliberately leprechaunish, cast of thought. In *Man and Superman* he took the legend of the Don Juan of Mozart's *Don Giovanni*, and made it into a dramatic parable of the universe's determined and eternal movement towards higher and higher life forms; Shaw considered this theory more satisfactory than Darwinism, restoring the divine element to man and his world.

Shaw had a genius for isolating and representing the forces at work and at war in day-to-day society. *John Bull's Other Island* expressed his view of the Irish character. In *Major Barbara*, the Salvation Army heroine of the title comes to understand that although her father, a munitions manufacturer, may be a merchant of destruction, his unorthodox principles and practice are

Top left George Bernard Shaw (1856–1950). *Top right and above* scenes from the National Theatre of Great Britain's 1981 production of *Man and Superman*.

religious in a higher sense – the Salvation Army requires the donations of the armourers and the distillers against whom it wages its war. The medical profession came in for Shavian satire in *The Doctor's Dilemma*, religious exaltation in *Androcles and the Lion*. In his comic masterpiece, *Pygmalion*, he produced a humane work about love and class. (It is the source of the musical *My Fair Lady*.) Acknowledging Chekhov, he wrote *Heartbreak House* to expose the spiritual bankruptcy of the generation he accounted responsible for the bloodshed of the First World War.

In England, Shaw's reputation lagged, in comparison to the fame he enjoyed on the Continent. In 1904–7 he backed Harley Granville-Barker's management at the Royal Court Theatre in Sloane Square, London, with his own capital and his plays. During the years of their association, Shaw became a public figure. A Fabian socialist and a vegetarian, the advocate of a forty-letter phonetic alphabet and promoter of the Shakespear (his spelling) versus Shaw contest for Champion Playwright of the World, he was also one of the great self-publicists of the new century, with a formidable public persona.

The 1920s further raised his standing. In October 1923 Shaw travelled to Birmingham to see Sir Barry Jackson's repertory company present his *Back to Methuselah*, an enormously long series of plays – it took four nights to perform – which the playwright considered his masterpiece. 'I have written a play with intervals of thousands of years (in the future) between the acts; but now I find I must make each act into a full-length play,' he reported in July 1918. The work was submitted to the Lord Chamberlain as 'a play in eight acts'. *Back to Methuselah* is a vast chronicle of mankind's failure, but at the centre of it lies what now seems a simplistic perception: that life is too short for human beings to learn any useful lessons. The theatre has admitted its scale and power, but has treated it as a kind of dramatic megalomania, best respected from a distance.

In the same year of 1923, Shaw surprised his public with a play quite different from anything he had previously written, his *Saint Joan*. Of course his Joan was Shavian, a saint at odds with her humanity. In this play, as in no other, Shaw allowed his characters rather than their ideas to speak, and the result is greater feeling and expression. In 1925 his achievements were rewarded by the Nobel Prize for Literature. He died, a monument to vegetarian longevity, at the age of ninety-four, on 2 November 1950.

Because of his bold and commanding intelligence, Shaw was not easily imitated, nor did he leave disciples who could claim to write in his style. As a playwright, he almost always sought to entertain, and his serious purposes never curbed his wit. Coming in the wake of Ibsen himself, he helped to restore literacy to the theatre, and to create an atmosphere in which change was possible. On the other hand it may be partly owing to Shaw that a host of modern playwrights, not gifted with his sharp intelligence and humour, have been able to persuade themselves that the stage makes a useful soapbox and the audience a target. For some of his descendants the theatre is a forum for political and social ideology, rather than what Ibsen made it, a crucible for the human conflicts which ideologies attempt to rationalize. Ideas not people were Shaw's passion. And it must also be said that few of his plays would not be improved by judicious cutting.

Bernard Shaw was not the only playwright to come under Ibsen's sway, nor was he the most important as an influence on the theatre of the twentieth century. In Ibsen's later years the portrait of a Swedish dramatist looked down at him from above his desk. He kept it there, he said, because to have 'that madman staring down at me' helped him to work. August Strindberg was a student when he first read *Brand*, three years after its publication, and described Ibsen as 'the voice of Savonarola'. He wrote a play in imitation called *The Freethinker*, and so began his frenzied career as a dramatist.

Strindberg's temperament varied all through his life from neurotic to unstable to clearly disordered. The stresses he lived under gave him a perspective on the world which revealed it to him in a glaringly pure light but with its relationships shifted and its proportions distorted. His eyes saw the surface in clinical detail, but they also saw beneath it, for his power was to peel away the carefully arranged exteriors of middle-class life. He was to become the archetype of his own creations. He drank too much. He suffered from persecution mania. He was fascinated by alchemy, and burned his hands while trying to make gold. He was forever on the breadline. Tortured and despairing, he typifies that urge in certain artists of the modern movement which drives them to the end of the springboard, and then starts it oscillating. He said of himself: 'Prospects brilliant. Situation desperate.' This is how he explained his own theatrical imagination:

> I do not believe in simple characters on stage... My souls are conglomerations from past and present stages of civilization; they are excerpts from books and newspapers, scraps of humanity, pieces torn from festive garments which have become rags – just as the soul itself is a piece of patchwork.

It happens that Strindberg, like Ibsen and Shaw, was blighted in childhood by a father's bankruptcy. Carl Oskar Strindberg was an aristocrat, variously described as a steamship agent or a shipping merchant, who married his former maidservant (also alternatively described as a former waitress). Their son August was born on 22 January 1849. When the boy was four, the bankruptcy occurred, when he was thirteen his mother died, and the following year his father remarried. His childhood and adolescence were marred by neglect, by emotional insecurity, and by his grandmother's religious mania. He studied intermittently at the university of Uppsala, first reading medicine and then, after failing as an actor at the Royal Dramatic Theatre, Stockholm, studying modern languages and political science. He never took a degree. To earn his living, he worked as a freelance journalist in Stockholm, and for the eight years after 1874 as a librarian in the Royal Library there.

In 1875 he met a guards officer, Baron Carl Gustaf Wrangel, and his unhappy wife, Siri von Essen, a Finnish actress. Siri and Strindberg fell in love, and two years later they married, the first of Strindberg's three tempestuous marriages. His intense but ultimately destructive relationship with Siri ended in divorce in 1891, and he lost the custody of their four children. His other wives were Frieda Uhl, an Austrian, and Harriet Bosse, a Swedish actress. All three of these women were strong-minded and dominating, the kind he feared but to whom he was irresistibly attracted, and who were to haunt his plays.

Though often close to total mental breakdown, he continued to write obsessively, and produced a large number of plays, novels and stories. He first came to the public attention with his satirical novel *The Red Room*, in 1879. The publication in 1884 of the first volume of his collected stories, *Married*, led to a prosecution for blasphemy. But his chief preoccupation was with the female as predator. He saw men and women in perpetual sexual conflict. 'I detest mankind,' he lamented, 'but I cannot live alone.' His outstanding works derive from this same vicious circle. In 1887 he produced *The Father*, in which a Captain is driven insane by his wife, Laura. But Strindberg is not content with describing this cruelty alone; he charges his play with an atmosphere of feminine power bearing down on the male protagonist. In the final scene, the Captain's old Nurse is whispering motherly words into his ear as she eases him fondly into a straitjacket.

The following year, when Strindberg was thirty-nine, he completed what is probably his best-known work, *Miss Julie*. Like *The Father*, it was written in a fortnight. The heroine of this bitter drama is described by Strindberg as a 'half-woman, the man-hater'. She is a neurotic child of a degenerate aristocracy, an hysteric driven to satisfy her uncontrollable sensuality. She abandons herself to her valet, Jean, who forces her to steal money from her father, and in the end persuades her that suicide is the only way out of the trap.

In the same year of 1888, he wrote *The Creditors*, another demonic account of the sex war. In this play, economy of style tightens the screws on his characters and the drama which confines them. Tekla, a voracious woman writer, has gained her power by sucking the life of one man and is engaged in destroying another. The emotional drive of the play is intense and unrelenting.

These plays represent a turning point in modern drama. Ibsen had broken with the tradition of the poetic tragedy, setting down dialogue that was muscular and spare, close to colloquial speech. Strindberg went still further:

> I have avoided the mathematically symmetrical construction of French dialogue and let people's brains work irregularly as they do in actual life, where no topic of conversation is drained to the dregs but one brain receives haphazard from the other a cog to engage with. Consequently my dialogue too wanders about, providing itself in the earlier scenes with material which is afterwards worked up, admitted, repeated, developed, and built up, like the theme in a musical composition.

August Strindberg (1849–1912), and Cheryl Campbell and Stephen Rea in the 1983 production of *Miss Julie* at the Lyric, Hammersmith, London.

Strindberg was attempting, in this period of his writing life, to make a dramatic language out of the terse broken rhythms of speech. Although these were thought to be natural and real in his play they were in fact carefully composed and orchestrated.

After 1896, a year in which he lived perilously close to complete insanity, he found consolation in the works of the eighteenth-century mystic and theologian Emmanuel Swedenborg. They helped him to believe that life was orderly even when he suffered, since that was his due retribution for sin; all was predestined by a just and merciful God. By 1897 Strindberg was well enough to write *Inferno*, an account of the torture he had endured. At one point he was convinced that he was in hell. He felt that his life was controlled by what he called 'the powers', creatures from another world.

From then until his death in 1912 he concentrated on plays in which he tried, as he put it, 'to imitate the inconsequent yet transparently logical shape of a dream. Everything can happen, everything is possible and probable. Time and place do not exist; on an insignificant basis of reality the imagination spins, weaving new patterns... The characters split, double, multiply, evaporate, condense, disperse, assemble. But one consciousness rules over them all, that of the dreamer.' Once his young son asked him if God could see in the dark. 'No,' said Strindberg, 'but Daddy can.' Night, the time of nightmare and confusion, was Strindberg's domain. In that heightened state, he produced *To Damascus*, *A Dream Play* and *The Ghost Sonata*.

It would take a book in itself to give an adequate glimpse of Strindberg's vast output. There were sixty-two plays (many of them bad), countless novels, volumes of essays, short stories, poems, memoirs, scientific and philosophical treatises. His collected works run to over fifty volumes. But somewhere in that manic flood lies the manifesto of the modern theatre. His distorted vision, intense and fiercely subjective, anticipated German Expressionism as though what he was and what he wrote set the rhythm for the coming age. The American dramatist Thornton Wilder claimed that Strindberg was the fountainhead of all modern drama. His influence is pervasive, and has been acknowledged by many playwrights, among them Tennessee Williams, Eugene Ionesco and Harold Pinter.

Ibsen and Strindberg are the master builders of our twentieth-century theatre. Each influenced the other. Their relationship was one of mutual hostility and mutual respect. Strindberg was critical of the Norwegian's view of women and called him a 'male blue-stocking'. Ibsen thought the Swede 'remarkable' and 'mad'. Both were in pursuit of psychological truth. And in the Vienna of their day, Sigmund Freud was beginning to explore the idea of the unconscious and the logic of dreams, and to recognize that artists in general and playwrights in particular have trodden that territory for as long as they have existed.

All the omens showed that the theatre had radical changes in store. In response to the problems of staging Ibsen, for example, a realistic approach seemed to offer the way forward – recognizable rooms, furniture, clothing, and a naturalistic acting style. These must replace the reigning forms and styles of melodrama, *mise-en-scène* and that 'grand manner' in acting which could sometimes make histrionics and hysterics seem near neighbours. In medicine, science and art, man was searching for a fuller understanding, and values more satisfying than those of the growing consumer society which was seen as threatening and destructive. It was the role of the theatre to confront reality, but not merely by reflecting the dominant material or institutional values, and this led to a search for another theatrical language at the opposite pole from realism – the language of symbols. Unfortunately there were some legacies of the nineteenth century that were not so readily disowned. One of them was the positivist belief that all things could be explained, rationalized and codi-fied – surviving in the twentieth century in the hopeful faith that there is a technological fix for every problem. Since the 'scientific' approach works so well in its proper place, and so ludicrously badly out of it, and there are no rules for telling one from the other, its presence in the theatre is more noticeably a plague than a comfort.

In Russia, Vsevolod Meyerhold believed that the theatre must be a harmony of movement, gesture, colour and sound that point towards a symbol. The figure of the director was edging towards centre-stage. It was an English designer, Gordon Craig, who tried to encourage and define the new pheno-menon. He wanted to reduce the importance of the actor, and that was ironic, since Craig was the son of a great actress, Ellen Terry, and in childhood had been an admirer of her leading man, Sir Henry Irving. Yet he came to regard actors, and everything they stood for, as trivial and fortuitous. Like George Bernard Shaw in later life, he would have preferred marionettes.

Craig's designs were an attempt to free the actor from the clutter of reality, just as he believed society must be freed from the weight of materialism. Meyerhold was an apostle of form: in design he brought the new artistic movement of Constructivism into the theatre; in acting, he invented the grotesque term 'biomechanics' to describe the process he wanted. But jargon aside, he was a vital force in the theatre, searching earnestly for ways to communicate understanding between people. He fell foul of Stalin, and appears to have been executed in 1940, though there is some doubt about the circumstances and even the date of his death.

If the drama came to accommodate so much bleakness and dislocation, it did not reject colour and verve, and a reaction against the gloomier implications of the most powerful contemporary work brought a return to dazzling theatricality. In Austria, Max Reinhardt seemed to combine all the aspirations of the avant-garde. He was a director *par excellence*, who delighted in mechanical devices and was ready to present symbols on the grand scale. After the First World War, when he founded the Salzburg Festival in 1920, he transformed the whole town into the setting for his production of *Everyman*. He turned the great exhibition hall of Olympia, in London, into a Gothic cathedral, and produced *Oedipus* in a circus. At the same time, the majority of playgoers all over the world still vastly preferred the escapist theatre of drawing-room melodrama, light comedy, farce and operetta. It took the impact of the 'Great War' to prove the need for the theatre to confront serious themes.

Germany at the turn of the century saw a flowering of theatrical life which was enlivened by the work of two writers in particular, one German and the other Austrian, born within two years of each other. Frank Wedekind (1864–1918) was a restless, rebellious writer who worked in cabaret in Munich, contributed to the famous satirical weekly *Simplicissimus*, and was imprisoned in 1899 for the German equivalent of *lèse-majesté*. Like Strindberg, Wedekind was at one moment a merciless critic of the world around him, at the next a creator of stark symbolic abstractions. He too was obsessed by the terrible power of sexual relationships. His first play, *Spring's Awakening* (1891), told the story, outrageous for a theatrical piece, of a love affair between a sixth-form schoolboy and a fourteen-year-old girl who dies after an abortion. In Lulu, the heroine of his plays *Earth Spirit* (1895) and *Pandora's Box* (1903), Wedekind created a figure of uncontrolled female sensuality which has entered the fictional portrait gallery of the twentieth century. The film director G.W. Pabst and the composer Alban Berg were both inspired by these dramas of a woman fatal to her first lovers, whose fascination with the destructive power of passion takes her into prostitution and then to her death in London at the hands of Jack the Ripper.

In Austria, Arthur Schnitzler (1862–1931) was more detached and mannered in his attitude towards love, sex and social injustice. He took a medical degree, though he never practised, and there is a deliberate clinical aloofness in some of his plays, which escapes falling into cynicism only because he never condescends to the characters he embroils in what are sometimes artificial plots. In *Liebelei* (1895) he has his principal male character, Fritz, go out for an evening during which he meets and apparently falls in love with a girl from the Vienna suburbs. That same evening Fritz agrees to fight a duel with the husband of his current mistress. His new love, Christine, loses him before their affair can begin. Schnitzler is best known for his play *Reigen* (1903), which introduces five women and five men, one after the other, in successive scenes during which a woman goes to bed with a man, that man with the next woman, she with the next man, and so on. The play is more familiar under its French title, *La Ronde*. It works because of the wit and elegance with which Schnitzler handled the theme. All of Schnitzler's plays show the same genius for writing sparkling talk, often in the lively dialect of his native Vienna.

What emerges from Europe in the years before the First World War is that the movement towards a vision of man as standing alone even in his own society was beginning to gather strength. But the story of the theatre is not one of single strands each spun in isolation. Nor is it the story of avant-garde movements which are bound to become the future's orthodoxy. In the theatre these forces coexist and overlap. Theoretical descriptions like expressionism, symbolism, naturalism and so on, which abound in the histories of the period, create barriers between artist and audience and have the effect of laying too much stress on form and of minimizing content. Ibsen and Strindberg are masters because each had his own imaginative vision of mankind and understood what the theatre could do. It was not styles and methods that dictated their work, but rather the work's tough substance that forced acting, direction and staging through the changes necessary to contain it.

THE ACTORS DO NOT UNDERSTAND

The undisputed queen of the nineteenth-century theatre, a formidable, flamboyant star of the old order, Sarah Bernhardt was born in Paris in 1844, sixteen years after Ibsen and only five years before Strindberg. And though their new order was to supersede her own, Bernhardt was still making her repeated farewell tours when both of them were dead. For more than fifty years, starting in the late 1860s, she was the most famous actress, and perhaps the most famous woman, in the world. Her influence was pervasive because she was a tireless traveller not only in Europe but also in Africa, North and South America and in Australia, at a time when the longer of these voyages were measured in weeks and months of monotony and discomfort.

Bernhardt was renowned for the beauty of her voice and the emotional power of her acting. Her style was grandiose and extravagant, and earned her the title of '*La reine de l'attitude*', and from Oscar Wilde the description which has stuck – 'the divine Sarah'. Although she was acclaimed as Phèdre, as Doña Sol in *Hernani*, and even as Hamlet, most of the plays she appeared in were melodramas, some specially written for her, since Bernhardt believed in the part, not the play. She was at heart a solo performer. The effect of her personality on audiences, whether or not they understood French, was, by all accounts, electrifying. She captivated and inspired artists, poets, and musicians, and her private life was a constant source of fascination and scandal. Gossip said that she learned her lines – and made love – while lying in a silk-lined coffin. She went on acting even after her leg was amputated in 1915, and made her last appearance on stage in 1922, only a year before her death, in a play written for her by Edmond Rostand.

The power of Bernhardt's reputation alone, backed by the world's theatrical managements and trumpeted by what were then the sole mass media, the newspapers, must have made it very difficult to see past her to other alternatives. Add to that the impact of her personal magnetism, and a Bernhardt performance would be overwhelming. In 1881, at the height of her powers, she visited Moscow, and this is the account of one Russian:

Two days ago, Moscow knew of only four elements: today she cannot stop talking of a fifth. She only knew of seven wonders of the world, now, every thirty seconds, she proclaims the existence of an eighth. A sort of primitive folly reigned in our heads. But we, ourselves, are far from admiring Sarah Bernhardt's talent. She lacks the flame that alone can move us to tears. Highly intelligent, this lady possesses an extremely effective technique – her acting is a well-learned lesson, but smacks less of genius than of immensely powerful hard work.

The piece was signed 'Antosha Chekhonte'. Its implicit criticisms must have been echoed by Constantin Stanislavsky, one young member of the theatrical profession. In 1881 he was eighteen years old, and in Russia, as elsewhere, the theatre was a means of passing an evening, a place to be seen, though audiences needed to be more well-to-do than in Western Europe.

Sarah Bernhardt (1845–1923) in *Iseyl*, by Morand and Sylvestre: and Constantin Stanislavsky (1863–1938), in Gorky's *Lower Depths*.

Yet the Russian drama had produced a generation of playwrights who had more to say than most of their contemporaries in the supposedly more developed West. In 1836 Gogol had produced *The Inspector-General*, a biting satire on small-town officialdom. Alexander Ostrovsky had come into prominence in 1848, at the age of twenty-five, with a play called *The Bankrupt*, which exposed bogus bankruptcy. He was dismissed from the Civil Service, and the play was banned for thirteen years. His best-known play is *The Storm* (1860), which ends with the heroine's suicide. Both of them are seen in the context of Russian literature as 'realists', which is to say that they described a recognizable middle-class society. Early in his career, the novelist Turgenev wrote satires and short plays with unequivocal titles like *Where It's Thin, It Breaks*, and in 1850 he produced one work of outstanding brilliance, *A Month In The Country*, to which we shall return.

Stanislavsky knew and admired these plays, and realized instinctively that the tradition represented by Sarah Bernhardt was too artificial to do them justice. Four years after seeing her act in Moscow, he attended performances by a foreign company with a very different concept of the theatre. He remembered the deep impression these visitors made:

> During Lent, Moscow was visited by the famous ducal players of Meiningen, headed by the stage director, Kronek. Their performances showed Moscow for the first time productions that were historically true, with well-directed mob-scenes, fine outer forms and amazing discipline. I did not miss a single one of their performances. I came not only to look but to study as well.

Ibsen had seen and admired the Saxe-Meiningen productions of his plays. Now Stanislavsky was fired by their example. He felt that their methods would suit not only epic drama such as Shakespeare's, but also the native tradition of Russian comedy, with its deep roots in the Slav character, or rather in those patterns of behaviour which are so frequently demonstrated in Russia's literature and drama that they are conventionally referred to as temperament by Russians themselves. This temperament is one of extremes. Great joy and deep sadness are constant companions. Russians as a nation have grown used to suffering, and its acceptance has inspired faith and fed hopelessness. At the turn of the century their writings invariably portray men and women with a deep streak of fatality and mysticism, a stoic ability to accept as God's design what life may have in store for them. There is an overwhelming sense of a nation possessed by a collective soul. This commonalty has produced a people unafraid of emotion or of its display, able to declare friendships and take pleasure with one another, and in the same breath to suffer remorse.

In art, and especially in the theatre, the sadness of life is often viewed with a comic eye. A typical Russian farce has been said to be the story of a man who searches all his life for a precious vase. Through a series of ludicrous adventures, at long last he finds the object. As he lifts it up it slips through his fingers and shatters. Russians have been known to cry with laughter at the recitation of this tale. In a more refined form, the Russian comic tradition, where tragedy hovers, can be approached by turning back to Ivan Turgenev's *A Month In The Country*, written in 1850, heavily revised and published in 1869, but not staged until 1872. Pain and tears counterpoint its pleasure and laughter. It is the first drama of the Russian theatre which develops psychological insights into the characters, but another feature is more important still: the play has no heroic figure. Family and friends, husbands, lovers and wives, masters and servants – the group is the hero of the Russian theatre. It was probably this quality which Stanislavsky related to the strengths of ensemble playing.

Vladimir Ivanovich Nemirovich-Danchenko was born in 1859, four years Stanislavsky's senior. He became a novelist, critic, writer of light comedies and stage director, sharing Stanislavsky's dissatisfaction with the theatre in general and the art of acting in particular, and in the 1890s he was in charge of the drama course of the Moscow Philharmonic Society, where the pupils included three notables of the future: Ivan Moskvin, Olga Knipper and Vsevolod Meyerhold. He wanted to transform the actor's approach to the art, and was forever exploring new ways to extend and school it:

> Psychological development, various features of social environment, problems of morality, attempts to find ways of merging with the author, striving after simplicity and truthfulness, search for greater expressiveness of diction, mimicry, plastic pose, individual surprise, discoveries, fascination, infectiousness, daring, confidence – these were some of the hundreds of ingredients of an exciting classwork.

Yet the theatre was dominated by popular, conventional products. The impact of Ibsen had yet to be fully felt. Plays had ceased to shock or disturb except at the stock level of melodrama. The disruptive spirit of Dionysus, no stranger in Russian society, was absent from the theatre. Nemirovich-Danchenko heard about Stanislavsky's ideas, and decided that the two of them should meet. They made an appointment for 10 o'clock on a June morning in 1897, at the Slavyanski Bazaar, a Moscow restaurant. As in Paris and Vienna, restaurants, cafés and nightclubs played a key part in Moscow's artistic development. There, people talked philosophy and politics, art and literature, poetry and the theatre. No one hurried them. One cup of coffee, a few vodkas, could last an afternoon.

The Slavyanski Bazaar, decorated in the colours of a Russian Easter egg, with its high vaulted ceiling, would be thick with the smoke from strong Russian cigarettes and cigars. Heady smells and constant chatter stoked a warm, seductive atmosphere. The place was open all day and night, with free newspapers and magazines lying around on the tables, but principally there was talk. Constantin Stanislavsky and Vladimir Nemirovich-Danchenko talked for seventeen hours.

'I want to put on stage life as it really is,
people as they really are, and not stilted.'

Above portrait of Anton Chekhov, in
Chekhov's house, Moscow.

Above top The Seagull, Act I: the historic
1898 performance.
Above a scene from the Moscow Art
Theatre's first *Uncle Vanya.* Stanislavsky as
Astrov stands holding his hat: Olga Knipper-
Chekhova is seated in the swing as Elena.
Right Olga Knipper as Mme Ranevskaya in
The Cherry Orchard.

Above Chekhov in our own time. Celia
Johnson as Madame Ranevskaya and Tom
Courtenay in the 1966 Chichester Festival
production of *The Cherry Orchard*.

In later years, Stanislavsky wrote of that meeting that the Versailles Peace Conference did not consider great world questions with as much clarity as he and Nemirovich-Danchenko devoted to the foundations of their future collaboration. They discussed their artistic ideals and how to realize them. They talked about the kind of actors and the sort of drama they admired. They debated practical details like the condition of dressing-rooms and how to heat them so that actors would not have to wear heavy overcoats in order to rehearse comfortably. But chiefly they thrashed out the ethics they would apply to the theatre of the future:

There are no small parts, there are only small actors.

One must love art, and not one's self in art.

Today Hamlet, tomorrow a walk-on, but even as a walk-on you must become an artist.

The poet, the actor, the artist, the costumier, the stage-hand serve one goal, which is placed by the poet in the very basis of his play.

All disobedience to the creative life of the theatre is a crime.

Lateness, laziness, caprice, hysterics, bad character, ignorance of the role, the need to repeat anything twice are all harmful to our enterprise and must be rooted out.

In the minutes of the meeting, Stanislavsky entered: 'The literary veto belongs to Nemirovich-Danchenko, the artistic veto to Stanislavsky.' Between them they fostered the idea of an ensemble, a group, a company.

They had started to talk at 10 o'clock in the morning of one day, and finished at 3 in the morning of the next. With the slogans of their theatrical revolution written down, they emerged from the restaurant, no doubt exhausted, but elated and full of hope. Stanislavsky had been in despair before their meeting. How could the theatre be taken seriously when the popular boulevard play was rehearsed for only two or three days and then thrown on the stage with neither thought nor care? Yet if they were to form a company, and try out their new methods, they still lacked the creator of the characters they wished to see on stage – they lacked a playwright.

Anton Chekhov was the playwright, and again it was Nemirovich-Danchenko who found him. He himself was awarded the Griboyedor Prize for the best play of the season, and as an honourable man he informed the judges that they should have given it to a play called *The Seagull*, whose production had been a dreadful failure. Its author was a young medical doctor already well known for his stories, some of which he had adapted as farces.

The grandson of a serf, Chekhov was born in Taganrog, on the sea of Azov, in 1860, the third of five children. Their mother was kind and loving, but their father, a struggling grocer, was a pious despot, and Chekhov's childhood always remained a painful memory. The local *gimnaziya* gave him a good education, and he grew up as a lively, sociable boy, with a talent for comic impersonations of teachers and priests. His last three years there were marred by his father's bankruptcy – the same canker that blighted the childhoods of Ibsen, Shaw and Strindberg – which caused the family to move to Moscow to make a fresh start while Chekhov stayed to finish his studies. In 1879 he joined his family in Moscow. There he enrolled at the university medical faculty, and in 1884 he qualified as a doctor.

Since his father could only find poorly paid employment, the responsibility of supporting the family fell on Chekhov's shoulders. His brothers – one a journalist, the other an artist – led Bohemian lives, which is another way of saying that they contributed nothing to the family's finances. Chekhov accepted his role as breadwinner cheerfully and diligently, and augmented his income by journalism and by writing comic sketches. By his late twenties he was a prolific writer of short stories, and won the Pushkin Prize for one of them. And he was the 'Antosha Chekhonte' who had criticized Bernhardt.

The previous year had seen the production of his first full-length play, *Ivanov*. He had difficulty in conveying his ideas to the cast about the way they should interpret it. 'The actors do not understand,' he complained. 'They talk nonsense, don't take the parts they should.' *Ivanov* was first performed at the Alexandrinsky Theatre in St Petersburg in January 1889, and to Chekhov's astonishment it was enthusiastically received. In a letter to Maria Kisselev he exulted that the play was 'still a colossal success, a phenomenal success!' Two weeks later he wrote to the writer Ivan Leontyev: 'I received more praise than I deserved. Shakespeare himself never heard the kind of speeches I had to listen to. What more do I want?' But Chekhov was not a complacent man, nor was he ever to be deceived by popular success. He was already at work on another play, which he had decided to give a happy ending. *The Wood Demon* was facetious and inept, though, and he was wise enough to put it aside.

Miraculously, some time during the next six years, mostly by cutting, Chekhov transformed this fiasco, *The Wood Demon*, into a work of genius, *Uncle Vanya*, but it was not yet to be performed. During that long period of revision he started work on a new play. 'I want to put on stage life as it really is,' he declared, 'people as they really are, and not stilted.' This play was *The Seagull*.

Like *Ivanov*, the new work was to be presented by the old-fashioned Alexandrinsky Theatre in St Petersburg. At rehearsals Chekhov was in despair. 'They act a lot,' he lamented. 'I wish there was not so much acting.' Most of the blame for the way *The Seagull* was first presented belongs to the producer, E.P. Karpov. Years later, he wrote an account of the rehearsals and gave a fascinating glimpse of the playwright:

Chekhov winced at every false note uttered by the actors and at their conventional intonations. In spite of his natural shyness, he would stop the rehearsal, interrupting a scene in the middle, and trying to explain to the players in an excited, confused fashion what he wanted to say by a certain sentence, adding invariably: 'The chief thing, my dear fellows, is to play it simply, without any theatricality: just very simply. Remember that they are all ordinary people.'

But to act simply was the one thing that those actors of the old school could not do. The play was almost hissed off the stage. After its failure, Chekhov withdrew in disgust and pain. He wrote to his sister: 'The moral is, never write any more plays.'

Chekhov called *The Seagull* a comedy, a description which has puzzled playgoers, actors, directors and even critics ever since. It is probably best to accept that he was simply appropriating the word to describe his own ironic vision of life. To describe as a comedy a play that deals with thwarted love and passion, and the pain of young creative artists, and which ends with a suicide, may simply be Chekhov's insight into the perverse nature of the Russian temperament, which he more or less shared. But this was not the only feature to baffle the first audiences of the ill-fated St Petersburg production.

Many of the now familiar complaints made against Chekhov as a dramatist were first made about *The Seagull*. The play has no plot, it was said, yet there are three complex love triangles; nothing happens, but there is a suicide, admittedly at the very end of the play, when the news is imparted in what must be one of the most devastating curtain-lines in modern drama – 'The fact is, Konstantin Gavrilovich has shot himself.' That the characters talk only of trivialities is an unfounded criticism which ignores the poetic language of the central theme, the struggle of young artists confronted by the successful establishment. The symbolism, too, caused confusion, but it is simply and exquisitely introduced. At the end of Act Two, Trigorin, the famous writer, catches sight of a dead seagull. He confides to Nina, a young aspiring actress, that it has given him an idea for a short story: 'A young girl has lived in a house on the shore of her lake since her childhood, a young girl like you; she loves the lake like a seagull, and she's as free and happy as a seagull. Then a man comes along, sees her, and, having nothing to do, destroys her, just like the seagull there.' After the first performance, the Theatrical Literary Committee described the symbolism as unnecessary Ibsenism.

In short, *The Seagull* is the herald of what is to come from the playwright: the minute observation of character, the eye for dramatic detail, the revealing silences and non-sequiturs, the distinctive atmosphere of time passing, of aimlessness. Chekhov's compassion is for the whole group, without exception. It was these qualities, and the symbolism in particular, that drew Nemirovich-Danchenko to the play, and made both him and Stanislavsky so anxious to revive it for the new company they formed.

In the eighteen months after they met, the two men set about organizing their venture. They chose the actors, who included Nemirovich-Danchenko's former pupil, Olga Knipper. A barn in the country was their first home, but they soon moved to the old Hermitage Theatre in Moscow. They called themselves The Moscow Art and Popular Theatre, expressing their seriousness and optimism. In October 1898 the company was launched with a production of *Tsar Fyodor Ivanovich* by Aleksey Tolstoy. Before the curtain rose, Stanislavsky told the cast: 'We strive to brighten the dark life of poor people, to give them happy and aesthetic moments. We are striving for the first sensible, moral, popular theatre, and to this high goal we dedicate our lives.' The words failed to inspire the company. Stanislavsky was disappointed with the acting, and perhaps with the play. He and Nemirovich-Danchenko continued to work on Chekhov, trying to persuade him to allow a revival of *The Seagull* and promising a new and faithful production. Chekhov, still smarting from the play's initial reception, was reluctant, but Nemirovich-Danchenko persisted – 'If you won't give me your play I am undone, for *The Seagull* is the only modern play that appeals to me strongly as a producer, and you are the only living writer to be of any interest to a theatre with a modern repertoire.' Eventually Chekhov gave in, and the play was put into rehearsal; it was to be the fifth production mounted by the Moscow Art Theatre.

The Moscow Art Theatre in 1898. Chekhov reads, with Stanislavsky seated to his right. Nemirovich-Danchenko stands to the left of the photograph.

By the time the company started work, Chekhov was ill. He had suffered a lung haemorrhage caused by tuberculosis whose symptoms could easily have been diagnosed earlier, but were ignored by Doctor Chekhov himself. He moved to the warmth of Yalta, and it was there that Nemirovich-Danchenko wrote to keep him informed of how things were going: 'Yesterday we had two readings of *The Seagull*. If you had been with us in spirit, you would have — well, you would have started writing another play on the spot.'

Stanislavsky was about to put into practice his theories about the art of acting and the creation of a dramatic character. He wanted the stage to hold not actors who projected the externals of the roles, but living people, each with an individual inner world. Nemirovich-Danchenko was enthusiastic and encouraging when he wrote again to the ailing author:

You would have witnessed such intense, such growing enthusiasm, such deep and thoughtful efforts to understand your play, such interesting interpretations, and such an atmosphere of general tension, that you would have fallen in love with yourself just by spending the one day with us. Today we all loved you very dearly for your genius: for the amazing delicacy and sensibility of your soul. We go on planning, trying out the tones, or rather the half-tones in which *The Seagull* has to be played, discussing by what scenic methods we can make the audience as enthusiastic about your play as we are ourselves. Never have I admired your genius more than I do now having delved deep into your play.

On the first night Chekhov had not yet recovered from his illness and remained in Yalta. The actors were aware of their heavy responsibility; their thoughts were with the playwright. They had steeled themselves to the reception of the first act which ends with Masha and Dorn, the doctor, alone:

Masha: Oh, I'm so unhappy! Nobody knows how unhappy I am. (*Leaning her head against his breast; softly.*) I love Konstantin.

Dorn: How distraught they all are! How distraught! And what a quantity of love about!... It's the magic lake! (*Tenderly*) But what can I do, my child? Tell me, what can I do? What?

Curtain

Stanislavsky, who played the writer Trigorin, tells what happened next:

There was a gravelike silence. Olga Knipper fainted on stage. All of us could hardly keep our feet. In the throes of despair we began moving to our dressing rooms. Suddenly there was a roar in the auditorium, and a shriek of joy or fright on the stage. The curtain was lifted, fell, was lifted again, showing the whole auditorium our amazed and astounded immovability. It fell again, it rose; it fell, it rose, and we could not even gather sense enough to bow. Then there were congratulations and embraces like those of Easter night, and ovations to Lilina, who played Masha, and who had broken the ice with her last words, which tore themselves from her heart, moans washed with tears. This it was that held the audience mute for a time before it began to roar and thunder in mad ovation. We were no longer afraid of sending a telegram to our dear and beloved friend and poet.

Nemirovich-Danchenko hoped he could communicate the excitement to Chekhov:

The play created a terrific sensation in Moscow... And as for the production: well, I think you'd have gasped at the first and, especially in my opinion, the fourth act. It is difficult to put into words – you must see it. I am beside myself with happiness. Are you giving me Uncle Vanya?

Not everyone was so enthusiastic. Tolstoy dismissed *The Seagull* as 'nonsense', 'utterly worthless', and concluded that it was written 'just as Ibsen writes his plays'. He is also supposed to have said to Chekhov: 'Anton Pavlovich, Shakespeare's plays are bad, but yours are worse.' Yet *The Seagull* was the making of the Moscow Art Theatre, and to acknowledge the debt the company insignia is a seagull. It decorats the curtain both of the Kamergeski Playhouse, to which the company moved in 1902, and of their newer house, built in 1968.

Because of his poor health, Chekhov spent most of each year in Yalta. His personal life was outwardly calm and uneventful and his personality is described as detached and reticent; he did not show much emotion. Although he was attractive to women he did not pursue them. The names of two mistresses are known, but Olga Knipper, whom he married, may have been the only deep love of his life. Because she continued her acting career, husband and wife were often apart. The marriage was childless.

Chekhov was the catalyst of the Russian theatrical transformation whose effects were to be felt all over the world, and yet his particular contribution to the drama is not easy to assess. If Ibsen and Strindberg are the fathers of modern drama, then Chekhov stands outside the great movement which was gathering force. We know from Stanislavsky that Chekhov did not admire Ibsen, even though he recognized his talents. He thought him 'dry, cold, a man of reason'. The antipathy is understandable, for Chekhov is a diviner of emotion, an attentive observer of behaviour, a disciple of the irrational and inexplicable in human affairs. His plays embody compassion in the true sense: a profound understanding and sympathy. He forgives; he never condemns. There are no villains in Chekhov's plays, and no romantic heroes. He noted the fact himself: 'I have not introduced a single villain nor an angel ... I accused nobody, justified nobody.' He said that the writer's role is not that of a judge, but of an impartial witness.

He is praised for his realism, but he loathed the idea, and ironically enough he detested Stanislavsky's productions of his plays. He wrote to a friend:

You tell me that people cry at my plays. I've heard others say the same. But that is not why I wrote them. It is Alexeyev [Stanislavsky] who made my characters into cry-babies. All I wanted was to say honestly to people: 'Have a look at yourselves and see how bad and dreary your lives are!' The important thing is that people should realize that, for when they do, they will certainly create another and better life for themselves. I will not live to see it, but I know that it will be quite different, quite unlike our present life. And so long as this different life does not exist, I shall go on saying to people again and again: 'Please, understand that your life is bad and dreary!' What is there in this to cry about?

Chekhov often clashed with the two directors of the Moscow Art Theatre, and particularly during the production of his last play, *The Cherry Orchard*. Writing to his wife, he asserted that Nemirovich-Danchenko and Stanislavsky saw in his play 'something I have not written, and I am willing to bet anything you like that neither of them has ever read my play through carefully'. He said to a colleague:

Take my *Cherry Orchard*. Is it my *Cherry Orchard*? With the exception of two or three parts nothing in it is mine. I am describing life, ordinary life, and not blank despondency. They either make me into a cry-baby or into a bore. They invent something about me out of their own heads, anything they like, something I never thought of or dreamed about. This is beginning to make me angry.

He specially disliked all the sound-effects that Stanislavsky believed made drama more true to life. It is said that in *The Cherry Orchard* Chekhov deliberately set the railway station miles away from where the main action takes place, because he did not want the director introducing shunting trains and whistles. Chekhov deserves admiration for that. Unfortunately, no script could be long enough to proscribe all the directorial embellishments that playwrights might prefer to exclude.

If he was vexed by the way his fellow countrymen produced his plays during his own lifetime, he would probably have felt outraged by the interpretations of later generations. In a recent production of *The Seagull* by Yefremov, the director of the Moscow Art Theatre, it is conceivable that Chekhov might have forgiven the casting of actors at least twenty years too old in the parts of Konstantin and Nina; what he would not have forgiven was the distortion of the final curtain. Instead of the play ending with Konstantin's suicide, Nina was allowed to quote lines from the first act, from Konstantin's play, the speech about the creatures of the earth having completed their mournful cycle. That sort of alteration seems to me indefensible.

Nor, I suspect, would Chekhov had admired many foreign productions of his work. Anglo-Saxon directors appear to experience special difficulties with it, in the belief that gloom and melancholy are the pervasive moods in all his plays. In England, Chekhov's characters are mostly played as if they were members of the languid English upper middle class, more at home on a vicarage lawn, swinging a croquet mallet, than on huge isolated estates or in provincial towns. The vitality, the abrupt changes of mood, the Russian temperament, are nearly always absent. Although many English playwrights – Shaw and J.B. Priestley among them – claim to have been influenced by Chekhov, his work remains elusive, and his position in world drama splendidly isolated.

He wrote five major plays: *Ivanov, The Seagull, Uncle Vanya, Three Sisters* and *The Cherry Orchard*, during whose first performance Chekhov coughed uncontrollably, already a dying man. He died in the German spa of Baden-weiler in 1904, at the age of forty-four. He once said: 'The stage demands a certain amount of convention. You have no fourth wall. Besides, the stage is art, the stage reflects the quintessence of life. Nothing superfluous should be introduced on stage.' Between these two worlds, of art and reality, Chekhov

The first production of Chekhov's *Three Sisters* in 1901.

discovered a theatrical truth of subtle objectivity, scrupulously fair to the characters he created. He was the least dogmatic of playwrights, and perhaps the most human.

Since this is a history of the theatre and not of theatrical criticism, I have tried to steer clear of stylistic definitions which are likely to come between the audience and the work of playwright, actor and director. In the late nineteenth century, realism, naturalism and symbolism, portmanteau notions applied to several of the arts, came to preoccupy the theatre too. The twentieth century has given birth to a horde of schools and styles – the absurd, the cruel, the ridiculous. Very few playgoers sit in the theatre full of anticipation because they are about to see a specimen of this or that theatrical tendency – if anything, these labels tend to put people off with their implication of intellectual exclusiveness. The theatre can move an audience to tears or laughter, thrill the imagination, take us 'out of ourselves' and into a broader, shared experience. None of these responses requires a knowledge of stylistic categories. In Russia, Chekhov, extending the process begun by Ibsen, wrote plays in which the characters were recognizable individual human beings. That made actors and directors look for a style of performing that would present his characters as truthfully as possible, and what they discovered was to have its repercussions on the theatre everywhere, but not because they admired style as such.

By a freak of chance, in the same year, 1898, that the Moscow Art Theatre was launched, another meeting took place between three people who also wanted to reassert the truth and to change the theatre in their own country, almost two thousand miles away. They met, not in a restaurant, but in Duras House, Kinvara, on the west coast of Ireland. The three were the dramatists W.B. Yeats, Lady Gregory and Edward Martyn, and later they were joined by George Moore, George Russell and John Millington Synge. They too were to create a theatre, the Abbey Theatre, in Dublin. Their aim was to reach back to the roots of their own culture, obscured by hundreds of years of English rule, and to reawaken the dormant Irish genius. They felt that their own dramatic tradition had been too anglicized, and that the Irish character had been grievously misrepresented, distorted and caricatured. Here too, as in Russia and so often elsewhere, the theatre was prefiguring social upheavals yet to come.

Compared to the Russian experience, Ireland's theatrical movement was more directly political, although the participants may not have fully realized it at the time. In 1891, Yeats was the co-founder, with T.W. Rolleston, of the Irish Literary Society in London, and the following year brought the foundation of the National Literary Society in Dublin. Later, Yeats was to insist that 'no political purpose informed our meetings', but Irish Nationalists recognized that a cultural revival would assist their cause. Yeats and the others were determined to tap the dramatic potential which had produced Farquhar, Congreve, Sheridan, Goldsmith, Boucicault, Wilde and Shaw, who all wrote in English. In fact an aim of the Abbey Theatre's founders was to provide opportunity for English-speaking actors and writers. Above all, Yeats intended to preserve intellectual freedom, which he thought essential to creative artists. But as Professor Hugh Hunt explains, in his definitive history of the Abbey:

> The founders of the Irish theatre were particularly vulnerable to the distrust of those mistaken nationalists who held that the only true hallmarks of an Irishman were Gaelic ancestry and the Catholic faith. Yeats, Lady Gregory, Edward Martyn, George Moore, George Russell and Synge were all of Anglo-Irish descent; Martyn was an ardent Catholic, but Moore was decidedly a lapsed one; the others were either Protestants, atheists, agnostics, or – worse still – dabblers in the occult sciences.

Yeats expressed their particular brand of nationalism and poetry in verse:

> John Synge, I and Augusta Gregory, thought
> All that we did, all that we said or sang
> Must come from contact with the soil, from that
> Contact everything Antaeus-like grew strong.
> We three alone in modern times had brought
> Everything down to that sole test again,
> Dream of the noble and the beggar-man.

The dream was first given reality by the publication of a manifesto:

> We propose to have performed in the spring of every year certain Celtic and Irish plays which, whatever their degree of excellence, will be written with high ambition, and so to build up a Celtic and Irish school of dramatic literature. We hope to find in Ireland an uncorrupted and imaginative audience trained to listen by its passion for oratory, and believe that our desire to bring upon the stage the deeper thought and emotions of Ireland will ensure for us a tolerant welcome, and that freedom of experiment which is not found in the theatres of England, and without which no new movement in art or literature can succeed.

The company set to work first as the Irish Literary Theatre, then, after an association was formed with a group of actors, as W.G. Fay's Irish National Dramatic Company, and later as The Irish National Theatre Society. Between 1889 and 1904, plays were presented in concert rooms, public halls and any available theatres. Works by Yeats, Moore, Lady Gregory and J.M. Synge were in the repertoire. All concerned wanted a theatre of their own which would give the company a practical as well as a symbolic centre. Consequently money was desperately needed, and as with all such enterprises the financial problems were to prove the least difficult to solve. In the Abbey's case, the funds came from an extraordinary Englishwoman, Miss Annie Horniman, heiress to the Horniman tea fortune.

Annie Horniman loved the theatre and was a generous patron of the arts. In passing, it is worth noting that she had a hand in establishing the repertory theatre system in Britain: she was founder and manager of the Gaiety Theatre, in Manchester, where the first repertory theatre was launched, under B. Iden Payne's direction. She had come to the Irish through her friendship with Yeats, though she had little sympathy for Irish nationalism, and often stated her opposition to 'those wicked politics which teach you to hate each other so intensely'. In 1904, while on a visit to Dublin, she confided to the actor Willie Fay that she had shares in the Hudson Bay Company, and if they were to 'do anything exciting, I shall have enough money to buy the Society a little theatre in Dublin'. The Hudson Bay Company did what was required of it, and Miss Horniman remained true to her word. The lease of a theatre on the corner of Lower Abbey Street and Marlborough Street was bought for £170 a year, and the Abbey Theatre opened on 27 December 1904 with *On Baile's Strand* by W.B. Yeats and Lady Gregory's *Spreading the News*, together with a revival of Yeats's *Cathleen Ni Houlihan*.

The new Irish theatre expressed its nationalism in plays which set out to embody the deeper reality of Irish life. Gone were the caricatures, the top-o'-the-mornin', broth-of-a-boy, comic cuts characters; in their place was the darker side of peasant life, and the speech and rhythms of the countryside. The Abbey Theatre was midwife to many talented writers, and especially to the outstanding gifts of J.M. Synge and later of Sean O'Casey, though it was Synge whose work first tested the theatre's strength and resolve.

The Playboy of the Western World had its première at the Abbey in 1907, and it told its Irish audience a lot that they did not want to hear. The playboy of the title is Christy Mahon, a weak and worthless man who becomes a hero because his boast that he has killed his father is believed. The father turns up, of course, and when Christy tries to reassert himself by attacking the old man, the village so recently bewitched by tales of Christy's valour is horrified. Synge intended to annoy his audience and critics, and he got his way. The language, which is tough and poetic, was thought to be unrealistic, offensive, even blasphemous. Rumours spread through Dublin that the play was obscene and that 'the womanhood of Ireland was being slandered'. There were riots in the theatre. Yeats defended his colleague in an open debate, the Abbey's finances were badly damaged, and Synge was famous.

Years later, a play by Sean O'Casey was to be the cause of another riot. O'Casey had written *The Shadow of a Gunman* (1923) and *Juno and the Paycock* (1924), both of them brilliant tragicomedies, and the latter with an unmistakably universal quality. In 1925, *The Plough and the Stars* was produced. The director, M.J. Dolan, disliked both the play and its author. In a letter to Lady Gregory he complained: 'the language is – to use the Abbey phrase – "beyond the beyond". The song at the end of the second act, sung by "the girl-of-the-streets" is impossible.' Again the rumour spread that the Abbey was to produce an immoral play, and although the first three

John Synge (1871–1909), drawn by W.B. Yeats's brother, Jack: and a scene from *The Playboy of the Western World*, with Sarah Allgood, at the Abbey Theatre, Dublin.

performances went by without incident, on the fourth night there was pandemonium. For the rest of the week, the play was performed under police guard, to full houses. Yeats commented: 'From such a scene in this theatre went forth the fame of Synge.'

It is always difficult for a later generation to understand why passions should have been so inflamed by what seems to them acceptable enough, and inoffensive by their own standards. But until the advent of the Abbey Theatre, audiences had been used to seeing the Irish character portrayed on stage as shallow and comic. The sound of powerful voices expressing a darker side of the national psyche, and revealing uncomfortable insights, disturbed public opinion, and not only in Ireland. The discovery that the Irish had acquired an uncompromising voice of their own brought violent reactions from the ruling class in Dublin and London. Dionysus was inside the city. O'Casey left Ireland after these events, and went to live in England. The Irish lost a playwright who knew them better than they had been prepared to admit, and gave them back their own speech as a vital dramatic language.

Both Ireland and Russia exported their theatrical revolutions to the United States, and the Abbey Theatre took on the journey its power to provoke a riot.

The Abbey toured America for the first time in 1911, with *The Playboy of the Western World* in their repertoire. It caused a furore in Philadelphia, and some protesters were arrested, but so too were the company – charged with presenting plays likely to corrupt public morals. Irish expatriates nursing fond and misty memories of the old country heard Synge's words and sensed personal danger. In the present safety of their adopted homeland, they were jolted out of romantic illusions by the playboy's reminder of the poverty and brutality they had left behind. The arrest of the entire Abbey company led Bernard Shaw to comment: 'All decent people are arrested in the United States. That is why we refused all invitations to go there. Besides, who am I to question Philadelphia's right to make itself ridiculous?'

A much more significant effect of the Abbey Theatre tour was on Eugene O'Neill, who was then twenty-three years old. It confirmed his ambition to be a playwright:

> It was seeing the Irish players that gave me a glimpse of my opportunity. I went to see everything they did. I thought then, and I still think, that they demonstrate the possibilities of naturalistic acting better than any other company.

In his own plays, O'Neill was to require the same degree of truthfulness in acting as Chekhov or Synge demanded for theirs. The actors – and the directors – had to be made to understand. It seems that each succeeding generation requires more naturalism or realism from the theatre, but then it also seems that styles of actual behaviour in the real world change. The theatre has to sense and express these changes, and by reflecting and defining them it gives them form and currency in the world. The result is that however 'natural' or 'real' Stanislavsky's actors – for example – may have seemed in their own time, in the changed reality of the next generation they would have appeared mannered, if not slightly grotesque. Of course the defence of 'the method' is that it is a means of arriving at a style, and not a style in itself. Stanislavsky knew perfectly well that it is the content of the play and the time in which it is produced that must dictate its performance. The dominance of style itself can produce short-term sensations, but in the longer term it produces dead theatre.

The Russian impact on the United States came twelve years after the Abbey's first tour, in 1923, when the Moscow Art Theatre was greeted as 'the theatre of feeling'. The acting was a revelation, and Stanislavsky became a theatrical guru overnight. In the search for a style of its own, the American theatre had always looked to Europe, and it was first the Irish and then the Russians who satisfied the need to express individual and collective identity. In New York City, Stanislavsky's method was eventually to find its Western home, and to become naturalized in the process.

Stanislavsky's system of preparing an actor for performance is much less dogmatic than his disciples, and many of his critics, have allowed. He has suffered the fate of many other brilliant theorists before and after him, by having disciples he never enlisted institutionalize laws he never made. In his book, written in an awkward semi-fictional style in 1926, *An Actor Prepares*, he is at pains to make clear that he is not legislating for genius or inspiration; he discourages discussion of the subconscious. The result is that Stanislavsky's detailed ideas are of greatest use to the intelligent student, and to the teacher who can sort out useful techniques and insights from the welter of jargon – objectives, super-objectives, emotion-memory, and so on. In practice, Stanislavsky was too inventive, and too much a man of the theatre, to have put up with the kind of self-absorption which can be produced by the doctrinal excesses of 'the' method – the definite article is not his. His monument is not in any latter-day orthodoxy, but in the influence of the Moscow Art Theatre in its heyday, and in the fact that it was he more than any other single person who brought about the changes which flow from the recognition that 'there are no small parts, there are only small actors.'

RAZZMATAZZ
AND REALISM

Broadway runs the length of Manhattan, slashing across the otherwise orderly arrangement of streets and avenues. South of Central Park it collides with Seventh Avenue: the point of impact is called Times Square. Here, and in the shattering of surrounding streets, is a floating population of pimps and whores, winos and junkies, unkempt policemen, street vendors and street musicians, eccentrics and derelicts, as well as conventional people going about their conventional business, and sightseers going about theirs. By day and by night the area vibrates with energy, danger and exuberance; it is tawdry, blatant and shameless. Only in the small hours of the morning, when the neon signs dim with the approach of day, and the people and the traffic ebb a little, does a sort of desolate beauty emerge. For most of the rest of the time, the place seems possessed by a frenzied demon. Peddling their own wares in this compact, pressurized arena of manic activity are the theatres of New York.

Exciting and garish, drab and squalid, these are the twin aspects of razzmatazz and realism which converge in Broadway, and it is this collision of apparently irreconcilable forces continually renewed in the heart of a great city which has caused one of the great theatrical explosions of the twentieth century. In that sense, Broadway is the crucible of the American theatre.

Razzmatazz, razzle-dazzle, show biz, hype, are American inventions which work in a habitat of outlandish publicity, noisy spectacle, and boastful pride in financial profit and also, inexplicably, in spectacular loss. Central to razz-matazz is the love of stars, of their vitality, energy and glamour, and this also has its two sides, because while creative originality can produce great artists, frantic novelty gives rise to what can best be described as freaks. The ethic of razzmatazz is to 'punch-'em-in-the-eye-and-run'. Yet it is one essential part of the story which has its roots in the mid-nineteenth century, in a youthful nation's exuberance and optimism before civil war levied its toll on innocence. To trace the history of this national phenomenon in theatrical terms, we can start in the proper American style with an extraordinary individual, Phineas Taylor Barnum, who was born on 5 July 1810, in Bethel, Connecticut. He was the prophet of much of what is now regarded as razzmatazz, and although a lot of his professional life went over the edge of this story, his style set a pattern for future generations of showmen, who brought to the theatre the same unabashed intention to entertain that they brought to vaudeville, the circus, and then the cinema and television.

Barnum's first recorded show carries all the hallmarks of his special gifts of imagination, impudence, and a genius for gulling the public. In 1835 he exhibited a withered and ancient black woman, Joice Heth, who according to Barnum was 160 years old and had been nurse to George Washington. He proceeded to invest his energies in all forms of entertainment, barnstorming with theatrical troupes, presenting vaudeville acts and venturing into melodrama. All this eventually took him to New York City, where in 1842 he bought John Scudder's American Museum, now to be known as Barnum's, and replaced the conventional exhibits with more eyebrow-raising attractions. Here you could see Ethiopian Minstrels, orang-outangs, the Anatomical Venus and the Living Skeleton, as well as Barnum's prize exhibit, Charles Sherwood Stratton, a.k.a. Tom Thumb, a midget then four years old and less than two feet tall, whom Barnum later displayed to many of what used to be known as 'the crowned heads of Europe', including Queen Victoria.

He presented 'legitimate' plays in what he called the Lecture Room, which seated 3,000 people and was furnished in the 'most voluptuously luxurious style'. Barnum specially favoured the Melodrama With A Moral, and his production of *The Drunkard, or, The Fallen Saved* broke all records for a long run in New York. Fire destroyed his museum in 1865 and again in 1868; in the twenty-six years of its existence it was estimated to have attracted more than 82 million visitors. When Barnum was over seventy, he combined his famous circus, the original Greatest Show on Earth, with James Bailey's, and Barnum and Bailey are now legendary names from the heyday of the travelling circus. Show biz, as American as P.T. Barnum, had come to stay.

The United States were to produce another form of entertainment, the minstrel show, which had less straightforward beginnings. It originated in the patter songs of a white performer, Thomas Dartmouth Rice, who blacked his face to perform the song-and-dance routine which made his name after 1828, and which he claimed to have learned from watching a crippled black stableman:

> Weel about an turn about and do jis so,
> Eb'ry time I weel about I jump Jim Crow.

Rice bought the man's clothes, added topical verses to the traditional songs, and became an international celebrity.

There is no doubt that Rice's popularity owed a lot to its disparaging version of the black American slave, or that the travesty he created spawned a whole range of black caricatures who, like stage Irishmen, became accepted theatrical types, their image a part of the ideology of their oppression. Here again, whether the theatre creates or is simply quick to reflect such images it is impossible to decide, but there is no doubt that it can sanction them. Nevertheless, Rice, whose act had begun with burlesques of Shakespeare and opera, inevitably drew on both the real music and real dialect of black slaves. From 1840 to 1880, the show which developed from his solo act became the most popular form of entertainment in the United States. His appearance at

'A collision of apparently irreconcilable
forces: Broadway is the crucible of the
American theatre'.

Above with characteristic pizzazz, Barnum
and Bailey's 'Greatest Show on Earth' strut-
ted its stuff throughout the 1880s.

Above Count 'em. The original
Ziegfeld girls in formation.
Some costumes were (*left*) more
successful than others: the
Arabian Nights.

Right The advance of the
American musical: the original
productions of *Showboat*, 1927:
Oklahoma!, 1943, and *West Side
Story*, 1957.

The 1970s saw the illusions
undermined; by Elaine Stritch
in Sondheim's *Company*, 1970:
and, collectively, by the cast of
A Chorus Line. Undaunted,
Carol Channing sang on (*right*)
in the title role of *Hello, Dolly!*

It was a time for re-examination. Sondheim, affectionately or acidly, reviewed the revues in *Follies*, 1971. And the grand-daddies of it all, Gilbert and Sullivan, were given the Broadway treatment when *The Pirates of Penzance* (*right*) was restaged a century after its première.

Two giants of postwar American theatre.
Tennessee Williams' *Cat on a Hot Tin Roof*
(*left*) played here in 1975 by Elizabeth Ashley
and Kier Dullay: and (*right*) Arthur Miller's
View from the Bridge, the 1982 production,
with Tony Lo Bianco and Rose Gregorio.

the Surrey Theatre, London, in 1836 began the enormous vogue of the minstrel show in England which persisted in the theatre and on television into the 1970s.

Unlike vaudeville and music hall, which were intended for adults only, the minstrel show was essentially family entertainment. Although Rice himself never became part of a troupe, the minstrels based their impersonations on the stereotype he had created. Later on, blacks themselves were to take part. Sitting in a semicircle with banjos, tambourines, one-stringed fiddles, and bones, they sang plaintive 'coon' songs and sentimental ballads interspersed with soft-shoe dances and volleys of backchat between the 'Interlocutor' and 'Bones'. Minstrel shows were a formative influence on American song and dance, which therefore came to contain some of the feeling and vitality of the slaves.

Black Americans were to provide a second and equally important strand in the development of the American theatre. In the year when Harriet Beecher Stowe first published her novel, *Uncle Tom's Cabin*, a dramatization by C.W. Taylor was mounted at the National Theater in New York City, on 23 August 1852. It ran for only two weeks. A month later, in Troy, New York, the play was revived and was an immediate hit, running for a hundred performances. The manager of the National Theater was persuaded to try the piece again, and on 18 July 1853 it reopened and turned into one of the greatest hits in the history of world theatre. Productions toured the length and breadth of the United States. Towards the close of its long run in New York, the company was playing eighteen performances a week, and the actors were eating their meals in the theatre. In less than four months after the opening at the National, Barnum mounted a rival production at his Museum, using a version by H.J. Conway. By mid-January 1854 the Bowery Theater had staged yet another version, starring the original minstrel, T.D. Rice, as Tom. Later in the century the play proved to be a standard vehicle for touring companies in every corner of the country.

Uncle Tom's Cabin was more than a national phenomenon: it swept the world. Shortly after its New York success it was brought to London and was played for several years throughout the British Isles under titles like *The Slave's Life In America*, *Eliza and the Fugitive*, and *Life Among The Lowly*. Paris was the next European capital to be conquered by *La Case de l'Oncle Tom*, which caused such rivalry that several versions were played simultaneously, each theatre using its own adaptation of the original novel or of some previous dramatization. In Germany it became *Onkel Toms Hütte*, in Denmark *Onkel Tomas*, in Holland *De Negerhut*. The play does not rank as great theatre: many of the productions were vastly extravagant, silly and sentimental, and part of its foreign appeal was simply the exotic quality of slave life. Yet although the subject matter can seem with hindsight like white condescension, in its time it aroused universal sympathy for the downtrodden. *Uncle Tom's Cabin* caught the world's conscience and proved to be America's first and most successful theatrical export. It also matters because it shows the American theatre trying to respond to a serious and tragic theme, one that was vital to the future of the United States.

American audiences loved, and they still love, novelty. Theatre managers had to come up with all sorts of diversions to entertain the people who bought the tickets. In between acts of fixtures like Shakespeare's *Richard III*, for example, you might find 'Jim Crow' Rice performing. The New York waterfront was the location chosen by an ex-actor called H.S. Chapman for his Floating Theatre, a large steamboat remodelled for theatrical use. It seated 1,200 people, drawn as much by the original setting as by what it contained. But the harbour of New York was no stranger to the history of American theatre, because it was here that the great European stars disembarked in the hope of conquest and wealth.

From as early as 1752, English actors and actresses had hoped to open up the theatrical goldmine of the American colonies, often after failed careers in England. Lewis Hallam the elder, for example, had gone bankrupt at Goodman's Fields in 1750 before arriving in the New World two years later, with his wife, children, and a company of ten actors, on board the *Charming Sally*. The troupe rehearsed on deck during the six-week voyage, and opened in Williamsburg, Virginia, with *The Alchemist*, by Ben Jonson, and *The Merchant of Venice*, in which young Lewis Hallam, then aged twelve, was struck by stage fright, burst into tears and left the stage, though not for ever. He was to become one of the leading actors of the new United States, and his company staged the first American comedy, Royall Tyler's *The Contrast*, in 1787.

Not all these English exports were as welcome as the Hallams. In 1810 George Frederick Cooke set out to capture what he still thought of as a dissident colony. He is often described as a colourful character (theatrical jargon for drunk and/or unreliable), and had gained some reputation as a tragedian in England, despite being usually in debt, often in prison, and almost always legless – though it was said in his defence that he played better drunk than sober. After two years in America, this was Cooke's reply to being informed that President Madison would attend a performance: 'What?!? George Frederick Cooke, who have acted before the Majesty of Britain, play before your Yankee President? No! It is degrading enough to play before the rebels, but I will not go on for a king of rebels, the contemptible King of the Yankee Doodles!' Cooke died in 1812 and was buried in New York, where a monument was later erected to his memory by the great English actor Edmund Kean, no pillar of respectability himself.

Kean, the idol of Drury Lane, renowned for his Shylock, Richard III, Iago, and Sir Giles Overreach, in Massinger's *A New Way To Pay Old Debts*, was acclaimed on his first visit to the United States, in 1820–1, until a house of only twenty people during a late-season visit to Boston caused him to refuse to continue the performance. He apologized, but his reputation suffered, and once on a later tour he was hissed off stage. But this was not Kean's most distinctive effect on the American stage. His influence on the theatre, and at a further remove on American history, arose out of a chain of events which had started not long before his first visit.

In London, in 1816, a handsome young actor called Junius Brutus Booth was promoted by press, public and a rival theatre as a challenger to Kean's crown as leading actor of the day. The atmosphere was something like the kind of ballyhoo which nowadays surrounds a fight for the world heavyweight championship. Kean agreed to accept the challenge: he would play Iago to Booth's Othello at Drury Lane on 20 February 1817. He inflicted what amounted to a first-round knockout, and the young actor was so deeply humiliated that he fled not just from the stage but from England. In 1821 he emigrated to the United States, and there he founded a theatrical dynasty. Three sons followed in their father's footsteps. The second, Edwin, was to become the leading American classical actor of his time, and one of the greatest of all American actors.

Edwin Booth (1833–1893), as Hamlet.

Edwin Booth, who was born in 1833, was the first American actor to achieve a European reputation. On a tour of England in 1880–2, he alternated Iago and Othello with Henry Irving. Hamlet was his most famous part: in 1864 he gave a hundred consecutive performances. Together with the Drews and the Barrymores, Booth was part of the fabric of the 'legitimate' theatre in the United States. Unfortunately the family suffered from a streak of instability. Junius Brutus was an alcoholic with symptoms of mental illness. Edwin also drank, and was a habitual depressive. He lived in a house in Gramercy Park, New York City, which during his lifetime he turned into a club for actors and other professional men, the Players' Club. There he died in 1893.

Apart from Edwin Booth's personal weaknesses, his life and career were the lesser victims of an historical disaster beyond his control, but which overshadowed the rest of his career. On the night of 14 April 1864, at 10.22 pm, during a performance of *Our American Cousin* at Ford's Theater, Washington, DC, Edwin's younger brother, also an actor, John Wilkes Booth, assassinated Abraham Lincoln.

I observed earlier that there were two converging themes in the history of the American theatre. While immigrant European actors were founding and inspiring a breed of gifted American actors, the country had been opened up, in the last two decades of the nineteenth century, to vaudeville and burlesque, which in England is known as variety, and which was the truly popular native form of entertainment. The ethic of P.T. Barnum flourished. Charles Frohman, a producer of flair, drowned when the liner *Lusitania* was sunk by a German submarine on 7 May 1915, justified the lighter side of the American theatre:

> Over here we regard the workman first and the work second. Our imaginations are fired not nearly so much by great deeds as by great doers. There are stars in every walk of American life. It has always been so with democracies.

And:

> To be a success, no matter how splendidly served, the menu should always have one unique and striking dish that despite its elaborate gastronomic surroundings, must long be remembered.

In championing stars and spectacle, Frohman was stating a well established creed, founded on long commercial experience: large numbers of people paid to see what he and his colleagues were serving. One fabled Broadway producer, Florenz Ziegfeld, made the even more basic discovery that as well as stars and spectacle, the public would also pay to see shapely girls. In 1907 he started a tradition of spectacular revues, the Ziegfeld Follies, famed for their gorgeous women and lavish staging – in 1927 the production cost $300,000, nearly half of it spent on costumes.

So by the end of the nineteenth century America had adequate playhouses and many first-class actors, but serious drama, a native American drama, had not surfaced. Commercialism, razzmatazz, had suffocated dramatic invention. One foreign playgoer visiting Broadway in 1905 asked: 'Are you all children in America? There is not a serious thought, not a suggestion of intellect in anything I have seen. I predict there will be no dramatic art in America for another twenty years.'

Yet if drama is the way a community takes its own measure, America as a community had hardly had time to come together, with its older components more divided than united by the Civil War, millions of new immigrants pouring in from the slums and ghettoes and backward rural areas of Europe, and vast territories still to be integrated. In that perspective, twenty years might have seemed an optimistic timescale, but the United States were in a hurry, as usual, and dramatic art came in ahead of schedule in the person of Eugene Gladstone O'Neill, born in 1888 in New York City, the son of an Irish-born romantic actor of the old school. His father, James, made his name in the title role of *The Count of Monte Cristo*, and toured extensively with the play, so Eugene's early education was fitful. He attended Princeton University, but only for a year, and afterwards signed on as a seaman on voyages to South America, Africa and elsewhere. After the encounter with the touring Abbey Theatre in 1911 which confirmed his vocation as a dramatist, in 1912 he came down with tuberculosis, but in the next two years he wrote several one-act plays and two longer works, and in 1914 he went to study under George Pierce Baker, the first Professor of Dramatic Literature at Harvard, and a vital influence through the playwriting workshop he had established there in 1906.

In 1916 O'Neill joined the Provincetown Players, a theatrical company centred on Provincetown, Cape Cod. That summer he wrote a one-act play drawing upon his experiences as a seaman, *Bound East for Cardiff*, which the Players staged as their first production at the Wharf Theater. Four years and several productions later, *Beyond the Horizon* became his first full-length play to be staged on Broadway. It won O'Neill the first of four Pulitzer prizes. His creative energy was compulsive. Over the next twenty years he completed more than a play a year, many of them complex and very long.

O'Neill is the first major playwright of the American theatre. He claimed to be influenced by Strindberg, but his theatrical ancestors were the ancient Greeks. In *Desire Under the Elms* (1924) and *Mourning Becomes Electra* (1931) he explored the themes of incest, infanticide and fateful retribution, which he used and re-used to express deeply personal conflicts arising out of the disturbing relationship with his own parents and with his brother James which haunted him all his life, and gave him his tragic view of the world. He was also preoccupied with the disintegration of personality, and in *The Iceman Cometh* (1946), perhaps his most complex work, with self-delusion, here seen almost as a saving grace, not to be lightly removed from people who have little else.

O'Neill's later life was tragic. He married three times. His elder son

Eugene O'Neill (1888–1953), and a scene from the 1971 production of *Long Day's Journey Into Night*, at the National Theatre of Great Britain: Laurence Olivier and Dennis Quilley.

committed suicide at the age of forty, his younger son was plagued by emotional instability, and his daughter Oona he cut out of his life, aged eighteen, when she married Charlie Chaplin, who was her father's age. His final years were dogged by illness which made it impossible for him to write. Angry, frustrated, and in pain, he longed to die. Seeing no one but a doctor, a nurse, and his third wife, Carlotta, he waited for death in a Boston hotel room. It came on 27 November 1953. It was not until 1956 that his great autobiographical play, *Long Day's Journey Into Night*, was first produced.

It does not diminish the stature of O'Neill as a great playwright to say that from the viewpoint of American drama he was not a revolutionary figure. The genius acknowledged by the award of the Nobel Prize for Literature in 1936 seems to me to stand in the European tradition, and although his work showed his countrymen the power of the theatre as a medium capable of handling themes as vital as any in American poetry and fiction, the American theatrical explosion as I perceive it does not stem from O'Neill. Yet paradoxically we have to go back to his theatrical beginnings to find the clue that leads to a theatre in the American grain.

During the first fertile decades of this century, small ensemble companies sprang up in several countries – Ireland, Russia, Germany, France – in reaction to the star system, the high production costs and the moth-eaten artistic ideals of the opulent established theatre. In the United States, the Provincetown Players were not unique, and other small companies, many of them amateur, were formed. The Washington Square Players pre-dated Provincetown by a year. It too produced new American plays, and it gave experience to talented young enthusiasts such as Katharine Cornell, who was to become one of America's legendary actresses. Some of its members went on to found the

Theater Guild, in 1919. It was to become the major producing organization in the modern theatre, as a literary and artistic influence. So serious drama was claiming its audience, in a modest but promising way. And if these pioneers saw commercialism as a threat to what they were aiming for, it would have amazed them to learn that their colleagues on the other side of the tracks were laying the basis of a theatrical form that was ready to turn itself into an art.

From a strictly academic angle, it can be argued that the American musical arose out of the ashes of European operetta, the work of Gilbert and Sullivan, music hall and the revues of the English impresario C.B. Cochran. No doubt these influences are all there, because the musical too is a kind of cultural melting-pot. But I would argue that this same love of keeping open house is part of the musical's national character, its American character: the art of the musical owes its vitality and brilliance to forces that existed nowhere else. The tradition of Barnum, Frohman and Ziegfeld, the minstrel shows, the vaudeville skills, the vulgarity, the energy, the stars, the razzmatazz – all these were to become bonded, in a way that no one could have sensibly predicted, with the legitimate theatre's drive towards realism and towards dealing with what mattered in the contemporary world. Realism is not necessarily reflected in a naturalistic style of performance, any more than entertainment can handle nothing heavier than a moral vacuum. The union of the two was made possible by the cut-throat commercialism of Broadway.

In the early days of this century, until after the First World War, the musical was aimed at a traditional figure, 'the tired businessman', which meant that shows had undemanding plots tenuously held together by music with a Strauss or Schubert flavour, as many laughs as possible, and, most important, chorus girls. An old Broadway joke had it that the average member of the audience could tell whether he enjoyed the show by the time the curtain was halfway up. But in December 1927 any tired businessmen who paid to see the new musical at the Ziegfeld Theatre were in for a surprise: no pretty girls to sing the opening chorus; instead, black workers carrying bales of cotton moved across the stage and sang about their work to a melody that was to become famous and which signalled a new age in the development of the musical. The melody was 'Ol' Man River' and the musical was *Show Boat*.

The music for *Show Boat* was by Jerome Kern, but from the point of view of this history the key figure was the lyricist, who also wrote the libretto – which in musicals is called The Book – Oscar Hammerstein 2nd. He came from a thoroughly theatrical background: his grandfather, Oscar Hammerstein 1st, had been a producer of opera and a builder of theatres. The younger Oscar was thirty-two years old when *Show Boat* was produced, but he had already collaborated successfully with Rudolf Friml on *Rose Marie* in 1924 and with Sigmund Romberg on *The Desert Song* in 1926. It is Hammerstein who was responsible for the innovations that opened the way to the serious musical theatre, because *Show Boat* was not a musical comedy but something new, a musical play.

Bearing in mind that the marriage between razzmatazz and realism had also involved a divorce between serious and solemn, *Show Boat* may be described as a serious musical because it dealt with real human problems and even contained elements of tragedy. Hammerstein had adapted Edna Ferber's popular novel set in the Deep South, published only a year before, in 1926. The specific setting of a showboat plying on the Mississippi in the mid-nineteenth century provided a logical reason for the presence of singers and songs, but Hammerstein's genius was to integrate the book with the lyrics: the songs grew out of the action and even advanced the story. In addition, the many changes of setting which *Show Boat* required produced a format composed of episode, song, set-change, episode, song, set-change, and so on, which was to prove durable. Such techniques seem commonplace today, but in 1927 they were new and startling.

The story concerns Cap'n Andy Hawks and his wife, Parthy Ann, who own the showboat *Cotton Blossom*, and what happens when their daughter Magnolia falls hopelessly in love with Gaylord Ravenal, a handsome, irresponsible gambler. Other central characters are Julie, the mulatto leading lady of the *Cotton Blossom*, and her husband Steve, the leading man, who are forced to leave the show because their mixed marriage is considered unlawful. The romance between Magnolia and Gaylord ends unhappily; so does the marriage between Julie and Steve, which was the first appearance of the explosive theme of miscegenation in what had been the marshmallow world of the musical theatre. The story ends on a bittersweet note. In passing it is worth pointing out that more than fifty years later the book of *Show Boat* holds up unusually well, and is certainly superior to many of the plays that were then being written. Even some of Eugene O'Neill's work of the same period seems a good deal more stilted and melodramatic.

Show Boat is historically important because it introduced elements of genuine human concern. Its realism contains the main charge of the American explosion, and the origin of my proposition that over the years the Americans have taken the most lavish and entertaining of theatrical forms and made it the home of themes pertinent and relevant to their own time. *Show Boat* was the forerunner, but it was sixteen years before anything so powerful appeared again on the musical stage. The link is Oscar Hammerstein 2nd. Between 1927 and 1943 he had written fifteen shows, many of them flops. He had lived through the Depression, and had seen his country enter the Second World War. Now he had a new collaborator, the composer Richard Rodgers.

Rodgers and Hammerstein's musical *Oklahoma!* opened on 31 March 1943. The curtain went up on a lone woman in a rocking-chair, and an unaccompanied tenor voice off-stage sang a song of lyrical gladness – 'Oh, what a beautiful mornin'!' By the time the final curtain came down, *Oklahoma!* had irrevocably changed the entire concept of musical theatre, and captured the audience in the process. Shortly after the opening night, Hammerstein took out an advertisement in *Variety*, the trade newspaper, reminding his colleagues of the theatre's unpredictability. Having listed all his recent failures, he concluded by saying 'I did it before and I can do it again.'

Oklahoma! was presented by the Theater Guild, that small and earnest group which had been formed in 1919. In the season of 1930–1 the Guild had produced a play by Lynn Riggs, *Green Grow the Lilacs*, with Franchot Tone and June Walker in the leading roles. At some point it was decided that the play needed music, and Western songs, cowboy ballads and chorus numbers were added, but did not do the trick. The play ran for sixty-four performances which covered the subscription period for Guild members. But one member, Theresa Helburn, persisted in thinking that the piece would make a good musical comedy. The circumstances which brought Rodgers and Hammerstein together are unclear. Hammerstein may have been offered the play for adaptation and asked to name a composer. One version says that Hammerstein had originally sent *Green Grow the Lilacs* to Jerome Kern, who turned it down, saying: 'It's a Western. I don't like it. Westerns don't make money.' What happened next is disputed, but whether it was Miss Helburn who suggested the collaboration, or Rodgers who chose Hammerstein, they decided that they could work together on the play.

Right from the start, the Guild ran into problems. It was hard to find backers to invest in the production, and for all sorts of good reasons. The Guild itself was in financial difficulty and the cast contained no stars. *Green Grow the Lilacs* had not been a successful play. Hammerstein had not written a hit for more than a decade. Richard Rodgers had never worked with any other lyricist except Lorenz Hart. Agnes De Mille had been chosen as choreographer, but she came from the world of ballet and had never before worked on a musical. The director, Rouben Mamoulian, had staged for the Guild George Gershwin's opera *Porgy and Bess*, an artistic triumph but a financial disaster. The omens were not good.

In one respect only did the production bow to tradition: it opened out of town, in New Haven, under another title, *Away We Go*, and went through the whole routine of re-writes, new songs added, old lyrics replaced, dialogue tightened – all the hallmarks of a Broadway production. In Boston the title was changed to *Oklahoma*, but the exclamation mark was not added until just before the New York première. Punctuation notwithstanding, the show was given little hope of success. One out-of-town critic, going for the quick kill, wrote: 'No legs. No jokes. No chance.' Others felt that the show suffered because it transgressed: a man was killed on stage, and chorus girls did not appear until the first act was almost forty-five minutes old. Yet *Oklahoma!* broke the world record for consecutive performances of a musical production previously held by *Chu Chin Chow* in London during the 1914–18 War.

Oklahoma! marks the turning-point. After such a thunderous success, any future musical production would have to match up to it. And in compensation for the early forebodings, now it was held to have been responsible for blazing the trail in almost every aspect of presentation. Because a man was killed on stage, it was said to have been the first musical to tell a serious story. Because Agnes De Mille's choreography was in key with her creation of the ballet of Aaron Copland's *Rodeo* in 1942, it went down as the first time ballet had been introduced to a Broadway show. Another part of the mythology of *Oklahoma!* is that it was the first musical to be recognized for its literary quality. The fact is that *Show Boat*, sixteen years before, had told a serious story. Both Marilyn Miller and Vera Zorina had danced balletic numbers in Broadway shows: Zorina, a former prima ballerina, had danced 'Slaughter on Tenth Avenue' in the 1936 Rodgers and Hart musical *On Your Toes*. And while the Critics' Circle did vote *Oklahoma!* best drama of the year, and the Pulitzer committee awarded it a special citation, *Of Thee I Sing* had won the Pulitzer drama prize in 1931. The triumph of *Oklahoma!* was that it fused all these elements: the necessary fragments had existed before, but now the theatre had made them into a new whole.

Until *Oklahoma!* the music, book and lyrics were regarded as the chief, and perhaps the only necessary, creative factors. It is Agnes De Mille who holds the credit for the role which dance now plays in the musical form. Here too, the musical has played host to a number of traditions, bringing together the technical discipline of ballet, the snap and dynamism of American modern dance, and the emotional expressiveness of jazz dancing, part descendant of the slave tradition that the minstrel shows once tapped. The best musical dancing and choreography now rivals any in the world for its excitement, colour, intensity and theatricality. Nowadays choreographers such as Jerome Robbins, Bob Fosse and Michael Bennett may direct the show so that dance is central to its development. In De Mille's work in *Oklahoma!* the dance numbers were both original and integrated with the story, growing naturally out of the action. She introduced a note of comic realism in the first number, 'Many A New Day', by having one of the dancers appear unable to keep pace with the others; the girl falls, quickly gets up again, as if embarrassed, and goes on dancing. The dream ballet dramatized the struggle between the two male protagonists, Curly and Jud Fry. The dance is set not to music specially composed but to fragments of tunes previously heard in the show. The spirited square dance performed to 'The Farmer and the Cowman' was an electrifying dance tribute to the sheer energy that developed the American West.

Although it might be said that *Oklahoma!* was simply first-class entertainment which gave respite for a few hours from the horror of war, the fact remains that it raised the musical to a level unequalled by its predecessors. In the forty years since it was first produced, the American musical has grown into a unique theatrical form. No subject is taboo. Pogroms and Nazis, the protest of a generation against the Vietnam War, the adaptation of a Shakespeare tragedy to gang warfare in New York, the personal agonies of the gypsies who are dedicated to the making of musicals, all have found expression on the Broadway stage with a tough and loving professionalism that has become the paradigm and yardstick of the genre. The musical is now recognized all over the world as a form whose expressive potential is no longer limited to petty themes. While the history of the theatre proves over and over again that the drama has an unrivalled power to influence and provoke, in the twentieth century it has seldom been truly popular. Though still in its infancy, the musical has become an enormously popular medium; it has yet to prove whether it could contain the pressures generated by the greatest creations of the legitimate theatre.

With the coming of peace in 1945, the recurring problem of the American theatre was in danger of reasserting itself. It looked as if the razzmatazz might once again stifle the realism. Of course there were notable playwrights – Lillian Hellman, Elmer Rice, Kaufman and Hart, William Saroyan, Robert Sherwood: serious or poetic, experimental or just solidly commercial. The 1930s had also seen the formation of the Group Theater, founded by Harold Clurman, Lee Strasberg and Cheryl Crawford, which evolved from the Theater Guild, and whose other members included Elia Kazan and Walter Fried. Group Theater had been responsible for producing the work of the young dramatist Clifford Odets, who wrote plays of social protest in the great era of social protest, in particular *Waiting for Lefty* (1935) and *Golden Boy* (1937). By the time of his death in 1963, aged fifty-seven, his influence had declined. Or perhaps it would be truer to say that his star had been eclipsed, for soon after the war's end, two outstanding and enduring voices were raised for the legitimate theatre. Arthur Miller and Tennessee Williams have come to epitomize the postwar years, although that is their only connection.

John Garfield and Lee J. Cobb in the American National Theatre's 1952 production of *Golden Boy*, by Odets.

If we accept Ibsen and Strindberg as the fathers of modern drama, then the ancestry of Miller and Williams is plain. Arthur Miller is Ibsen's child. He concerns himself with ideas, with the practical function of society, with people's failings and aspirations. He was born in New York City in 1915, graduated from the university of Michigan in 1938, and then joined a Federal Theater writing project which occupied him for four months before it was purged by Congress. This would not be the last time that Miller suffered at the hands of the US government. He wrote radio scripts, and during the early years of the Second World War he worked as a steamfitter in the Brooklyn Navy Yard. For six months he was attached to the infantry to gather material for Ernie Pyle's film, *The Story of GI Joe*. The experience resulted in a book, *Situation Normal*, published in 1944. His only novel, *Focus*, a haunting story of antisemitism, was published the following year.

As a young man in New York, Miller had admired the work of the Group Theater which had reflected his own social awareness. Although the Group had disbanded in 1941, it was to its former members that he turned when he completed his first play, *All My Sons*, in 1947. Harold Clurman, Elia Kazan and Walter Fried were the three producers. Kazan directed. The play centres on Joe Keller, a manufacturer who has sold the government aeroplanes with defects which have caused the deaths of twenty-one pilots. His son returns from the war and decides to inform the government about his father's crime. Joe kills himself. The last line of the play, spoken by the son to his mother, encapsulates the theme: 'Once and for all you can know that there's a universe of people outside, and you're responsible to it.' Miller was denounced as a Communist by fanatical patriots who believed that any criticism of American life was Soviet-inspired. *All My Sons*, they said, was a smear on the American business community. The theatre had not lost its power to disturb the collective conscience, or the community its readiness to shift its guilts back on to the playwright.

In his masterpiece, *Death of a Salesman*, produced in 1949, Miller created an archetype of American society: at home, Willy Loman is a good family man, dreaming the commonplaces of the American dream; in his work, selling merchandise on the road, he postures and bluffs his way into believing in the mythology of success while drowning in his own failure. It falls to Willy's wife to speak his epitaph:

> I don't say he's a great man. Willy Loman never made a lot of money. His name was never in the paper. He's not the finest character who ever lived. But he's a human being, and a terrible thing is happening to him. So attention must be paid. He's not to be allowed to fall into his grave like an old dog.

In form, *Death of a Salesman* was thought to be experimental, but by the standards that were to be set a decade later the story unfolds in a simple narrative style in which the protagonists were thoroughly realistic in speech and action, apart from a ghostly figure to whom Willy is allowed to express his innermost thoughts and feelings. But it demonstrates Miller's gift for exploring social themes through the personal lives of his characters. The play is universal because it is particular.

Above: Arthur Miller (born 1915) and *overleaf*, Tennessee Williams (1914–1983).

The importance of the theatre was soon to be thoroughly tested. In 1950, Senator Joseph McCarthy launched his campaign to undermine the highest ideals of American life in the guise of defending them as a dedicated patriot. His wild charges of Communist infiltration in all walks of life were never substantiated. Using fear, intimidation, and techniques of character assassination ranging from innuendo to straightforward fabrication, McCarthy induced a fever in his fellow countrymen which led to the accused being denounced, losing their jobs, and being generally condemned and disowned by the society that most of them believed in.

The theatre's response was framed by Arthur Miller. First, he adapted Ibsen's *An Enemy of the People*, which embodies the courage of one man to stand against the mob. Then in 1953 Miller hit upon a devastating metaphor for what was happening around him. He dramatized the Salem witch-trials of 1692 in *The Crucible*, and no one was in any doubt about its meaning. His play caught the hysteria that reinforces itself with greater hysteria, and made it possible to discuss the prevailing mood in the context of a notorious historical incident. So it came as no surprise when Miller was himself summoned before the House Un-American Activities Committee in 1956 and ordered to name people he had seen ten years earlier at an alleged meeting of Communist writers. He refused and was convicted of contempt, but the decision was reversed on appeal. His best work belongs to the decade that followed the war.

The plays of Tennessee Williams are the children of Strindberg's drama, and belong to the world of the neurotic, the sexually obsessed, social and spiritual disablement, intangible perceptions. Like Strindberg's, his vision of man springs from the knowledge of a tortured self, and his plays are never didactic in the manner of Arthur Miller. Williams's father really was a salesman. Cornelius Coffin Williams sold smart shoes and lived for a time in Columbus, Mississippi, where his second child, Thomas Lanier Williams, to be known as Tennessee, was born in 1914. The boy's mother was a Southern lady, a woman to whom society meant manners, gossip, marriage and scandal. Tennessee's early years were blighted by his overbearing father's disapproval – he even took to calling the boy 'Miss Nancy'. Tennessee escaped briefly to the universities of Missouri and Washington. When the Depression interrupted his education for two years, he obeyed his father's command to work as a clerk in the International Shoe Factory. He wrote in his spare time, and performances of his work by local amateur groups encouraged him to study dramatic writing at the University of Iowa, where he graduated in 1938.

The American Blues, a collection of one-act plays, brought him some recognition, but it was in 1945 that he was hailed as a promising dramatist with the success of *The Glass Menagerie*, which he described as a 'memory play'. A work of delicate feeling, tenderness and subtlety, the play is in no way a literal autobiographical record of what happened to Williams, his sister and his mother in St Louis. 'Yes, I have tricks in my pocket,' says Tom, the author figure in his play, 'I have things up my sleeve. But I am the opposite of a stage magician. He gives you illusion that has the appearance of truth. I give you truth in the pleasant disguise of illusion.' That statement can be said to stand for much of the playwright's work, but his plays always contain a deep sense of pain and loneliness. *Summer and Smoke* has the epigraph from Rainer Maria Rilke: 'Who, if I were to cry out, would hear me among the angelic orders?'

The play which made Williams's name, and for which he will probably be best remembered, was *A Streetcar Named Desire*, which was written after *Summer and Smoke*, but was produced before it, in 1947. It is an agonizing study of the psychological and moral disintegration of Blanche Du Bois, a former Southern belle, whose pursuit of emotional and sexual fantasies is smashed when confronted with the real and brutal world represented by her brother-in-law, Stanley Kowalski, played on Broadway by the stunningly powerful young Marlon Brando. This play, and several that followed, developed Williams's obsessions with rejection and longing, cruelty and suffering. His probings of private sexuality before such themes had become part of the conventional literary domain repeatedly shocked, until that intention became habitual to a point that sometimes neared self-parody. His later plays disappointed. In 1969 he suffered a severe mental and physical breakdown, and although his play *Small Craft Warnings*, written in 1972, displayed some of his former brilliance, he spent the rest of his life trying unsuccessfully to regain a reputation which was receding into the past. He died in 1983.

Both Williams and Miller gained worldwide reputations, and their plays are still performed and revived in many languages. Yet they are exceptions to the Broadway rule whose ruthless commercial logic has made it more and more difficult for playwrights to pursue a long relationship with their audience, and often stops them being heard at all. The saying that Broadway is not interested in plays, only in hits, has an uncomfortable ring of truth. New York has therefore had to develop other venues, and a theatre of account rather than of accountants has grown up off-Broadway, and even off-off-Broadway. New plays, revivals, bizarre experimental work, all find a place in halls, converted rooms and cellars or with luck small theatres. There is also a passion for revitalizing the classics, especially Shakespeare. Joseph Papp, who founded the New York Shakespeare Festival in 1954, produces the English playwright in an unequivocally American style which works just because it knocks down some dispensable preconceptions. It happens that Papp is also a producer and director of musicals, and was responsible, as producer, for *A Chorus Line*. His example clinches my point that in the United States there is no necessary dividing line between razzmatazz and realism. In the best American drama, they can coexist.

ADMIT ME, CHORUS, TO THIS HISTORY

Throughout the two thousand five hundred years of this history, I have argued the necessity of the theatre in its own time. We cannot know how an Athenian audience responded to the first tragedies, but we can be certain that its response involved an excited recognition that here was a new way to look at the contemporary world. No playwright ever addressed his work to posterity and lived. Plays survive in the mystery of the imaginative world they create, and its continued availability to the special community which is formed when one group of men and women, or perhaps just one man or woman, suspend their ordinary selves to become actors, and another group finds its minds tuned well enough together to become an audience. People do this for pleasure, not instruction. If the theatre does not please you, then unless you are a critic you do not go to it. Not that all pleasures are necessarily lighthearted, and with luck the playgoer discovers that the theatre can create deep satisfactions even in the badlands of human experience that some playwrights are compelled to explore.

Now that the story has brought us more or less to the outskirts of modern times, it is possible to see how far the theatre has come since its ritual beginnings. Gods and religions have made war in drama, people have killed and made love in it, forces of order and revolution have spoken through it, new ideas about human society and human psychology have expressed themselves on stage, sometimes before they have been formulated in the everyday world. If today the theatre is what it has always been in the past, then it must be dealing with what matters in our century, or else it must be helping audiences to look the other way, as it did through so much of the nineteenth century. The modern playgoer is bound to wonder whether the theatre will retain the work of the present age, as it has retained the drama of fifth-century Athens, Elizabethan England, seventeenth-century France, or whether it will consign it to the archives and the academics, as it has with the 'sentimental comedy' of the eighteenth century, and the melodramas and 'well-made plays' of the nineteenth.

To illustrate the difficulty of proceeding with this chapter, before going on to proceed with it nevertheless, take the case of Stephen Phillips. Between 1900 and 1908 he had six plays presented in London, five of them in verse. His

Herod, and then his *Ulysses*, were presented by Sir Herbert Beerbohm-Tree at Her Majesty's Theatre in 1900 and 1902. On 6 March 1902, Phillips's *Paolo and Francesca* was staged by Sir George Alexander at the St James's Theatre. The next morning the critics decided unanimously that Stephen Phillips was Shakespeare's successor. Only the dissenting voice of William Archer was raised to argue that, on the contrary, the young dramatist spoke with the voice of Milton. Poetry had been restored to the theatre, they all said, about blank verse such as:

> I have fled for ever; have refused the rose
> Although my brain was reeling with the scent.
> I have come hither as through pains of death;
> I have died, and I am gazing back at life.

And:

> So still it is that we might almost hear
> The sigh of all the sleepers in the world.

Phillips was regarded as a poet-dramatist of genius, the greatest of living English playwrights. Until 1908 he enjoyed the commercial success which that status brought. By 1910, after *Nero*, *Faust*, and a prose play, *The Lost Heir*, he was almost forgotten. He died unknown and poor.

Had this chapter been written in the first decade of the twentieth century, it must have given first place to Stephen Phillips, but others would have had to be included. Bernard Shaw was a towering theatrical and literary figure. John Galsworthy, J.M. Barrie and W. Somerset Maugham (four plays running in London simultaneously in 1908) were clever, talented and much admired. Again, if this were being written between the wars, then in England I might have had to take account of J.B. Priestley (time theorist, socialist, grudgingly respected by the intelligentsia), John Drinkwater (poet-dramatist), Noel Coward (beloved by theatregoers, almost always critically abused), or James Bridie (a Scot who wrote stunning first acts). And what about R.C. Sherriff, and that brilliant writer of farces, Ben Travers? In the years immediately after the Second World War, Terence Rattigan, T.S. Eliot and Emlyn Williams were being lauded. The names of Anouilh, Cocteau and Giraudoux were similarly prominent, in London as much as in Paris. When I began my London theatre-going, in the early 1950s, the leading playwright in the English-speaking world was undoubtedly Christopher Fry. He too was greeted as Shakespeare's heir. John Gielgud, Laurence Olivier, Edith Evans and Peter Brook contributed their talents to his work. He was the subject of essays and critical analysis.

I do not mean to say that any of these are burned-out stars, but time is a severe judge of playwrights, and critical fashion a poor theatrical yardstick. Our 2500 years of theatre are not teeming with great dramatists: they are numbered in platoons, not in battalions. Yet today most contemporary theatrical histories for the years 1956–80 will insist that there are, or have been, at least fifty or sixty theatrical giants at work, from Albee and Arrabal to Weiss and Williams. That such a doubly dramatic population explosion could have taken place seems to me inherently unlikely, and I do not intend to further overcrowd the theatrical pantheon.

Nevertheless, since anybody who has an interest in the art of their time is bound to take an attitude towards it, even if only for fear of being submerged, what follows will express my view of where the growth is taking place in modern theatre. In recent years, attitudes to art have become coloured by a number of notions, one of them inane but perennial, the second modish but fraudulent, the third familiar in other guises, but always tyrannical. They are, in the same order: first, that if the individual or a group of individuals likes a play, a novel, a painting, it is therefore good; second, that if an artist says that his or her work is art, then it is art; third, that if a given work of art does not meet the requirements of a particular ideology or belief, then it is not art, or it is bad art. I see these notions as obviously false, because none of them satisfies the objective technical criteria which govern art (but do not govern self-expression) and because none of them seems to have much to do with the way the human race has chosen what to keep and what to lose in the course of time.

In trying to diagnose the state of the contemporary theatre, I have tried not to allow my personal taste to be too obtrusive and not to be overawed by fashion. I do not make out a case for any single playwright or actor or director or theatrical experience. But be warned: I am not trying to second-guess posterity either. The evidence I present will be selective, and therefore suspect. I have already omitted the drama of whole countries – Spain is the most conspicuous absence – and important figures such as Gorky, Kleist, Lorca, Marivaux, Pushkin, because their work is not in today's international repertoire or merely because the organization of a television series, and of the book that derives from it, made it inconvenient to take account of them. Yet the theatre as I have seen it all over the world in the making of this series, and as a playgoer, is diverse and all-embracing. Everywhere there is an appetite for the drama, one which has to be fed, and the result is an enormous amount of theatrical activity, impressive for its energy, invention and enthusiasm. All this is valuable for its own sake, but that does not mean that the theatre is meeting my first and most important criterion: is it dealing with what matters in our century? what has it contributed to our understanding of ourselves?

Over the centuries, successive layers of drama have built up a complex vision of human identity. The playwright, one of the secular heirs to the ancient priesthood, has been at the centre of a long process of revelation. The Greeks saw humanity as a plaything of the gods, but also as their challenger. Was man a god in his own right? Like Dionysus, god of the theatre, was man both human and divine? Throughout the ages, the drama has placed humanity at the apex of its own imaginative world, as angel, demigod, superman, tragic hero, the force which can decide to create or to destroy a moral, just and rational reality. People are painfully human, Ibsen acknowledged in the later nineteenth century, but their own aspirations could redeem them. Chekhov, writing at about the same time, saw his characters as simultaneously vulnerable and destructive, yet capable of redemption through work and the acceptance of their own fallibility. It was Strindberg who pointed to inherent psychological flaws and stubborn sexual antagonisms capable of undermining the whole structure of human personality.

The theatre in our own time has taken a new and sombre direction, and I cannot help hearing it as a powerful voice insisting that there are no gods, and that we ourselves are without divinity. Man is placed in the animal kingdom, the possessor of insatiable, compulsive appetites served by the same powers of intellect and emotion that used to be his pride. He is a homicidal predator living in a world where there is no reason and only a pretence of moral order. Nothing can be explained: our actions can be reported but not rationalized. We are an accident of random circumstance, living on the dung-heap.

I do not say that I myself take that view, but I do assert that this is the vision the theatre has projected. Never before has man held so bleak a view of himself. Honour, nobility, heroism, sacrifice – all romantic twaddle or the catchwords of cynical manipulators. There is no meaning outside the individual existence. The theatre, the drama, has not only diagnosed that condition but also has planted it as a powerful image in our minds. This concluding chapter in the history of the theatre could justifiably be entitled The Descent of Man.

Some of the impetus behind this theatrical descent comes from Strindberg – his use of dreams and nightmares, his preoccupation with a neurotic inner world. But there is always in his work the sense of a struggle for order, a battle – lost, perhaps, but still fought – for sanity. There is no one point of surrender to chaos, but the urge is unmistakable in these words of the French playwright Alfred Henri Jarry, written at the end of the nineteenth century.

> Every man is capable of showing his contempt for the cruelty and stupidity of the universe by making his own life a poem of incoherence and stupidity.

Jarry was born in Laval in 1873. When he was six, his mother deserted her husband and took her son and daughter to live in Saint-Brieuc. In 1888 Jarry entered the Rennes *lycée* and struck up a friendship with a fellow pupil, Henri Morin, whose favourite sport was baiting the physics master, Monsieur Hébert. Their victim was variously known as 'P.H.', 'Ebé' and 'Père Heb', and was soon to be immortalized as 'le père Ubu' when Jarry developed a sketch by Morin into a playlet for marionettes. A few years later this became the basis of the trilogy eventually known as *Ubu Roi*, *Ubu Cocu* (written last and published posthumously) and *Ubu Enchaîné*. Jarry was also the author of a novel, *Les Gestes et Opinions du Docteur Faustroll, Pataphysicien*, in which he invented the 'Science of Pataphysics' – 'the science of imaginary solutions' – which examined 'the laws governing exceptions and will explain the universe supplementary to this one'.

With *Ubu* Jarry broke both theatrical and social convention together. They are not first-rate plays but give the impression of still being in an experimental stage of development. Jarry employed slapstick, placards, crude pantomime. *Ubu Roi* is an outrageous parody of *Oedipus Rex* in which the language is coarse and often infantile, the action unpredictable and extreme, the characters symbolic caricatures. Man is mocked and debased, depicted as amoral and mindless.

In January 1896, Jarry met the resoundingly named Aurélien-François Lugné-Poë, actor, director and manager of the Théâtre de l'Oeuvre, in Paris, where in December *Ubu Roi* received its first performance and the audience was presented with the spectacle of the actor Firmin Gémier, playing Ubu, marching down to the footlights to bawl out 'Merdre!' By the end of the evening the stunned spectators had resorted to violence, as they had on the famous first night of Hugo's *Hernani*, only with greater provocation. Next morning the critics continued the assault and abuse in their columns. With Ubu the chief topic of café conversation and debate, Jarry was famous

Ubu Roi, by Jarry: a caricature by De Lasques after the 1908 Théâtre Antoine production.

overnight. His friends took to calling him 'Père Ubu' and he responded by adopting the language, manners and physical attributes of his fictional creation, until his early death in 1907.

Because of the starkness of his characters and the outlandish construction and brute anarchic power of his dramatic work, Jarry is sometimes described as a symbolist, and as one of the founders of a kind of drama known as the Theatre of the Absurd. In discussing his work, as in seeing his plays, neither classification is very much use. And I feel that it is worth pointing out that it is possible to spend some time – in my own case, thirty years – without ever hearing anybody who works in the theatre use the term 'Theatre of the Absurd'. It is an academic label frequently pasted on to plays most distinguished by their lack of form, and even more often of content. Jarry is important not as a 'symbolist' or 'absurdist' but as a playwright who anticipated and helped to create a nihilistic view of mankind. During this narrative, the theatre has often given the early warning of disturbances in the moral climate, as dreams may give clues to an individual's mental state. Jarry's nightmare was of mankind stripped of reason and moral purpose.

The war that started in August 1914, and which was known as 'The Great War' until subsequent events demoted it to 'The First World War', introduced our century to horror and disgust on an unprecedented scale. Humanity succumbed to a universal sickness which continues to rage, because the lesson of the Great War was that man was demonstrably mindless, savage, cruel and helpless. The theatre, like the rest of life, was infected by the idea that man could no longer make any claim to divinity, and it was to make that notion felt by means of indelibly vivid imagery. I believe that all subsequent dramatic work of the first importance has been written in the fevered sickness The Great War caused, and in reaching this conviction I am indebted to an extraordinary work of cultural history, Paul Fussell's *The Great War and Modern Memory*, in the author's words, a book 'about the British experience on the Western Front from 1914 to 1918 and some of the literary means by which it is remembered, conventionalized and mythologized'. In particular I would single out the following observations:

> ... the Great War was more ironic than any before or since. It was a hideous embarrassment to the prevailing Meliorist myth which had dominated the public consciousness for a century. It reversed the Idea of Progress....

> I am saying that there seems to be one dominating form of modern understanding; that it is essentially ironic; and that it originates largely in the application of mind and memory to the events of the Great War.

The history of the drama for the greater part of the twentieth century was the exploration of two main themes: man in conflict with the old mythology and learning that there is no escape from despair; and man against the pitiless social and technological machinery which he himself has created.

The Czech playwright, Karel Čapek, depicted man as a machine, the victim of technology, and gave the word 'robot' to the world. His ferocious satire, *R.U.R. – Rossum's Universal Robots* – was written in 1920. Three years later, the American playwright, Elmer Rice, completed *The Adding Machine*. To dramatize his concern that man was just a cipher in the rule of the machine age, he called his main protagonist, a colourless book-keeper, Mister Zero. Both these plays are pointers towards the theatre's future: recognizable reality was being abandoned in favour of means of expression that would not be consistent with rounded characters or accurately reported speech. Furthermore, the theatre was becoming unashamedly theatrical.

Hostility to all naturalism and realism was formulated by the French actor, director and poet, Antonin Artaud, who was born in 1896. In 1932 he published what he called the first manifesto of the Theatre of Cruelty – another of those generic terms which seek to define and focus on an extremely narrow band of theatrical activity. 'We cannot,' he declared, 'go on prostituting the idea of theatre whose only value is in its excruciating magical relation to reality and danger.' Artaud believed in the theatre as an instrument of devastating power, one by which people could be freed from moral restraints as they were during the great plagues of history. Here is Dionysus again, the invader, the god of licence, loosing the repressed subconscious so that audiences could see themselves as they really were. For Artaud, the drama was inside man himself: not man against the gods, or fate, or circumstance, but pitted against the forces contained in his own being.

For the last ten years of his life, Artaud was confined to a mental institution. He died in 1948. His influence was enormous, in particular on the plays of Jean Genet and Albert Camus, and on the directors Jean-Louis Barrault, Jean Vilar and Peter Brook, who all followed Artaud in his search for a new theatrical language:

> ...instead of continuing to rely upon texts considered definitive and sacred, it is essential to put an end to the subjugation of the theatre to the text, and to recover the notion of unique language half-way between gesture and thought.... It is not a question of suppressing the spoken language, but of giving words approximately the importance they have in dreams.

The text, the word, the conscious mind – these were too rigid for Artaud. Smash them and you freed the dreams they imprisoned, even if that meant the nightmares too.

There was a playwright at work in the 1920s and 1930s who may have been marginally more conventional in his formal intention than Artaud, but who was quite as radical in content. Luigi Pirandello was born in Sicily on 28 June 1867. He did not start writing for the theatre until the Great War had begun, and he too rejected narrative. 'All descriptive and narrative props should be banished from the stage,' he wrote, criticizing the practical concerns of his colleagues. For Pirandello, art was life, not a series of ideas: 'A play doesn't create people, people create a play.' He believed that the characters in a play should not be slaves to the author's plot and purposes, but free to express their individual natures, which will ultimately drive them to what he called specific actions. This belief he fulfilled in *Sei personaggi in cerca d'autore* (*Six Characters in Search of an Author*), written in 1921. In this play he invented the 'theatre within a theatre', and provided a metaphor for the shifting nature of personality by dramatizing the ambivalent relationship between the actors and the characters they play. The play is part of a trilogy: its companions are *Ciascuno suo modo* (*Each in His Own Way*) and *Questa sera si recita soggeto* (*Tonight We Improvise*).

More central to the modern movement is Pirandello's tragedy *Enrico Quattro* (*Henry IV*, 1922), perhaps his masterpiece. Its hero has suffered a riding accident while playing a character in a pageant, and lives under the delusion that he is that character. Eventually he recovers, but chooses to pretend to be mad, and goes on living as if he were the eleventh-century king. Figures from the past re-appear in his life, and play along with the illusion. One of them is the man who caused the original riding accident, Baron Belcredi, another is a love from the past, the Marchioness Matilda Spina, who guesses the pretence. When the 'king' kills Belcredi, he is condemned to continuing his masquerade or being found guilty of murder. His plight is a perfect metaphor for Pirandello's view of the futility of our notions of character and the impossibility of achieving a truly integrated personality.

In 1934, two years before he died, Pirandello was awarded the Nobel Prize for Literature, and in him the prize committee found a playwright whose influence was to prove deep and long-lasting. His pessimism may be detected in the work of Jean Anouilh and Jean-Paul Sartre, and in the plays of Eugene Ionesco and Samuel Beckett. In 1920 he wrote this comment on his philosophy and his art:

> I think that life is a very sad piece of buffoonery; because we have in ourselves, without being able to know why, wherefore or whence, the need to deceive ourselves constantly by creating a reality ... which from time to time is discovered to be vain and illusory ... My art is full of bitter compassion for all those who deceive themselves; but this compassion cannot fail to be followed by the ferocious derision of destiny which condemns man to deception.

He died in Rome on 10 December 1936, requesting in his will that there should be no public ceremony, only 'a hearse of the poor, the horse and the coachman'.

As a corrective to this account, it must be remembered that Jarry and Artaud were a long way from the mainstream of theatrical life. Even Pirandello, who had an international reputation, was forced to close his Teatro d'Arte in Rome because it lost too much money. Yet all over Europe the theatre thrived and

Richard Burbage (c1530–1597)

Edward Alleyn (1566–1626)

Anne Oldfield (1683–1730)

Kitty Clive (1711–1785)

Peg Woffington (c1714–1760)

David Garrick (1717–1779)

Although actors remain, by temperament and by choice, rogues and vagabonds; although society's attitude towards them remains largely equivocal: their legends are prone to outlive them. And of those, what follows is purely a personal selection.

Friedrich Schröder (1744–1816)

Sarah Siddons (1755–1831)

Edmund Kean (1787/90–1833)

George Frederick Cooke (1756–1812)　　William Macready (1793–1873)　　Elisa Rachel (1820–1858)

Sir Henry Irving (1838–1905)

Jean Mounet-Sully (1841–1916)

Ellen Terry, D.B.E. (1847–1928)

Sir Johnston Forbes-Robertson
(1853–1937)

Eleonora Duse (1858–1924)

Marie Tempest, D.B.E. (1864–1942)

Sir Gerald du Maurier (1873–1934)

John Barrymore (1882–1942)

Sybil Thorndike, D.B.E. (1882–1976)

Edith Evans, D.B.E. (1888–1976)

Helen Hayes (1900–)

Katherine Cornell (1898–1974)

Eugene Leontovich (1900–)

Helene Weigel (1900–1971)

Sir Ralph Richardson (1902–)

Madeleine Renaud (1903–)

Sir Donald Wolfit (1902–1968)

Sir John Gielgud (1904–)

Lord Olivier (1907–)

Peggy Ashcroft, D.B.E. (1907–)

Sir Michael Redgrave (1908–)

Jean-Louis Barrault (1910–)

Lee J. Cobb (1911–1976)

Sir Michael Hordern (1911–)

Sir Alec Guinness (1914–)

Zero Mostel (1915–1977)

Paul Scofield (1922–)

Margaret Leighton (1922–1976)

Alan Badel (1923–1982)

James Earl Jones (1931–)

Peter O'Toole (1933–)

Alan Bates (1934–)

Maggie Smith (1934–)

Albert Finney (1936–)

Tom Courtenay (1937–)

Vanessa Redgrave (1937–)

Luigi Pirandello (1867–1936).

playgoers had a varied diet to choose from. In this century and most noticeably in recent years there has been a curious separation between what might be called Serious-Popular and Serious-Esoteric Theatre, sustained and encouraged by an awful snobbery which makes many critics and academics disdain what is available and engrossing, but champion what is obscure and rarefied. Throughout his career, from his first success, *The Vortex*, in 1924, when he was twenty-five years old, until his death in 1973, Noel Coward, the author of at least two classic comedies of manners, was constantly belittled, and yet he was a brilliant and vastly popular playwright, as well as an actor, lyricist and composer. (Perhaps it was this suspect versatility that condemned him.) Coward's career exemplifies the fact that the majority of playgoers (or readers, viewers, listeners) may be perfectly prepared to be enlightened, but they also want to be entertained; faced with a choice between the two, they go for entertainment, and the preference is not shameful.

The academic prejudice against what is popular may spring from the age-old suspicion that the theatre is not respectable, and is certainly backed by an excessively high valuation of the academic qualities themselves, in particular

Noel Coward (1899–1973), with Gertrude Lawrence in his *Private Lives*, at the Phoenix Theatre, London, in 1930.

the literacy of long sentences, long words and complex cultural references. In minds of that cast, only the printed word, the text that lends itself to theory, interpretation and dissertation, can raise real interest. I take an opposite view. It is not really my concern whether a play is literature. What matters most to me is that it should work in the theatre, acted by live actors in front of a live audience. If the necessary mystery takes place, then the play succeeds. Of course I also care, and admittedly care more, about plays which catch or illuminate the human condition, but I see them as part of a dramatic spectrum, not as mutually exclusive. The modern 'serious' theatre was not born in a culture-dish; it owes a lot, especially in England, to the popular theatre which was responsible for keeping alive the habit of theatre-going and a sense of professional standards.

When I entered the theatre in 1953, the English popular theatre was ruled from an office at the top of the Globe Theatre in Shaftesbury Avenue. From his managing director's desk at H.M. Tennent Ltd, Hugh 'Binkie' Beaumont commanded an empire. He presented a great variety of plays, and believed passionately in star actors, elegant sets and costumes, well-tried formula plays and sumptuous revivals. All the leading actors of the day worked for him – John Gielgud, Ralph Richardson, Michael Redgrave, Edith Evans, Alec Guinness, Peggy Ashcroft, Paul Scofield and a host of others. He produced all-star revivals of Shakespeare, Molière, Congreve, Ibsen, Wilde and Chekhov. He presented the plays of Noel Coward, Terence Rattigan and Christopher Fry. It was Binkie Beaumont who helped to make London's West End theatre shine again after the Second World War. The audience was middle-class and upwards, yet young people without much money could see the theatre's classics superbly staged and acted.

To enter this dazzling West End world, an aspiring actor had to be properly trained. He or she had to learn to speak what was then called 'standard' or 'received' English – received with proper deference by those who did not speak it! – and it was necessary to move gracefully and to be charming. The Royal Academy of Dramatic Art produced something called the 'RADA voice', which implied a mannered artificiality of tone. RADA had been founded by Sir Kenneth Barnes in 1906, and the institution had produced many of England's leading players. Sir Kenneth was still Principal when I entered the Academy in 1952, and the teaching methods were not much different from those employed in its earliest years. Sir Kenneth wanted his students to be ladies and gentlemen; the atmosphere was like a Finishing School for Gentlefolk.

Of course there were other influences at work. South of the River Thames, Michel Saint-Denis, Glen Byam Shaw and George Devine had founded the Old Vic School. Here another approach to the art of acting was offered – more serious, and perhaps more intellectual. Certainly the emphasis was on the inner life of characters and plays, and not on acting for effect; the ideal was the company, not the star. Saint-Denis was a brilliant trainer of actors, and a great influence on English acting generally. Yet the Old Vic School seemed to be preparing students for a theatre that was either foreign or not yet born. Opposition to its methods was vociferous and effective, and the school was forced to close in 1951. But the theatrical establishment, from RADA to H.M. Tennent, was soon to change, under the impact of a number of different events.

Shortly after I left the Academy in 1953, Sir Kenneth was gone, and so were the ladies and gentlemen. A new and alarming breed of student suddenly appeared. Three of them exemplify the change: Albert Finney, Peter O'Toole and Tom Courtenay. They did not worry much about perfectly-formed vowels or Standard English, and they stuck to their regional accents, mostly northern. It was as if they were training for a very different kind of theatre from the one presided over by Binkie Beaumont.

Beaumont was a great theatrical producer, but he had a flaw that was to prove fatal: he could not see around the status quo. For example he did not raise his voice against the archaic official called the Lord Chamberlain, who still had to vet all plays. Beaumont's own taste was for plays that were safe and comforting, and in which he could parade his stars; the classics were palatable because they offered such good parts to leading actors. The theatre is too volatile a medium to be stagnant for long. By the mid-1950s, it was ready to take off again.

On the night of 3 August 1955 an audience assembled at the Arts Theatre, Great Newport Street, in London, to see Peter Hall's production of a play which had got there by an unusual route. It had been written by an Irishman in French and translated by him into English. When first performed at the Théâtre de Babylone in Paris it caused a *succès de scandale* which was to be repeated in countries throughout the world. The play was *En attendant Godot*, and was translated by its author, Samuel Beckett, as *Waiting for Godot*. It helped to change not only the face of the theatre, but also its heart and soul. In *Waiting for Godot*, the forces of Jarry, Artaud and Pirandello converged. If Jarry's statement that every man is capable of making his own life a poem of incoherence and stupidity is to be taken literally, then *Godot* bears it out. If Pirandello's pessimism needed a more piercing voice, *Godot* was a cry of despair. If Artaud's search for a language halfway between gesture and thought had halted, then *Godot* pursued and fulfilled it.

The unforgettable images of Samuel Beckett: *Waiting for Godot*.

Précis is a clumsy instrument for describing narrative plays; for a non-naturalistic play such as *Waiting for Godot* it is especially awkward. Beckett describes the setting as 'A country road. A tree.' (The starkness of the description sets the mood.) Two tramps, Vladimir and Estragon, are the principal figures. They are waiting for someone called Godot, talking aimlessly and sometimes exchanging music-hall crosstalk. Time passes. A master, Pozzo, enters with his servant, Lucky. A boy brings messages to say that Mr Godot is unable to keep his appointment. The effect is cumulative. One is aware that the play is richly symbolic, but one cannot be certain of what. There is a sense that the climax is being deliberately and eternally delayed. The ending is full of the terrible irony that Paul Fussell diagnoses.

Vladimir: Well? Shall we go?
Estragon: Yes, let's go.
      (*They do not move.*)

CURTAIN

The effect is one of doom and despair with no hope of redemption. Futility is the clarion of modern drama. The reception that greeted *Waiting for Godot* veered between bewilderment and outrage. Some theatregoers thought it was a hoax. The critics complained that nothing happened. Beckett kept silent and offered no clues. His work was his statement.

Before *Godot*, Samuel Beckett was best known as a novelist. He was born in 1906 in Foxrock, a suburb of Dublin, and became Reader in English at the Ecole Normale Supérieure in Paris in 1928. In Paris he became part of the circle around his fellow countryman, the novelist James Joyce. After a return to Ireland in 1930, and several years of restless travel, in 1937 he settled in France. *Waiting for Godot* (1952) was his first play. Those that followed, and notably *Endgame* (1957), *Krapp's Last Tape* (1959) and *Happy Days* (1961), all work at a similar level of abstraction and all perform variations on the theme of futility. In 1969 Beckett was awarded the Nobel Prize for Literature.

The West End of Binkie Beaumont would have been astonished by that award, just as it was taken aback, but tried to ignore the event, when *Waiting for Godot* transferred to the Criterion Theatre. Yet it was *Godot* that laid the basis of the upheaval that was to come. Theatrically, the play was original because, in Artaud's terms, Beckett's language between gesture and thought was akin to the way Impressionist painters constructed their images. I believe that the theatre has made its greatest impact on the late twentieth century through stark, unforgettable imagery. It is not the words of plays that we now remember, but their visual imprint. Beckett was the first to demonstrate a new way of experiencing the theatre.

All through this century, as if by an unspoken agreement, the theatre was being prepared for change. In design, Gordon Craig, who was twenty-eight years old in 1900, echoed Artaud and Jarry in his *The Art of the Theatre*, originally published as a booklet in 1905:

The first dramatist understood what the modern dramatist does not yet understand. He knew that when he and his fellows appeared in front of them, the audience would be more eager to *see* what he would do than *hear* what he might say.

Craig, like the playwrights, dispensed with realism and favoured a setting more symbolic of the play as a whole, and therefore bound to be more abstract. He was an outcast in his own day, and lived out his years in self-imposed exile in France, but today his methods are generally accepted, and have enabled playwrights and directors to move the action rapidly and to smash the restrictions of space and time. This liberation from the old naturalistic tyranny was backed by startling advances in lighting. Adolphe Appia, a Swiss stage designer and pioneer of stage lighting following the invention of incandescent light bulbs in 1879, created the concept of light enhancing the play and enabling the actor to occupy his own illuminated space. The drama was being concentrated on the conflicts and tensions present in the individual.

Symbols, abstract settings, the use of light, visual imagery – taken together these represent a revolution in style. But the contemporary theatre had other revolutions in store, and one of them was political, didactic theatre, the theatre of polemics. Bernard Shaw, going some steps beyond the earlier 'social' plays of Ibsen, was the forerunner of the preacher-dramatist. He expounded his socialist views in brilliantly contrived arguments, witty dialogue, and with a sense of fairness which now seems quite old-fashioned. He stands like a father-figure over contemporary political drama, which has almost exclusively embraced the progressive thought of the century, in most of its varieties from apocalyptic to dogmatic. The effect of some of these plays has been to make an evening at the theatre feel like a session of the Inquisition, with the audience on the rack, but as I have already suggested, theatrical pleasures are not necessarily measured in smiles.

The loudest and most gifted voice of the political theatre belongs to Bertolt Brecht, who was born in Augsburg, Bavaria, in 1898. His military service in The Great War made him a pacifist for the rest of his life. In the late 1920s the influence of the great theatrical director Erwin Piscator and the rise of National Socialism were two of the forces which led him to become a Marxist. But for a pacifist and a man who claimed concern for humanity, Brecht's life and work betray contradictions whose own 'alienation effect' is as great as any that he produced in accordance with his famous theatrical theory. There are episodes in his life which force even lovers of his work to see him with a highly critical eye. At the time of the Stalinist trials conducted in Moscow in the mid-1930s, Brecht said of the accused: 'The more innocent they are, the more they deserve to die.' Yet it was the very innocence of the Gestapo's victims in Germany that most outraged him in anti-Nazi plays like *The Informer*. When his own mistress, the actress Carola Neher, was arrested in the Soviet Union, Brecht failed to intervene on her behalf. She was never seen

Mother Courage at the Deutsches Theater, Berlin. Helene Weigel stands in the title role. *Right* the author, her husband, Bertolt Brecht (1898–1956).

again. Since none of the other dramatists who appear in these pages faced dilemmas of this kind in their own lives, it is impossible, of course, to say that they would have behaved any better than Brecht. But these episodes serve as a further reminder that it is misguided to draw conclusions about a playwright's life from the content of his plays.

Through his theory of 'alienation' (the *'Verfremdungseffekt'*) Brecht looked for a way to disengage the audience from its emotional involvement with the action so that it could take a more rational view of what happened on stage. He wanted his audience to be entertained, but he also wanted them detached and critical, and used a variety of devices to interrupt the action and destroy the theatrical illusion. The loss of self was not what Brecht was aiming at. He also wrote about his ideas of 'Epic Theatre', and here he takes the example of what he called 'The Street Scene':

> ... an eyewitness demonstrating to a collection of people how a traffic accident took place. The bystanders may not have observed what happened, or they may simply not agree with him, may 'see things a different way'; the point is that the demonstrator acts the behaviour of the driver or victim or both in such a way that the bystanders are able to form an opinion about the accident.

Brecht's friend Walter Benjamin described the purpose of 'Epic Theatre', but showed how far Brecht meant to be from solemn propagandizing:

> It is less concerned with filling the public with feelings, even seditious ones, than with alienating it in an enduring manner, through thinking, from the conditions in which it lives. It may be noted by the way that there is no better start for thinking than laughter.

I have argued that the theatre removes the audience from the sphere of everyday life and into a wider one; Brecht's notion of alienating the public 'from the conditions in which it lives' came too close to the ancient function of the theatre not to have results quite different from what he anticipated.

In 1928 Brecht collaborated with the composer Kurt Weill on an adaptation of John Gay's *The Beggar's Opera* which he called *Die Dreigroschenoper* (*The Threepenny Opera*). It brought him his first public success. He had to leave Germany in 1933, and lived in Switzerland, Denmark, Finland and then the USSR before going to California in 1941. His finest plays belong to that American exile; during it he wrote *Mutter Courage und ihre Kinder* (*Mother Courage and Her Children*, 1941), *Leben des Galilei* (*The Life of Galileo*, 1943), and *Der gute Mensch von Sezuan* (*The Good Woman of Setzuan*, 1943).

Brecht's influence has been extensive, so much so that it seems to have been totally absorbed, for paradoxically the genius of the playwright defeated the aim of the theorist. Ernest Bournemann assessed these contradictions:

> Every device which he used to destroy the 'magic' of theatre became magic in his hands. The exposed stage lights, far from alienating us, communicated all of Brecht's love for the stage ... The very rhythm of interruptions became a poetic pattern and destroyed the purpose for which they had ostensibly been conceived.

And:

> The tragedy of Brecht's life boils down to this simple fact: he gained the admiration and respect of those whom he professed to despise – the poets, the intellectuals, the West; and he failed to gain the one audience for whom he claimed to write: the working class, the Party, the East.

What Brecht had not understood was that audiences *know* they are in the theatre, *know* this is not real life, that they enjoy the theatre's metaphors and pretences rather than being deluded by them. The theatre does not destroy the critical understanding that Brecht wanted; it expands that understanding by combining it with feeling and imagination.

The forces of twentieth-century drama were gathering strength, and although the bursts of theatrical energy which we have been observing tend not to occur in the same place twice, I have to argue that England is an exception. (Since England is where I live and work, and I obviously stand to be accused of adoptive chauvinism, I would point out that the playwrights I am about to discuss are translated and played all over the world, as leading figures in the international repertoire.) At about the same time that Beckett was being discussed and Brecht defended – in England, principally by the drama critic Kenneth Tynan – and when the new breed of actors were on the point of hatching, George Devine, one of the Old Vic School triumvirate, founded the English Stage Company. He wanted a theatre for new plays, and he took the Royal Court in Sloane Square, which happened to be where many of Bernard Shaw's plays were first performed. In May 1956 the company presented *Look Back in Anger*.

John Osborne's play was the focus of what was either a genuine theatrical explosion, or at the very least an extremely loud bang, and an historical turning-point for the theatre. Jimmy Porter, the hero of *Look Back in Anger*, gave voice to the frustrations, the unhappiness and sense of desperation of a whole generation. The phrase 'Angry Young Man' became current, and was thought of as standing for leftish politics, yet the play may have been misinterpreted at the time. There is a sense of loss inherent in the piece that was not then remarked upon, and Osborne, along with other so-called young angries like the novelists Kingsley Amis and John Braine, has since emerged as a rather conservative voice in English culture.

Look Back in Anger by Osborne, premiered in 1956 at the Royal Court Theatre, London, with Alan Bates, Kenneth Haigh and Mary Ure.

The English Stage Company helped to change not only the theatrical but also the political climate. The Royal Court spawned a host of new playwrights, among them John Arden, Edward Bond, David Storey and Arnold Wesker. Some were good, others not, but all were highly praised, not so much for the quality of their dramatic writing but because they conformed to a shifting centre of power in European society. An obsession with class, social conditions, and the destruction of the old order, was the badge of the new wave. The class of person about whom it was possible to write plays had changed again; what was not changed was the class of person who visited the theatre. In one sense, the Royal Court preached to the converted. The theatre continued to be filled by the middle class that seemed to enjoy watching plays in which the middle class was ritually jumped on. Hugh Beaumont may have been swept away, but his audience remained loyal, at least to the habit of theatre-going.

The Lord Chamberlain's long theatrical censorship came to an end in 1968. Dionysus lost his leash. Nudity, uninhibited language and political satire broke out. Yet, in the 'serious' theatre, a censorship quite as severe as any imposed by the Lord Chamberlain now came into force. Plays had to be 'committed' (so did actors, directors and scene designers) or 'pertinent' or else they were nothing. The new wave made Binkie Beaumont's exclusivity appear positively ecumenical. Peter Ustinov observed that the critics had become more avant-garde than the playwrights.

Two years after the inauguration of the Royal Court, another playwright raised his voice, far away from the West End and some distance even from Sloane Square. Not many ears were listening when Harold Pinter's *The Birthday Party* came to the Lyric Theatre, Hammersmith, in 1958. The play received disastrous notices from every critic except Harold Hobson, writing in the *Sunday Times*. Like John Osborne, Pinter was an actor, and perhaps accustomed to facing the critical muzak. Two years later, *The Caretaker*, one of the finest plays in English since the war, was produced and acclaimed. Since then, Pinter has written, among other works, *The Homecoming* (1964), *Old Times* (1971), *No Man's Land* (1975), *Betrayal* (1978) and *A Kind of Alaska* (1983). While there is no denying that his work is part of the framework of the modern theatre – he acknowledges the influence of both Strindberg and Pirandello – somehow he is also outside it. In critical studies he is often coupled with Samuel Beckett, but his theatrical ancestry may be older and more surprising, for Pinter – like the Greek dramatists, and more powerfully than any other contemporary playwright – expresses the irrational impulse in man's affairs. His sparse and poetic use of language, sinister silences and remarkable theatrical instinct for subterranean violence and grinding tension serve to dramatize the inarticulate and to show what cannot be merely explained.

I have identified the sources of modern drama in Ibsen and Strindberg, and described how to their achievements were bonded the work of Jarry, Artaud,

Pinter's *The Caretaker*, at the National Theatre in 1980, with Jonathan Pryce and Warren Mitchell.

Pirandello and Beckett, and the political insights of Shaw and Brecht. It is a shambling sort of figure I am describing, wandering across a desolate theatrical landscape, given to bursts of frenzy, intervals of black depression, and flashes of ruthless intelligence. Paradoxically, the management of this lawless figure has brought to centre-stage a complementary law-giver – the director. All over Europe and the United States the director's theatre flourishes. In an age when the ensemble is the ideal, in forms as various as Brecht's and Helene Weigel's Berliner Ensemble, Peter Brook's nomadic companies, and our own Royal Shakespeare and National theatres, the director is a seeming paradox, the dictator among the democrats. While paying great respect to living dramatists, directors more often than not subject the classical repertoire to the sort of treatment for which the old actor-managers are rightly criticized. Occasionally they usurp the role of author, to present their own theatrical vision without an orthodox dramatic text.

Directors are comparative theatrical newcomers, still exploring their powers. It is only since the Second World War that they have really proliferated. Egoism is their vice, but then it is the occupational disease of the theatre. Their virtues are many. They can give coherence to the performance, and unity to the interpretation, like a good conductor. They can bring invention and excitement to the stage. Best of all, they can create an atmosphere in which it is possible for actors to act.

This century has been particularly rich in the number and quality of its leading actors and actresses. The new breed who inhabited the Royal Court were not to have it all their own way. It was an actor born in 1907 who made the old theatre, Binkie Beaumont's theatre, face the brave new world when Laurence Olivier played Archie Rice in John Osborne's *The Entertainer*, produced at the Royal Court in 1957. In doing that, he seemed to bless the new generation, for it was Olivier who became the first Artistic Director of England's National Theatre and gave its hospitality to the contemporary drama. He was also ennobled, becoming a life peer in 1970 – the 1st Lord Rogue and Vagabond, inside the gates.

The National Theatre, with its three auditoria, is an example, if not an acme, of modern theatre building. Yet it can be seen as the misconceived result of pioneering work undertaken in the 1920s by William Poel, who fought against the ornate productions of Shakespeare and declamatory style of acting which were still popular. Poel wanted a simpler, more direct form of staging, a theatrical shape that harked back to the sixteenth-century Globe Theatre. Harley Granville-Barker and Tyrone Guthrie were Poel's heirs. They helped to dismantle the proscenium arch, so long the conventional frame of all forms of theatrical presentation. The audience need no longer feel that they were watching separate, formally grand events. The drama was being pushed out among them. Thrust stages, apron stages and theatre-in-the-round have become familiar in the United States, Canada, and all over Europe.

The greatest moments of theatrical activity occur when none of the constituent elements – plays, actors, directors, scenic effects, buildings – vie for supremacy, or when they have wrestled each other into a balance. To harness three of Dionysus' elements into a truism, when good actors act in good plays, great theatre emerges, something fierce and lively. Has that happened in our time? Have we experienced a dramatic explosion to rank with some of those described in this history? Or has the theatre been caught up in a flux of ominous events which it could neither foresee nor influence? The answers are locked, as we are locked, in the confines of our own involvement and our inability to distance ourselves in time. In any case, no matter how the future may see the present, I believe that the theatre of our own century has once again proved its power as a means towards understanding ourselves and the nature of our existence, but also as an end in itself, one of the vital forms of pleasure and creativity.

The theatre has the ability to change society, which is why it is scrutinized by democratic states and regimented by totalitarian ones. It also has the power occasionally to bless society, and a mysterious gift of revealing, anticipating or altering the collective consciousness. Strangely, it does not require a great mass of people to be present when these changes take place. A play does not need to be a great commercial success to turn the world upside-down. It may be seen at first by comparatively few people, yet it can affect the lives of entire nations. Television and the cinema, blunter instruments, have been indelibly influenced by what has happened in the modern theatre. But the bleak view of humanity that has been projected appears, to my eyes at least, to be changing, as though the theatre has begun to respect the past, not condemn it.

Fortunately for the theatre, it does not have to keep pushing to the edge of human experience. It must be remembered that the most popular forms of theatre are light comedy, farce, murder mystery and musical comedy – the musical without a message. These are some of the ways audiences enjoy themselves, and since that too calls for work and vitality, it belongs to this theatre which I have been trying to describe and celebrate. There is no exclusive form of theatre. It is not now, and never has been, the preserve of some intellectual minority. Academics may visit now and then, but it is not theirs either, and is not to be judged by literary standards. In the first instance, the playgoer comes not in order to understand a play, but to experience it. If we needed a test of theatrical response, it would be judged not by analysis but by enjoyment.

There is no one form of theatre – I have to repeat this – if the play works, it is valid. And plays are working everywhere: on the fringe, off Broadway, off-off Broadway, private and nationalized, avant-garde and commercial. The theatre, the drama, crude ritual or sophisticated production, is something we need. It reinforces our lives. It is not possible to guarantee that a visit to the theatre will capture its energy and excitement, but that uncertainty is part of the excitement that the audience has to contribute. For a theatre audience is no passive receiver. It has its own role to play. Each particular performance is a gamble, uncertain and dangerous. Of course there are dull and mechanical performances, but there are also those in which the audience lights on an experience that stays forever. That is the mystery that the theatre has preserved in all its transformations: enter it, and you can take out more than you took in.

BIBLIOGRAPHY

GENERAL

Burton, E.J., *The Student's Guide to World Theatre* (London, 1962).
Gascoigne, Bamber, *World Theatre* (London, 1968).
Hartnoll, Phyllis (ed.), *The Oxford Companion to the Theatre* (Oxford, 1972).
Nicoll, Allardyce, *World Drama* (London, 1976).
Speaight, Robert, *Shakespeare on the Stage* (London, 1973).

MAKERS OF MAGIC

Brandon, James R., *Theatre in Southeast Asia* (Harvard, 1967).
Frazer, J.G., *The Illustrated Golden Bough* (ed. Mary Douglas) (13 vols, London, 1978).
Hunt, Hugh, *The Live theatre: An introduction to the history and practice of the stage* (Oxford, 1962).
Rudgeway, W., *Dramas and Dramatic Dances of non-European Races* (Cambridge, 1915).
Schechner, Richard, *Environmental Theatre* (New York, 1973).
Sheldon, Cheney, *The Theatre: 3000 years of drama, acting and stagecraft* (London, 1952).
De Zoete, Beryl & Spies, Walter, *Dance and Drama in Bali* (Oxford, 1973).

ENTER DIONYSUS

Allen, James Turney, *Stage Antiquities of the Greeks and Romans and Their Influence* (New York, 1963).
Bieber, Margarete, *The History of the Greek and Roman Theater* 2nd edn (Princeton, 1971).
Bowra, C.M., *The Greek Experience* (London, 1957).
Dodds, E.R., *The Greeks and the Irrational* (Berkeley, 1951).
Kitto, H.D.F. *Greek Tragedy* (London, 1950).
Kott, Jan, *The Eating of the Gods* (London, 1974).
Pickard-Cambridge, Sir Arthur, *The Dramatic Festivals of Athens* (Oxford, 1953).
Shorter, Alan W., *Everyday Life in Ancient Egypt* (London, 1932).
Webster, T.B.L., *Greek Theatre Production* (London, 1956).

NOW COMES MY COMEDY

Dover, K.J., *Aristophanic Comedy* (Berkeley & Los Angeles, 1972).
George E., *The Nature of Roman Comedy* (Princeton, 1971).
Hope, Thomas, *Costumes of the Greeks and Romans* (New York, 1962).

MYSTERIES

Chambers, E.K., *The Mediaeval Stage*, 2 vols (Oxford, 1903).
Edwards, Francis, *Ritual and Drama* (London, 1976).
Hardison, O.B., *Christian Rite and Christian Drama in the Middle Ages* (Baltimore, 1965).
Kolve, V.A., *The Play Called Corpus Christi* (Stanford, 1966).
Nicoll, Allardyce, *Masks, Mimes and Miracles* (London, 1931).

Purvis, J.S., *The York Cycle of Mystery Plays* (London, 1957).
Southern, Richard, *The Medieval Theatre in the Round* (London, 1957).
Taylor, Jeremy & Nelson, Alan H. (eds), *Medieval English Drama: Essays Critical and Contextual* (Chicago & London, 1972).
Tydeman, William, *The Theatre in the Middle Ages* (Cambridge, 1978).
Wickham, Glynne, *Early English Stages 1300–1660*, 3 vols (London, 1959–1980).
——*The Mediaeval Theatre* (London, 1974).

A MUSE OF FIRE

Chambers, E.K., *The Elizabethan Stage* (4 vols, Oxford, 1923).
Halliday, F.E., *A Shakespeare Companion* (London, 1952).
Harrison, G.B., *Elizabethan Plays and Players* (London, 1940).
Holmes, Martin, *Shakespeare and His Players* (London, 1972).
Rowse, A.L., *The Elizabethan Renaissance: The Life of the Society* (New York, 1971).
Salingar, Leo, *Shakespeare and the Traditions of Comedy* (Cambridge, 1974).
Schoenbaum, S., *William Shakespeare: A Compact Documentary Life* (New York, 1977).

SUCH STUFF AS DREAMS ARE MADE ON

Bentley, Gerald Eades (writer of introduction), *A Book of Masques* (Cambridge, 1967).
Gibbons, Brian, *Jacobean City Comedy* (London, 1968).
Gurr, Andrew, *The Shakespearean Stage, 1574–1642* (Cambridge, 1980).
Hibbard, George (ed.), *The Elizabethan Theatre VII* (London, 1980).
Jung, Carl G., *Man and His Symbols* (London, 1964).
Nicoll, Allardyce, *Stuart Masques and the Renaissance Stage* (London, 1937).
Noyes, Robert Gale, *Ben Jonson on the English Stage 1660–1776* (New York, 1935).
Orgel, Stephen & Strong, Roy, *Inigo Jones. The Theatre of the Stuart Court* (2 vols, London, 1973).

THE VICES OF MANKIND

Arnott, Peter D., *An Introduction to the French Theatre* (London, 1977).
Brereton, Geoffrey, *French Comic Drama from the Sixteenth to the Eighteenth Century* (London, 1977).
——*French Tragic Drama in the Sixteenth and Seventeenth Centuries* (London, 1973).
Bryant, Arthur, *King Charles II* (London, 1931).
Fraser, Antonia, *King Charles II* (London, 1979).
Huxley, Aldous, *The Devils of Loudon* (London, 1952).
Lawrenson, T.E., *The French Stage in the Seventeenth Century* (Manchester, 1957).
Moore, W.G., *Molière: A New Criticism* (Oxford, 1962).
——*The Classical Drama of France* (Oxford, 1971).

SILK STOCKINGS AND WHITE BOSOMS

Hazlitt, William, *Dramatic Essays* (ed. Archer and Lowe) (London, 1895).
Holland, Peter David, *The Ornament of Action* (Cambridge, 1979).
Howarth, W.D. (ed.), *Comic Drama, the European Heritage* (London, 1978).
Little, David M. & Kahrl, George M. (eds), *The Letters of David Garrick* (London, 1963).
Morgan, Fidelis, *The Female Wits, Women Playwrights of the Restoration* (London, 1981).
Nicoll, Allardyce, *The Garrick Stage* (Manchester, 1980).
Smith, G. Gregory (ed.), *The Diary of Samuel Pepys* (London, 1929).

A WORLD TURNED UPSIDE-DOWN

Hamerow, Theodore S., *Restoration, Revolution, Reaction* (Princeton, 1958).
Irving, Laurence, *Henry Irving* (London, 1951).
Lewes, George Henry, *On Actors and the Art of Acting* (London, 1875).
Mayer, David (ed.), *Henry Irving and The Bells* (Manchester, 1980)
Pascal, Roy, *The German Sturm und Drang* (Manchester, 1953).
Price, Victor, *The Plays of Georg Büchner* (with introduction) (Oxford, 1971).
Prudhoe, John, *The Theatre of Goethe and Schiller* (Oxford, 1973).
Steiner, George, *The Death of Tragedy* (London, 1961).

THE MASTER BUILDERS

Craig, Edward, *Gordon Craig* (London, 1968).
Downs, Brian W., *Ibsen, the Intellectual Background* (Cambridge, 1946).
Marker, Frederick J. & Lise-Lone, *The Scandinavian Theatre: A Short History* (Oxford, 1975).
Meyer, Michael, *Henrik Ibsen* (3 vols, London, 1967, 1971).
——(ed.) August Strindberg, *The Plays (with introductions)* (London, 1975).
Pearson, Hesketh, *Bernard Shaw* (London, 1942).
——*G.B.S. A Postscript* (London, 1951).
Shaw, George Bernard, *Our Theatre in the Nineties* (3 vols, London, 1932).
——*The Quintessence of Ibsenism* (London, 1922).
Wilson, Colin, *Bernard Shaw* (London, 1969).

THE ACTORS DO NOT UNDERSTAND

Hunt, Hugh, *The Abbey: Ireland's National Theatre, 1904–1979* (Dublin, 1979).
Magarshack, David, *Chekhov the Dramatist* (London, 1980).
Nemirovich-Danchenko, Vladimir, *My Life in the Russian Theatre* (trans. John Cournos) (London, 1968).
O Haodha, Micheal, *The Abbey – Then and Now* (Dublin, 1969).

Stanislavsky, Constantin, *My Life in Art* (trans. J.J. Robbins) (London, 1924).
——*An Actor Prepares* (trans. E.R. Hapgood) (London, 1937).
Toumanova, Princess Nina Androikova, *Anton Chekhov* (London, 1937).

RAZZMATAZZ AND REALISM

Clurman, Harold, *The Fervent Years – The Story of the Group Theatre* (New York, 1945).
Connelly, Marc, *Voices Offstage* (New York, 1968).
Hewitt, Barnard, *Theatre U.S.A., 1668–1957* (New York, 1959).
Houseman, John, *Run-through* (London, 1973).
——*Front and Center* (New York, 1979).
Hughes, Glenn, *A History of the American Theater, 1700–1950* (New York, 1951).
Playfair, Giles, *Kean* (London, 1939).
Ruggles, Eleanor, *Prince of Players, Edwin Booth* (London, 1953).

ADMIT ME, CHORUS, TO THIS HISTORY

Artaud, Antonin, *The Theatre and Its Double* (London, 1970).
Bablet, Denis, *The Theatre of Edward Gordon Craig* (London, 1981).
Bell, Michael, *Primitivism* (London, 1972).
Bentley, Eric (ed.), *The Theory of the Modern Stage* (London, 1968).
Elsom, John, *Post-War British Theatre Criticism* (London, 1981).
Fussell, Paul, *The Great War and Modern Memory* (Oxford, 1979).
Inness, Christopher, *Holy Theatre* (Cambridge, 1981).
Saint-Denis, Michel, *Training for the Theatre* (London, 1982).
Trewin, J.C., *The Theatre Since 1900* (London, 1951).
Watson-Taylor, Simon, Introduction to *The Ubu Plays* (London, 1968).

NOTES AND SOURCES

Page

MAKERS OF MAGIC

13 'the theatre ... take place'/Interviewed by the author for *All the World's a Stage*.

16 ... at the beginning ... life./ibid.

17–18 'The pygmies ... and so on.'/Colin Wilson, *The Occult* (1971), p. 143.

34 'the Balinese sideways glance'/In de Zoete and Spies, *Dance and Drama in Bali* (1973), p. 170. Willing suspension ... poetic faith'/Coleridge, *Biographia Litteraria*, ch. XIV.

35 'When an actor ... the part.'/Interviewed by the author for *All the World's a Stage*.

ENTER DIONYSUS

38 'I think ... in art.'/Interviewed by the author for *All the World's a Stage*.

41 They were ... bare hands./Euripides, *Bacchae*, tr. Vellacott (1954), II, 730f.

43 Our constitution ... possesses./Pericles, funeral oration, quoted in Thucydides ii, 37.

46 'the imitation of one action'/Aristotle, *Poetics*.

NOW COMES MY COMEDY

56 Margarete Bieber suggests .../In *The History of the Greek and Roman Theater*, 2nd edn (1971), p. 45.
Now comes ... a winner!/Aristophanes, *The Clouds*, translated by Christopher Stace for *All the World's a Stage*.

65 'the poet ... the truth'/Quoted by A.W. Gomme in 'Aristophanes and Politics', *More Essays in Greek History and Literature* (1962).

65–6 The lout ... wine./Theophrastus, *Characters*, tr. C. Stace for *All the World's a Stage*.

66 'O Menander ... the other?'/Aristophanes of Byzantium, quoted in L.A. Post, *Transactions of the American Philological Association* 62 (1931).

67 He whom ... trouble./Quoted in Duckworth, *The Nature of Roman Comedy* (1952), p. 25.

67–8 I count ... enemies./ibid., p. 26.

69 as Horace pointed out/Horace, *Epistles*, ii, I, 156f.
According to ... Livy/In *History of Rome*, VII, 2.

70 If you want ... long one!/Plautus, prologue to *Pseudolus*, tr. C. Stace for *All the World's a Stage*.

70–1 In case ... himself .../Plautus, prologue to *The Pot of Gold*, tr. C. Stace for *All the World's a Stage*.

73 'Homo sum ... deterream.'/Terence, *Heauton Timoroumenos*, 77.

73–4 This play ... some respect./Terence, *The Mother-in-Law* (*Hecyra*), tr. C. Stace for *All the World's a Stage*.

76 Their hands ... a lyre./Quintilian XI, 3, 86f., quoted in E.K. Chambers, *The Mediaeval Stage* (1903), vol. 1, p. 4.

MYSTERIES

78 It is known ... redemption./Hardison, *Christian Rite and Christian Drama in the Middle Ages* (1965), p. 39.
For they be ... people./Kolve, *The Play Called Corpus Christi* (1966), p. 6.

79 Destroy ... worship./Bede, *Hist. Eccl.*, 1:30.

80 ... four brothers ... o coelicola./Chambers, *The Mediaeval Stage*, vol. II (1903), p. 14.

80–1 ... he rises ... now .../ibid., pp. 14–15.

83 I ... have not ... writers./Hroswitha, *Plays*, ed. Winterfeld (1901), Prologue.

87–8 Quotations from Chambers, op. cit., vol. II, pp. 138–42 and Appx W.

88 Oh, comely creature ... obedient be./Kolve, op. cit., p. 258.

97 'Alas ... hell pit.'/*The York Cycle of Mystery Plays*, ed. Purvis (1978), p. 309.

98 Richard Southern's brilliant study/*The Medieval Theatre in the Round* (1957).
Nathalie Crohn Schmitt challenges/In 'Was there a medieval Theatre in the round?', *Theatre News* 23 (1968–9).
Of worldly good ... dame./*Castle of Perseverance*, I: 580f.

99 Everyman ... guide./*Everyman*, I: 522. Fellowship: Sir ... no more./ibid., I:216f.

A MUSE OF FIRE

101 Margarete Bieber ... ancient Greece/In Bieber, op. cit., p. 1.
What tumult! ... boys./Quoted in Chambers, op. cit., vol. II, Appx N.
Some transform ... masks./ibid.

104 Glynne Wickham writes/In *Early English Stages*, vol. I (1959), p. 54. With lines ... amen!'/From John Bale, *Kyng Johan*, in *Elizabethan History Plays*, ed. Armstrong (1965), p. 41.

105 Leicester approached ... City of London'./Chambers, op. cit., vol. II, pp. 87–8.

107 *Mankind*: Go and ... drife./*Four Tudor Interludes*, ed. Somerset (1974), p. 36.
Tyb: Ah, whoreson knave ... to borrow!/*A Mery Play* ... (Chiswick Press, 1819), pp. 32–3.

107–8 Like when Apollo ... doth show./*The Poems of Henry Howard, Earl of Surrey*, ed. Paderford (1920), p. 131.

108 'the jigging veins ... mother-wits'/Marlowe, from the Prologue to *Tamburlaine the Great*.

110 Ah, Faustus ... soul!/From the final scene of *Doctor Faustus*.

111 He is the greatest ... Shakespeare./Quoted in F.E. Halliday, *A Shakespeare Companion* (1952), p. 395.
'All that is known ... buried.'/*Supplement to the Edition of Shakespeare's Plays*, ed. Jonson and Steevens (1778).

113 There is an upstart ... country./ibid.
The actors ... plaie'./S. Schoenbaum, *William Shakespeare: A Compact Documentary Life* (1977), p. 63.

113–14 'divers other persons ... woode'/Quoted in C.W. Wallace, 'The First London Theatre', *Nebraska University Studies* XIII (1913).

115 Thomas Platter of Basle/Quoted in Wickham, op. cit., vol. II, pt ii, p. 58.

118 Charles Lamb declared ... whatever'/Lamb, quoted in *Enc. Brit.*, 15th edn (1974).
'O! for a muse of fire'/This and following quotes are from the Prologue to *Henry V*.

119 But this rough magic ... book./*The Tempest*, V i 50f.

SUCH STUFF AS DREAMS ARE MADE ON

129 What a piece ... animals!/*Hamlet*, II ii 304f.

130 Until philosophers ... day./Plato, *Republic*, tr. H.D.P. Lee (1955), Book VI.

134 In their study ... England'./Orgel and Strong, *Inigo Jones: The Theatre of the Stuart Court* (1973), Preface.
Our revels ... a sleep./*The Tempest*, IV i 148f.

135–6 Samuel Daniel ... Mychanitiens'./See Lily B. Campbell, *Scenes and Machines On the English Stage During the Renaissance* (1923), p. 184.

145 *Ben Jonson*: Court masques ... mysteries./ibid., pp. 164–214 passim.

146 Oh, to make Boardes ... Age!/Jonson, 'An Expostulation with Inigo Jones', in *Poems of Ben Jonson*, ed. Johnston (1954), p. 304.

146–8 Text of *Salmacida Spolia* from *A Book of Masques: In Honour of Allardyce Nicoll* (1967).

149 'Cover her face ... young./Webster, *The Duchess of Malfi*, IV ii.

150 'I cannot see ... modesty!' Middleton and Rowley, *The Changeling*, III iv.
'the profitable ... God'/E.N.S. Thompson, *Controversy Between the Puritans and the Stage* (1903), p. 184.

THE VICES OF MANKIND

151 The effects ... miracles./Elie Konigson, quoted in Arnott, *An Introduction to the French Theatre* (1977), p. 73.

152 'far from edifying ... scandal'/Arnott, op. cit., p. 8.

154 Peter Arnott ... hostility'./ibid., p. 9f.

155 When we have ... hazard./*Henry V*, I ii 261f.

156 The common ... city./Corneille, quoted in Arnott, op. cit., p. 19.

157 The playwright ... buffoons'./ibid., p. 33.

157–8 'The generation ... order.'/Quoted in T. Lawrenson, *The French Stage in the Seventeenth Century* (1957), p. 184.

160 'One doesn't know ... acts it.'/Quoted in Arnott, op. cit., p. 140.

161 You people ... pleasure./Molière, *La Critique de l'Ecole des Femmes*, translated by T. Lawrenson for *All the World's a Stage*.

166 ... if you were ... laugh./ibid.

167 'The function ... mankind.'/Molière, *Dom Juan*, V ii.

SILK STOCKINGS AND WHITE BOSOMS

178 Described ... mind'/In John Palmer, *The Comedy of Manners*(1913), p. 36.

179 To the Duke's ... stage./Pepys, *The Diary*, ed. Latham and Matthews (1970).

180 The anonymous author ... Cit'./Quoted in Peter Holland, *The Ornament of Action* (1979), p. 15.
I come ... the Moor!/From Thomas Jordan, *A Royal Arbour of Loyal Poesie* (1660).

181 'I never ... for wit.'/Aphra Behn, *The Dutch Lover*, II iii.
'Come away; poverty's catching.'/*The Rover*, II i.

182 'Wit ... returned home.'/Margaret Cavendish, Duchess of Newcastle, *Plays Never Before Printed* (1668).
'Lord ... trust us.'/Wycherley, *The Country Wife*, V iv.

184 'unreproachful man'/John Gay, quoted in *DNB*, 'Congreve'.
'Every sentence ... terms.'/Hazlitt, *Lectures on the English Comic Writers*, ed. W.C. Hazlitt (1901), p. 92.

184 'Here she comes ... prose. Congreve, *The Way of the World*, II i.

184–5 *Millamant*: ... Positively ... reasonable./ibid., IV i.

185 Our ladies ... writ./Quoted in Bonamy Dobrée, *Restoration Comedy* (1924), p. 71.

187 'Nelly ... protection.'/Quoted in M. Summers, *The Restoration Theatre* (1934), p. 69.

188 2nd March, 1667 ... admire her./Pepys, ed. cit.

189 Mrs Bracegirdle's ... desire./A.M. Nagler, *A Sourcebook In Theatrical History* (1959), 'Bracegirdle'.
'By God ... cured?'/Both exchanges quoted in J.C. Lucey, *Peg Woffington* (1952), p. 106.

189–90 I have heard ... audience./T. Cibber, *Dissertations on Theatrical Subjects* (1756).

190 In *Macbeth* ... countenance?/Quoted in J.W. Krutch, *Comedy and Conscience After the Restoration* (1924), p. 113.

191 On Giffard, see Allardyce Nicoll, *The Garrick Stage* (1980), p. 4. 'the most extraordinary ... Occasion'/Quoted in ibid., p. 8.

192 'If this young ... wrong./Quoted in *The Oxford Companion to the Theatre*, ed. Hartnoll, 3rd edn (1967), 'James Quin'.

193 Little Garrick ... declamation./Richard Cumberland, *Memoirs* (1806), pp. 59–60.

194 The drama's ... sense./Quoted in Nicoll, *The Garrick Stage*, p. 79. 'he hammered ... minds'/ibid., p. 157.

196 'Indeed ... actor.'/Fielding, *Tom Jones*, Bk XVI ch. V.

A WORLD TURNED UPSIDE-DOWN

197 When the Lord ... Order'./See Cecil Price, *Theatre in the Age of Garrick* (1973), p. 186.

198 'the nameless ... bosom'/Quoted in Pascal, *The German Sturm und Drang* (1953), p. 186.

200 'Command ... alive!/Schiller, *Die Räuber*, tr. Lamport (1979), III i; V ii; III i.
The playbills ... love'./See John Prudhoe, *The Theatre of Goethe and Schiller* (1973), p. 53.

202 'the richest ... maelstrom'/Pascal, op. cit., p. 320.

203 One writer ... counter'./See Allardyce Nicoll, *A History of Late Nineteenth Century Drama* (1959), p. 68.

204 These our actors ... air ... /*The Tempest*, IV i 146f.

205 Mr Betterton ... orange-girls./Quoted in Nagler, op. cit., 'Betterton'.
'And so ... Betterton.'/Pepys, ed. cit.

209 *The Bells* ... fears./*The Bells*, by Leopold Lewis, Irving's script ed. D. Mayer (1980), Introduction.

209–10 Irving's biographer ... great.'/Laurence Irving, *Henry Irving* (1951), pp. 198–9.

210 'Are you ... life?'/Quoted in ibid., p. 200.

213 I feel ... blood./Quoted in *The Plays of Georg Büchner*, tr. Price (1971), Introduction.

214 *Woyzeck: When* ... Dead./Büchner, *Woyzeck*, tr. Price, pp. 108, 122.

THE MASTER BUILDERS

215 Anyone who ... sun!/Quoted in Felix Philippi, 'Mein Verkehr mit Henrik Ibsen', *Neue Freie Presse*, Vienna, 27 October 1902. I was born ... centre./Quoted in Meyer, *Ibsen* (abridged edn, 1974), p. 26.

216 'the clash ... individual'/Preface to the 1875 edition of *Catalina*.

217 I ... crossed ... sunshine'/From a speech by Ibsen quoted in Meyer, op. cit., p. 139.
'If I were ... me.'/Letter of 12 September 1865, quoted in Meyer, op. cit., p. 228.
'For some ... poem'/Quoted in Meyer, op. cit., p. 243.

218 *A comfortably* ... day./*A Doll's House*, tr. Meyer, opening scene.

219 There are two ... defeat./Quoted in Meyer, op. cit., p. 446.
'knew no ... ethics'/Halvdan Koht, quoted in Meyer, op. cit., p. 476.
'A Doll's House ... enemy.'/Koht, quoted in ibid., p. 476.
'the much ... life'/Quoted in Meyer, op. cit., p. 355.
'probably ... written it'/Quoted in ibid., p. 505.

221 'My new ... against.'/Letter to Ludwig Passarge, 22 December 1881, quoted in Meyer, op. cit., p. 506.
'Ghosts is ... Scandinavia.'/Quoted in Meyer, op. cit., pp. 508–9.
'My book ... future!'/Letter to Hegel, quoted in Meyer, op. cit., p. 512.

222 Ibsen's contemporaries ... onwards./Meyer, op. cit., p. 514.
'an open ... publicly'/Clement Scott, writing in the *Daily Telegraph*: quoted in G. Rowell, *The Victorian Theatre* (1956), p. 129.

222–3 The private ... about./Quoted in Meyer, op. cit., p. 548.

223 'most effective ... world'/Shaw, *The Quintessence of Ibsenism* (1926).

Laying hands ... lives./Shaw, *Mainly About Myself* (1898), Preface.

'I must ... themselves'/Shaw, *Widowers' Houses* (1898), Preface.

'once more ... profession'/Shaw, Apology to *Mrs Warren's Profession* (1902).

223–4 *Mrs Warren*: ... all ... likely./*Mrs Warren's Profession*, Act II.

224 'I should ... better.'/Apology to *Mrs Warren's Profession*.

'the man ... performances'/Quoted in Pearson, *Bernard Shaw* (1942), p. 165.

227 He kept it ... to work./In Meyer, op. cit., p. 165.

'the voice of Savonarola'/Quoted in ibid., p. 226.

'Prospects ... desperate.'/Quoted in Introduction to Strindberg, *Plays*, ed. Meyer (1975).

I do not ... patchwork./Ibid.

228 'I detest ... alone.'/ibid.

'half-woman, the man-hater'/ibid.

I have avoided ... composition./*Enc. Brit.*, 15th edn.

229 'to imitate ... dreamer.'/Introduction to *A Dream Play*, tr. Meyer.

230 Ibsen ... 'mad'./See Meyer, op. cit., p. 770.

THE ACTORS DO NOT UNDERSTAND

233–4 Two days ... work./Quoted in Sophie Lafitte, *Chekhov* (1970), p. 79.

235 During Lent ... well./Stanislavsky, *My Life in Art*, tr. Robbins (1948), p. 197.

236 Psychological ... classwork./Introduction to *The Seagull Produced By Stanislavsky*, tr. Magarshack (1925).

241 There are no ... rooted out./Stanislavsky, op. cit., p. 298.

242 'The actors ... should.'/Quoted in Magarshack, *Chekhov the Dramatist* (1980), p. 92.

In a letter ... want?'/Quoted in ibid., pp. 117, 118.

242–3 Chekhov winced ... people.'/Quoted in Magarshack, *Chekhov*, p. 184.

243 'The moral ... plays.'/Quoted in Lafitte, op. cit., p. 136.

244 'We strive ... lives.'/Stanislavsky, op. cit., p. 334.

'If you won't ... repertoire.'/Quoted in Introduction to *The Seagull Produced By Stanislavsky*.

245 'Yesterday ... the spot.'/ibid.

You would ... your play./ibid.

245–6 There was ... poet./Stanislavsky, op. cit., p. 356.

246 The play ... Vanya?/Introduction to *The Seagull Produced By Stanislavsky*.

Tolstoy dismissed ... worse.'/Quoted in Magarshack, *Checkhov*, pp. 16, 15.

He thought ... reason'./Stanislavsky, op. cit., p. 345.

'I have not ... witness.'/Chekhov, quoted in Ilya Ehrenburg, *Chekhov, Stendhal and Other Essays* (1943), p. 13.

247 You tell me ... about?/Quoted in Magarshack, *Chekhov*, p. 14.

'something ... carefully'/ibid., p. 282.

Take my ... angry./ibid., p. 282.

248 'The stage ... stage.'/Introduction to *The Seagull Produced By Stanislavsky*.

249 Later ... meetings'/Yeats, *Autobiographies* (1955), p. 396.

250 The founders ... sciences./Hunt, *The Abbey: Ireland's National Theatre* (1979), p. 15.

John Synge ... beggar-man./From 'The Municipal Gallery Revisited', *The Collected Poems of W.B. Yeats*, 2nd edn (1950), p. 368.

We propose ... succeed./Lady Gregory, *Our Irish Theatre* (1913), p. 20.

251 'those wicked ... intensely'/Quoted in Hunt, op. cit., p. 91.

she confided ... Dublin'/Quoted in W.G. Fay and C.

Carswell. *The Fays of the Abbey Theatre* (1935), p. 132.

Rumours ... slandered'./Hunt, op. cit., p. 75.

In a letter ... impossible.'/Lady Gregory, *Journals*, ed. Lennox (1946), p. 87.

252 'From such ... Synge.'/Quoted in Hunt, op. cit., p. 128.

253 'All decent ... ridiculous?'/Shaw, quoted in ibid., p. 95.

It was seeing ... company./Quoted in Louis Sheaffer, *O'Neill: Son and Playwright*, vol. I (1968), p. 205.

RAZZMATAZZ AND REALISM

256 Weel about ... Jim Crow./Quoted in R. Nevin, 'Stephen Foster and Negro minstrelsy', *Atlantic Monthly* XX (1867).

266 'What?!? ... Yankee Doodles!'/Quoted in A.H. Quinn, *A History of the American Drama*, vol. I (1923), p. 613.

268 Over here ... remembered./M.C. Crawford, *Romance of the American Theatre*, (1925), p. 120.

269 'Are you all ... years.'/Quoted in *The American Theatre As Seen By Its Critics*, ed. Montrose (1934), p. 216.

273 'It's a Western ... money.'/Michael Freedland, *Jerome Kern: A Biography* (1978), pp. 160–1.

276 I don't say ... dog./*Death of a Salesman*, Act I.

ADMIT ME, CHORUS, TO THIS HISTORY

282 I have fled ... in the world./Quoted in *Enc. Brit.*, 15th edn (1974), 'Stephen Phillips'.

284 Every man ... stupidity./Quoted in C. Innes, *Holy Theatre: Ritual and the Avant-Garde* (1981), p. 23.

286 ... the Great War ... War./Paul Fussell, *The Great War and Modern Memory* (1975), pp. 8, 35.

287 'We cannot ... danger.'/Antonin Artaud, *The Theatre and Its Double*, tr. Corti (1970), p. 68.

... instead of ... dreams./ibid., p. 86.

'All descriptive ... stage,'/Pirandello, quoted in *Enc. Brit.* 15th edn.

288 'A play ... play.'/ibid.

I think ... deception./ibid.

302 The first dramatist ... say./Quoted in Denis Bablet, *The Theatre of Edward Gordon Craig* (1966), p. 79.

'The more ... to die.'/Quoted in Robert Conquest, *The Great Terror* (1968), p. 501.

303 ... an eyewitness ... accident./Quoted in Eric Bentley (ed.), *The Theory of the Modern Stage* (1968), p. 85.

304 It is less ... laughter./Walter Benjamin, 'The Author As Producer', in *The Essential Frankfurt School Reader*, ed. Arato and Gebhardt (1978), p. 267.

304 Every device ... the East./Ernest Bournemann, *Brecht* (1978).

INDEX

PICTURE CREDITS

Picture research by Maggie Colbeck Rowe

Colour Photographs

Page 25 Mauro Pucciarelli; 26 Mauro Pucciarelli; 27 Scala/Eoliano Museum, Lipari; 28 top Scala/Archeological Museum, Ferrara, bottom Scala/Capitolini Museum, Rome; 29 Martin Stringer; 30 BBC/Peter Wineman; 31 Maurice Newcombe; 32 Maurice Newcombe; 57 Scala/Archeological Museum; 58 Scala/Archeological Museum, Siracusa; 59 top Mary Evans Picture Library, bottom Mauro Pucciarelli; 60–61 Scala/National Museum, Naples; 62 Mauro Pucciarelli; 63 Mauro Pucciarelli; 64 top Scala/Gregoriano Etrusco Museum, Vatican, bottom Giraudon/National Museum, Naples; 89 Mauro Pucciarelli; 90 Mauro Pucciarelli; 91 Giraudon; 92–93 Giraudon, (inset) BBC/Harry Rankin; 94 Mauro Pucciarelli/Burcardo Museum, Rome; 95 Mauro Pucciarelli; 96 top Mauro Pucciarelli/Theatre Museum, Monaco, bottom BBC/Harry Rankin; 121 British Library, (inset) BBC/Joan Williams; 122 top Robert Harding, bottom Robert Harding/Walter Hampden Memorial Library at the Players, N.Y; 123 E.T. Archive/Garrick Club; 124 Robert Harding/V & A; 125 Robert Harding; 126 Donald Cooper; 127 top Martha Swope, bottom Donald Cooper; 128 Martha Swope; 137 Scala; 138 Scala; 139 Scala/Biblioteca Manicelliana, Firenze; 140 Scala/ Biblioteca Nazionale, Firenze; 141 Scala/Bibliioteca Nazionale, Firenze; 142 top left Robert Harding, top right Robert Harding, bottom Scala/Biblioteca Nazionale, Turin; 143 Robert Harding; 144 Scala/Gabinetto Mediceo; 169 top Snark International, bottom BBC/Joan Williams; 170 Snark International; 171 V & A/Joan Williams; 172 Reg Wilson; 173 E.T. Archive/Garrick Club; 174 Reg Wilson; 175 John Frost Collection; 176 Donald Cooper; 237 BBC/David Clark; 238 Novosti Press Agency; 239 Novosti Press Agency; 240 Zoë Dominic; 257 Bettmann Archive Inc; 258 Bettmann Archive Inc; 259 top Bettmann Archive Inc, centre Bettmann Archive Inc, bottom Martha Swope; 260 top Zoë Dominic, centre and bottom Donald Cooper; 261 Zoë Dominic; 262 Martha Swope; 263 Martha Swope; 264 Martha Swope; 289 top left and top centre Dulwich Picture Gallery, top right Garrick Club/E.T. Archive, bottom left Garrick Club/Joan Williams, centre right Garrick Club/ Joan Williams, bottom right Garrick Club/Joan Williams; 290 top left BBC Hulton Picture Library, centre left Garrick Club/E.T. Archive, bottom left E.T. Archive, top right Garrick Club/ E.T. Archive, bottom centre Mander and Mitchenson Theatre Collection bottom right Roger Viollet; 291 top left, Garrick Club/E.T. Archive, bottom left and bottom centre BBC Hulton Picture Library, top right Roger Viollet, centre right and bottom right Garrick Club/E.T. Archive; 292 top left BBC Hulton Picture Library, centre left Garrick Club/E.T. Archive, bottom left BBC Hulton Picture Library, top right Mander and Mitchenson Theatre Collection, centre right BBC Hulton Picture Library, bottom right BBC Hulton Picture Library/Associated Press; 293 top left BBC Hulton Picture Library, centre left Compagnie Renaud-Barrault/Bernand, bottom left BBC Hulton Picture Library/Torrington Douglas, top centre A.D.N. Zentralbild, top right Donald Cooper, bottom right BBC/Joan Williams; 294 top left Zoë Dominic, centre left Compagnie Renaud-Barrault/Bernand, bottom left BBC Hulton Picture Library, top right Zoë Dominic, centre right BBC Hulton Picture Library, bottom right Zoë Dominic; 295 top left Donald Cooper, centre left Zoë Dominic, bottom left Donald Cooper, top right Zoë Dominic, centre right BBC Hulton Picture Library, bottom right Donald Cooper; 296 top left Zoë Dominic, centre left BBC Hulton Picture Library, bottom left Donald Cooper, top right Zoë Dominic, centre bottom Royal Exchange Theatre Manchester/Kevin Cumming, bottom right Zoë Dominic

Black and White Photographs

Page 17 BBC/Peter Wineman; 19 Royal Anthropological Society; 22, 23 BBC/Peter Wineman; 36 BBC Hulton Picture Library; 40 BBC Hulton Picture Library; 46 bottom left and centre Mauro Pucciarelli, bottom right BBC Hulton Picture Library; 51 top left Mauro Pucciarelli, top right Deutsches Archaeologisches Institut, Athens; 65 Scala/Theatre Museum, Milan; 68 left Mauro Pucciarelli right Ronald Sheridan; 72 BBC Hulton Picture Library; 79 BBC Hulton Picture Library; 82 J.C.D. Smith; 100 Mauro Pucciarelli; 102 J.C.D. Smith; 103 left Mauro Pucciarelli; 109 BBC Hulton Picture Library; 110 BBC Hulton Picture Library; BBC Hulton Picture Library; 114 left British Library, right BBC/Joan Williams; 119 BBC/Peter Wineman; 120 BBC Hulton Picture Library; 131 E.T. Archive/V & A; 133 Scala; 136 Robert Harding Devonshire Collection Chatsworth; 149 Royal Exchange Theatre/Kevin Cummins; 153 Roger Viollet; 159 left BBC Hulton Picture Library, right Bernand; 162 left BBC Hulton Picture Library, right Snark International; 163 Snark International; 164 left Rene Dazy, right Mansell Collection; 165 BBC Hulton Picture Library; 168 Roger Viollet; 181 BBC Hulton Picture Library; 183 BBC Hulton Picture Library; 186 BBC Hulton Picture Library; 188 BBC Hulton Picture Library; 191 V & A/Joan Williams; 192 BBC Hulton Picture Library; 195 BBC Hulton Picture Library; 199 BBC Hulton Picture Library; 201 left BBC Hulton Picture Library, right Landesbildstalle Wurttemberg; 206 Harry R. Beard Theatre Collection; 208 BBC Hulton Picture Library; 212 Buchners Samtliche Poetische Werke; 213 Donald Cooper; 220 Universitetbiblioteket, Oslo; 225 top left BBC Hulton Picture Library, top right and bottom Donald Cooper; 229 top left BBC Hulton Picture Library, top right Donald Cooper; 234 left BBC Hulton Picture Library, right Novosti Press Agency; 244 Society for Cultural Relationships with the USSR; 248 Novosti Press Agency; 252 left National Library of Ireland, right Irish Tourist Board; 267 BBC Hulton Picture Library; 270 top left BBC Hulton Picture Library, top right Donald Cooper; 275 Fred Fehl; 277 Camera Press; 278 Martha Swope; 285 Roger Viollet; 297 BBC Hulton Picture Library; 298 BBC Hulton Picture Library; 300 Houston Rogers; 303 top left A.D.N. Zentralbild, top right A.D.N. Zentralbild; 305 BBC Hulton Picture Library; 307 Zoë Dominic

Endpapers: Interior of Drury Lane Theatre, Henry E. Hunlington Library and Art Gallery.